IBM Data Files:
A BASIC Tutorial

David Miller

Reston Publishing Company
A Prentice-Hall Company
Reston, Virginia

Library of Congress Cataloging in Publication Data

Miller, David
     IBM Data files: a BASIC tutorial.

     1. IBM Personal Computer—Programming. 2. Basic
(Computer program language) 3. File organization
(Computer science) I. Title. II. Title: I.B.M. basic
files.
QA76.8.I2594M54 1983   001.64'2   82-25053
ISBN 0-8359-3026-2 (pbk.)

Editorial supervision by
Ginger Sasser DeLacey.
Cover design by
Joyce Thompson.

©1983 by
Reston Publishing Company, Inc.
A Prentice-Hall Company
Reston, Virginia

10   9   8   7   6   5   4   3   2   1

Printed in the United States of America

Train up a child in the way he should go: and when he is old, he will not depart from it. Proverbs 22:6

To Christy, Cindy, Mark and Paul—children of the personal computer age.

Contents

*A special note of appreciation
to Gil Rosa and Ted Isbell
for their timely suggestions
and generous assistance.*

Preface

The purpose of this book is to take some of the misery and mystery out of learning to use IBM's file structure. The book is aimed at people who would like to learn to use the computer to assist them at home or at work by using the file capabilities of the IBM Personal Computer.© *IBM Data Files: A BASIC Tutorial* is designed as a step-by-step tutorial. The book explains some things that, without adequate manuals, take many painful hours of trial and error to learn. Progress has been made in creating better file-handling techniques and an explanation of some of these techniques is included.

Upon completion of the book, you should fully understand what files are and how to use them. You will be able to create your own sequential or random access files. Examples of both of these file types are included throughout the book. Program examples include file creation programs for: the stock market, mailing lists, inventories, recipes, and medical records.

There are some very good data-base programs available commercially. If your needs require an elaborate data base structure, you should probably use one of those programs or pay a programmer to create one for you. Reading this book will not make you capable of creating complete commercial data base programs, but with practice, you will be able to effectively create and use any type of file you want.

I really enjoy programming and creating programs for my own use. I like the freedom programming gives me, because I can easily change or add to what the program does. I hope this book conveys some of that enjoyment and freedom.

IBM Personal Computer© is a copyright of International Business Machines Corporation, 1981.

Introduction

No book is magic in that, by possessing the book, you possess the knowledge of that book. Yet I have tried to make it relatively easy for *anyone* to learn to use the IBM Personal Computer.

No single book will suffice for everyone, and this book makes no claim to being the exception. But I have attempted to make it useful for the beginner as well as the more experienced IBM BASIC user. The program examples cover the areas of home, education, business, hobby, and investment.

Computer vocabulary has been introduced very gradually. Readers somewhat knowledgeable of the vocabulary may find the process repetitious at first, but I have found this to be the best method for acquiring a working knowledge of the multitude of "jargon."

The "system" approach has been used so the reader will not be overwhelmed with a large number of different application programs. The programs presented are intended to be useful, as well as instructive. The programs build upon themselves so that something that may appear awkward to an experienced programmer is used to help explain a concept needed in later chapters.

Information for the more experienced BASIC user includes a thorough discussion of DIF files with application programs. Other items are: automatic, initial use, file-creation techniques, an introduction to the MERGE and CHAIN commands, BATCH files, "protected" files, and tape files. The section on tape files briefly explains how this book can be useful to someone without a disk drive.

You cannot absorb this information. You must read the book and plan to re-read and/or study the text and programs of parts that are at first unclear. Invest time in learning how to get the most out of the

IBM. Experienced BASIC users may find that they can either skip parts or proceed quickly through certain sections. I would encourage everyone to finish the book.

Finally, a disk containing all the programs presented in the book is available. You can make the disk yourself by typing in all the programs. If you just want to see the programs in operation, you may want to purchase the disk.

I sincerely hope you enjoy the book and find it instructive.

IBM Keyboard

One of the nicest features about the IBM PC is its additional keys. Certain keys deserve special mention. With a printer, the PrtSc key is very handy. At just about any point, you can use this key by pressing on the shift key and the PrtSc key. Assuming the printer is properly connected and turned on, the contents of the screen will then be "dumped" to the printer. In other words, the printer will print an exact copy of whatever is on the screen at that moment.

The edit keys are just as useful. In addition to the arrow keys, IBM thoughtfully provided a key to allow for the insertion of material (Ins) and a key to delete material (Del). Brief practice with these keys and the arrow keys will greatly expand your ability to comfortably enter and edit BASIC program listings.

There are certain problems with the keyboard that seem to affect nearly everyone at first. The two shift keys are the same size as the other keys, and the left shift key is beyond its normal "American" position. The Num Lock key changes the "state" of the numeric keys, but nothing indicates what "state" the keys are currently in. They can either be used as numbers or as edit (arrow) keys. The Num Lock key shifts between the two states. The Caps Lock key locks the keyboard into either all upper case or all lower case. The shift keys then provide the opposite state for individual characters. The ESC key erases the line being entered if the key is pressed before the ENTER key.

Finally, I have observed many new users experiencing problems with the auto repeat feature of each key. Depressing any key for more than a fraction of a second causes the key to automatically repeat itself. For certain keys, this feature can be very useful. Until you get used to it, however, the auto repeat feature on all keys (especially the ENTER key) may cause a few problems.

With practice, the IBM keyboard is one of the best around. It spoils users with its additional key functions and editing capability. But like most things, it takes some practice to make full use of it.

Although the standard IBM Personal Computer Display allows 80 characters on a line, it was necessary in the printing of this book to limit the number of characters to approximately 57 per line. That is the reason you will see words split in two. When you are typing a line from a listing given in the book, it is preferable to continue typing the line for as many characters as the display will allow, regardless of where the break occurs in the listing given in the text. For example, on page 40, the book indicates that line 190 is broken in the middle of the word envelope with the characters ope." all appearing on the next line. Since the entire line actually contains less than 80 characters (63 counting spaces), there is no need to break the line anywhere when you are typing this line on the computer.

The programs in this book are available on disk with additional documentation.
To order your copy, please send $15.00
($17.50 outside North America) to:
AEN, 9525 Lucerne St., Ventura, Ca. 93004.
California residents, please add 6% sales tax.

I

IBM File Types

There are as many definitions of the word file as there are kinds of files. You can quickly become confused if your understanding of the term differs from an author's intended use, and dictionary definitions are of little use in the computer world of today. Before becoming involved with the computer, my understanding of a file was limited to information that was kept in a folder in a file cabinet. I think we often learn best by trying to fit that which is new into something we already understand. Therefore, following this idea, I will try to explain IBM file structure in terms of a file cabinet.

In a four-drawer file cabinet, one drawer might be for accounts payable, while another could be for accounts receivable, a third for personnel information, and the fourth for inventory information. These are used only as examples to show that each drawer might contain different file types. The file cabinet just as easily can contain game instructions in one drawer, receipts in another, name and address information in a third, and medical records in the fourth. The idea is of a file cabinet containing different types of information. *The IBM's file cabinet is the disk drive and diskette.* One type of file is a BASIC program file. A second file type contains only data. Other file types are identified by their "extensions" to their file names. Therefore, each diskette you use is like a file cabinet. It is set up to accept and classify many types of files.

How do you know what files are on your diskettes? We will begin the tutorial part of this book by going through all the steps necessary in order to find out just what files are on your diskette. If you are already acquainted with the procedure used to start up the computer and disk drive, sometimes called "booting the system," you can skip the next paragraph.

The first step to finding out what files are on your diskette is to take your DOS diskette and insert it into the disk drive. (If you have more than one drive, make sure to put the diskette into drive A—the drive on the left.) Then do one of the following: (1) Turn on the computer, or (2) If the computer is already on, press and hold down the keys marked CTRL and ALT, and then press the key marked DEL. The disk drive should make some noise, and the light on the disk drive should come on. Soon the disk drive will stop, and the light will go out. The command "Enter today's date (m-d-y):" should appear. (If you have not been able to get to this point with the computer, try another diskette, preferably the diskette marked "DOS diskette." If switching diskettes does not work, you will need to check the manuals for your particular system.)

Now, type today's date using numbers in the form of "8-5-83" or "12/25/83". (DOS 1.1 users will also be asked to type in the time in the form of 8:25:00.0 or 20:25:00.0) After you have entered a valid date (and time), the DOS prompt "A>" appears below some information about the IBM Personal Computer© and the copyright notice. At this point, type:

    DIR or dir

The Disk Operating System will recognize either upper case or lower case letters. Dir stands for directory. The disk drive will come back on, and you will see a list with four things (five with DOS 1.1) on each line of text:

1. the name of the file,

2. up to three characters for an extension (if the file name has one),

3. some number, and

4. a date.

    (DOS 1.1 adds a time also.)

The extension may indicate what type of file it is: BAS for a BASIC program file, DAT for a file containing only data, COM for a system command file, etc. The name, consisting of letters and/or possibly numbers, is the actual name of the specific file. The size of the file is given as the decimal number of characters or bytes in that file. The date (and time) indicate either the date (and time) of the file's actual creation, or the last date (and time) the file was changed. In our file cabinet example, this is the same information that might appear on each folder. You might label each folder with: (1) a name for the infor-

---

©International Business Machines Corporation, 1981.

mation within the folder, (2) an extension indicating which drawer it goes in, (3) how much information it contains, and (4) the date of the last addition to the file.

Most file cabinets do not have a list of all the files stored within them. It would be a time-consuming job to update that list every time you added, changed or threw away a file, but IBM's file management system does just that and does it automatically. The diskette's list of everything in the file cabinet is what you get when you type "DIR". *Typing "DIR" shows the list previously created by the file management system.*

How are these files used? What are they? How are they different? Returning to the file cabinet, the person in charge of that cabinet might put some rules or locks on the drawers. In other words, he or she might say that the BAS file could be used only in a certain way or only by certain people. The same could be true of the other file types or drawers. This is exactly what IBM's file management system has done. Each file type is used differently and can be used only in certain specific ways. *BAS files are instructions (also called programs) to the computer to do something.* Examples of such instructions would be:

```
20   CLS
40   IF  NUMBER  =  5  THEN  5000
50   GOTO  100
100  PRINT  "HELLO"
```

Most DAT files are not computer instructions but contain information of value to people such as names, addresses, zip codes, payroll deductions, pay rates, book titles, etc. Often DAT files are just lists of such information. Such lists, of course, would not make sense as instructions to the computer.

It should be clear that IBM files are used to store information just as you or I use a filing cabinet, that there are different types of files, and that they are used for different purposes. In the next chapter, we will look more closely at the file types and how they are used. In subsequent chapters, we will look at one of those file types, the DAT, or data file, and examine how information is kept, how that information is used, and how those files are created. The latter, creating files, is the main emphasis of this book and will occupy the remaining chapters. If you want to know how to create the BASIC files (programs), you will need to learn "programming." Effectively using the DATA files requires some knowledge of how to program in BASIC. The programs discussed in this book will be BASIC programs, and the discussion will be such that anyone willing to try the examples should learn to program, as well as learn to create and use DATA files. In other words, although the main emphasis of this book is on DATA files, you will learn a certain amount of programming—BASIC program files—in order to be able to create, display, and change DATA files. And I repeat, *anyone willing to try all the examples, and read carefully through the discussion of the examples, can and will learn to program and thus make effective use of DATA files.* Any individual, no matter what his or her age, background or experience, can learn the information presented in this book. Programming and file manipulation are a matter of learning how to give instructions to the computer in a manner the computer can understand or, more simply, programming is learning how to talk to the computer and tell it what you want it to do.

QUESTIONS

1. How are IBM file types identified?
2. What extension is used to identify BASIC program files?
3. What extension is used to identify data files?
4. Which file type will this book emphasize?
5. What word should you type in order to see a list of the files on a diskette?
6. Which files contain instructions to the computer?
7. Which files contain information of value to people?
8. What information is shown when you ask to see a list of the files on a diskette?

ANSWERS

1. By the extensions to their file names
2. BAS
3. DAT
4. DATA files
5. DIR
6. BASIC or other program language files
7. DATA files
8. The file name, the extension to the file name, the size of the file, and the date (and time) the file was created or last changed

2
BASIC Program Files

In this chapter, we are going to take a closer look at the first main file type. This would be the same as opening our file cabinet's top drawer for a quick look at what is kept inside.

We begin with what is probably the most common type of file, the BASIC file. Some of you might already be confused because you have always referred to BASIC "programs" rather than files. In reality, they are both. Suppose one drawer in the file cabinet is used for games. Each folder contains the rules or instructions for playing a different game. Most of the time, you would simply refer to the folders as games, not files; yet they are really both games and files. When you have taken one folder out of the file cabinet and are using the instructions to play the game, it is not a file; however, when you are finished with the game and want to put it back in its place, it becomes a file, one of many game files. The same is true of BASIC program files. The top drawer contains only BASIC programs or computer instructions (rules). When the computer is using the instructions in one of those BASIC file "folders," the instructions are a program, but when the computer is not using the instructions, the instructions are stored as files. The important thing to understand is that BASIC files contain only computer instructions (programs). Some of these files contain larger or longer sets of computer instructions than others, but a BASIC file can only be a set of instructions for the computer or, in other words, a computer program. The second limitation of the top drawer, or ".BAS" file, is that it can only be a certain kind of computer program, a BASIC computer program, not a FORTRAN computer program or a COBOL computer program, etc. (FORTRAN and COBOL are two other computer languages, just as BASIC is a computer language.)

Let's look at the rules for using these BASIC computer program files. In our mythical office, we have three main secretaries that can use BASIC program files. Secretary number one can only go and get the file (LOAD). Secretary number two can only put the file away (SAVE). Secretary number three can go and get the file and immediately begin execution or operation of the program (RUN). *These three secretaries, or commands, do not have access to other drawers or file types.*

Secretary number three (RUN) does two jobs by loading a program into memory from a diskette and then beginning the operation or execution of that program. In other words, the RUN command goes and gets a copy of the file from the disk, puts it in the computer's memory, and tells the computer to begin operation according to the instructions in the file (now program).

Secretary number two (SAVE) can only put the file (program) currently in the computer's memory in the file cabinet (disk).

Secretary number one (LOAD) is only able to get the file (program) from the file cabinet (disk) and put it on the boss's desk (in the computer's memory). The load command goes to the diskette and gets a specific file. In order to know which file to get, the LOAD command must be given the specific name of the file: LOAD "MATHDRIL or LOAD "CHECKER. (The quotation mark indicates the beginning of the file name). If the file name is not spelled exactly the way it is spelled in the DIRectory, which is the list of all the files in the file cabinet, then the LOAD command or secretary won't be able to find the file and will come back and tell you "File not found". (The LOAD command will add the extension .BAS and look for the file name with that extension.) On the other hand, if the LOAD command does have the exact name, it will go to the disk and get a copy of the file. Notice the use of the word "copy." The LOAD command does not actually go and remove the file from the diskette like a secretary would remove a file from the file cabinet. The LOAD command takes only a copy so that the original always remains on the disk. The copy of the file is loaded into the computer's memory, similar to a secretary getting a file and putting it on the boss's desk. You, the boss, must then decide what you want to do with the file. If you want to open it and look at it, you use some form of the LIST command. (Type LIST or LIST 100–200, etc.) If you want to see the program in operation, type RUN.

Secretaries, or BASIC file commands, must be given a specific file name. Usually, after using the LOAD command, you will want to look at the instructions (LIST) and perhaps change, add, or remove some instructions. When you have finished, you may want to keep what you have done by giving the file to secretary number two (SAVE) and telling the secretary the exact name under which you want to keep this file. If you have made changes but still want to keep the original currently on the disk, then the secretary must be informed of a new file name. If the secretary uses the same file name as the file currently on the disk, the secretary will throw out the file on disk (erase it) and replace it with the one you have changed. This may or may not be what you want, so be careful what name you use with the SAVE command.

Let's actually try some of these commands. You will need your DOS diskette and a new diskette. If you do not have a new diskette, you should: (1) wait until you do have a new diskette before doing the next steps, or (2) use a diskette that you know has some room on it and skip the first step below, or (3) use an old diskette that contains information you no longer need. Use your DOS diskette to get the computer working; i.e., to boot the system. (Review this procedure in Chapter 1, if necessary.) When you get the A> prompt on the screen, type the following carefully, and remember to press the key marked with the bent arrow (called the RETURN or ENTER key) after each entry: (You can use either upper case or lower case.)

FORMAT A:/S

You should see:

```
Insert new diskette for drive A:
and strike any key when ready
```

Remove the DOS diskette and insert a blank or new diskette. If you do not remove the DOS diskette you used to boot the system, you can destroy the information on it. Once you have chosen and inserted your blank diskette, press any key. The disk drive makes a noise and the light comes on. The message "Formatting ... " appears on the screen. The computer is transferring numerical information onto the diskette to enable the computer to find locations on that diskette later. It is also including a copy of DOS so that you can use this diskette to boot the system from now on. Eventually, you will be asked "Format another (Y/N)?" You should respond with an "n" unless you have other blank diskettes that you want to format at this time. *Remember, this first step destroys any existing information on an old diskette.* This step is used to format a new diskette or re-format an old diskette so that the diskette can store files. The FORMAT command is usually used only once on each diskette. *A second use erases whatever is currently on the diskette.*

The second step is to transfer a copy of the BASIC language onto the newly formatted diskette. Remove the just-formatted diskette and insert the DOS diskette. Type:

COPY BASIC.COM B:

Make certain that you have typed everything exactly as it is shown above, spaces included. The colon is necessary to indicate that we are specifying drive B. Remember to press the ENTER key. If you have only one drive, you should see:

```
Insert diskette for drive B:
and strike any key when ready
```

In this case, since we are assuming only one drive exists, drive B refers to the newly initialized diskette. We want this newly initialized diskette to contain a copy of the file BASIC.COM. (If you do have two drives, you can simply insert the initialized diskette into drive B and press any key.) When you have removed the DOS diskette and inserted the initialized diskette, press any key. The drive will come on and soon a copy of the file BASIC will be placed on the new diskette. To see that the BASIC language file does exist on this diskette, type:

```
DIR
```

You should see:

```
BASIC       COM      10880     08-04-81
```

or for DOS 1.1

```
BASIC       COM      11392     05-07-82    12: 00pm
```

Now type:

```
BASIC
```

This command loads the BASIC language from the diskette and displays a version number and copyright notice from IBM. Now type:

```
NEW
20 PRINT "HELLO"
40 PRINT "I am the IBM Personal Computer"
```

Check your typing to be sure you have typed everything exactly the way it is shown above. The word NEW erases any BASIC program that is already in the computer's memory. It does not do anything to the diskette or any information stored on the diskette. The numbers 20 and 40 are line numbers in a BASIC program. Line numbers can be any number from 0 to 65535. Usually, the numbers chosen are not consecutive, so other lines can be added, if needed. The word PRINT instructs the computer to display on the screen whatever follows it and is between the quotation marks. Now type the word RUN, and press the ENTER key. Below the word RUN, you should see just the words between the quotation marks.

```
Hello
I am the IBM Personal Computer
```

You have just written and executed a BASIC program. The program is still in the computer's memory, but if you were to turn off the computer now, you would lose that program. It would be lost because it has not been permanently saved on tape or disk. We will take care of that with our next step.

The third step is to save the program in the computer's memory out to a file on the diskette. This is easily accomplished by giving the file to the SAVE secretary and letting the secretary do all the work. Simply type:

```
SAVE "HELLO
```

You do not have to add the extension since this command, or secretary, knows to add the standard extension of .BAS for BASIC programs. The secretary, or SAVE command, has transferred a copy of the contents of the computer's program memory to the diskette and stored it in the file called "HELLO.BAS". If you want to see the names of the files on the diskette while working under the BASIC language, you need to type the command:

```
files or FILES
```

You should see:

```
COMMAND .COM BASIC    .COM HELLO    .BAS
```

(The BASIC command, FILES, displays a period before the extension. The DOS command, DIR, does not display the period, but indicates its existence with at least one space before the extension.) To see what is in the computer's memory, type:

```
LIST
```

The display should show:

```
20 PRINT "HELLO"
40 PRINT "I am the IBM Personal Computer"
```

LIST is similar to FILES in BASIC and DIR in DOS in that both FILES and DIR show what is on a diskette, and LIST shows what is in the computer's memory. Now type:

```
NEW
LIST
```

The program is now gone and there is nothing in the computer's memory. Type:

```
LOAD "HELLO
LIST
```

The program is back. Immediately after the LOAD "HELLO, the disk drive comes on for a brief time. The computer is instructed to go to the diskette, bring in a copy of the file called HELLO and store that copy in its memory. When you type LIST, you are telling the computer to show you what it has in its memory. Therefore, the program now actually exists in two places: (1) in the computer's memory, and (2) as a file on the diskette. Type carefully and add a third line like this:

```
60 PRINT "I am a smart computer"
```

Then type:

```
SAVE "HELLO2
FILES
```

Now the list shows:

```
COMMAND .COM BASIC    .COM HELLO    .BAS
HELLO2  .BAS
```

(With the IBM Personal Computer display device, up to six file names are displayed on each line with a single space separating each name.) There are four files on the diskette. The first file is part of DOS; the second file is the BASIC language file, and the other two are BASIC program files, or programs written using the BASIC language. After you type SAVE "HELLO2, the disk drive comes on briefly while the computer transfers a copy of the contents of its memory to the diskette. FILES shows the new list of files on the diskette. Finally, type:

```
NEW
LIST
```

The program is gone. Type:

```
RUN "HELLO2
```

and the screen shows:

```
Hello
I am the IBM Personal Computer
I am a smart computer
```

Now type:

```
LIST
```

and the full program is back. Type:

```
RUN
```

(this time without a file name, since the instructions are already in memory), and you should get the same message.

First, you erase the program in the computer's memory (NEW), and then ask to see if there is anything left in the computer's memory (LIST) in order to verify what you did. Next, RUN "HELLO2 tells the computer to access the diskette, load the file called HELLO2 into its memory, and begin operation according to the file's instructions. LIST shows that the program is back in memory. To prove it, RUN without a file name tells the computer to operate again according to the program's instructions.

Let's review from the viewpoint of the secretaries and file cabinet. Remember, so far we have three main secretaries: number one (LOAD), number two (SAVE), and number three (RUN). In order for these secretaries to do anything, they must be given a file name:

```
LOAD  "MATHDRIL
RUN   "CHECKERS
SAVE  "ANYTHING
```

BASIC file commands must be given a specific file name.

There are other BASIC commands that can be used with files. NAME can change the name of any file. KILL can remove or erase any file. MERGE can combine a program on disk with a program in memory. BLOAD and BSAVE are used to load and save binary data. These commands are generally less used but are good to have when you need them.

I have used the concept of secretaries for two reasons. First, I believe it gives the impression that BASIC file commands are there to help you. In the examples, the secretaries are really BASIC file commands. BASIC file commands do certain things for you that a number of personal secretaries might do. The only limitation is that you must be exact and specific with the secretaries (commands). File commands must be used with a specific file name. Second, the concept of secretaries may help clarify the use of a duplicate term. When the word RUN is used without a file name, it is no longer seen as a secretary or BASIC file command. Instead, it is simply one of many internal BASIC commands. Typing RUN, without a file name, instructs the computer to execute the instructions currently in memory. RUN, with a file name, instructs the computer to access the DISK, load the specified program into memory, and begin operation according to that program's instructions.

We've covered a lot of new information in this chapter. If something is not clear, you should review it and use the IBM Personal Computer and disk drive to better understand these concepts.

QUESTIONS

1. *True or False:* BASIC programs are stored on disk as files.

2. What BASIC word is used to show a list of files on a diskette?

3. What does DOS stand for?

4. How many main BASIC file commands are used with BASIC program files?

5. Which BASIC file command gets the program from disk and immediately begins execution or operation of the program?

6. Which BASIC file command stores programs on the disk as files?

7. *True or False:* The LOAD command actually removes the program from the disk and loads it into the computer's memory.

8. What happens when you save back to disk a program you have changed, and you save it under the same name?

9. Name other BASIC file commands that can be used with files.

10. *True or False:* LIST shows what is on the diskette.

11. What DOS command (not a BASIC command) is used to prepare a new diskette to receive files?

12. *True or False:* BASIC programs are never files.

13. Explain what NEW does.

14. What DOS command is used to transfer a file from one diskette to another diskette?

ANSWERS

1. True
2. FILES
3. Disk Operating System
4. 3
5. RUN with a file name
6. SAVE with a file name
7. False, it takes a copy.
8. The previous version is erased and replaced with the new version.
9. NAME, KILL, MERGE, BLOAD, BSAVE
10. False
11. FORMAT
12. False
13. Erases whatever is in the computer's memory
14. COPY

3

Data File Introduction

If you go back to the file cabinet example used in the last two chapters, this chapter is a quick look inside the DAT (DATA) drawer and a superficial look inside the two different kinds of file folders in this drawer. We will examine the characteristics that are common to both kinds of DATA files and look at how you can access those files.

Of the different types of files, we have seen that one type contains instructions, called programs, for the computer: BASIC program files. One of the other types usually contains information for people rather than machines. By this, I do not mean that the computer cannot make use of the information, but that the information usually is not in the form of direct instructions for the computer. An example of an instruction for the computer is:

    20 PRINT "HELLO, HOW ARE YOU?"

An example of information that is not in the form of a computer instruction would be:

    Title: IBM DATA FILES: A BASIC TUTORIAL
    Author: David Miller
    Publisher: Reston Publishing
    Address: Reston, Va.

This last example is the kind of information usually kept in a DATA file. Before we get into the process of actually storing and retrieving data files, we need to understand the main difference between the two kinds of DATA files.

Data files have two ways of storing and retrieving information. (Remember that the information really stays on the diskette and we are just getting a copy of the information.) These two ways of storing

15

and retrieving information are sequential access and random access. Sequential access basically means that the information stored in the file is kept in sequential order. Random access usually means that each part of the file is divided equally and can be reached directly and at random instead of going through all previous records. The process of looking at each record in order (sequence) to decide if it is the record you want is a characteristic of sequential files and can require more time than the direct method of random access files.

The basic difference between sequential data files and random data files is somewhat like the difference between a cassette tape and a phonograph record. If I want to find a specific song on a cassette tape, even using the best available tape deck, I must begin at the current location of the tape and proceed either forward or backward, passing over all intervening songs until I have found the song I want. The process proceeds in sequence, one song after another. For example, if I want to play only the fourth song on the tape, I would have to advance the tape through the first, second, and third songs until I get to the fourth one. On the other hand, if the songs are on a phonograph record, all I would have to do to play the fourth song would be to place the phono cartridge containing the needle at the start of the fourth division instead of at the start of the first song. I can do that because I am able to clearly see the divisions between songs and because those individual songs are directly accessible. I do not have to go through the grooves of the first three songs in order to get to the fourth, and moving the needle by hand only takes seconds. Using this example, imagine that the DAT drawer contains two basic divisions: the first division contains files that operate in a way similar to cassette tapes, while the second division contains files that operate like phonograph records in the way described.

Despite their differences, these two kinds of DATA files do have things in common, just like tapes have things in common with phono records. The most obvious common characteristic is that they both usually contain information that is not in the form of instructions for the computer. In other words, they contain information like lists of things, addresses, receipts, and inventories. Second, both files make use of some of the same BASIC file commands, but with different parameters.

Because these DATA files are not computer instructions, they cannot be used in the same manner as BASIC program files. In other words, you cannot RUN, SAVE, or LOAD a DATA file. Those three commands, when combined with a file name, are the computer's means of access to BASIC disk files. The obvious question, then, is that if RUN, SAVE, or LOAD cannot be used with DATA files, how does the computer get the information on the disk in a DATA file or back off the disk from a DATA file?

In order to gain access to DATA files, you must use certain BASIC file commands in specific ways, depending on the kind of DATA file you are accessing. Both sequential and random access data files primarily use four types of commands: (1) OPEN, (2) CLOSE, (3) some way of reading the file (INPUT # or GET #), and (4) some method of writing to the file (PRINT # or PUT #). Future chapters will examine in detail how each of these are to be used for either of the two kinds of DATA files. For now, you need only to understand the essential task of each command. Again, the example of the filing cabinet is useful. In much the same way that a secretary must open a file folder removed from the filing cabinet before making use of any information contained in the file, so also must all data files be opened before the information they contain can be put to use. And, just as the secretary should close the file folder before replacing it in the filing cabinet, so also should all data files be closed before ending the program or turning off the computer. If a secretary does not close the file folder, some information might drop out and get lost. The same is true if data files are not properly closed. This is usually only the case after new information has been written to the file and the file not closed. Loss of information should not occur after a data file has only been read and not closed.

INPUT #/PRINT # or GET #/PUT # are the main processes by which information is either read from or written to the file. If you only want to see information already in a data file, the BASIC file commands INPUT #, for sequential access, and GET #, for random access, are the commands you would use. If you want to add information to the file or create a new file, use either the BASIC file command, PRINT #, for sequential access, or PUT #, for random access.

At this point, let's try out some of this information on the computer. Take the diskette that you formatted in the last chapter and place it in the disk drive. Then, either turn on the computer, or, if the computer is already on, press CTRL ALT and DEL at the same time. (Refer to Chapters 1 and 2 if you are not sure what to do.) When the cursor (blinking line) appears, type carefully and remember to press the ENTER key after each entry. First, type the current date in the form:

    5-25-83

DOS 1.1 users will also need to type the time in the following form (only hours and minutes are necessary):

    11: 27: 00. 0

And you should see:

```
The IBM Personal Computer DOS
Version 1.00 (or 1.10) (C)Copyright IBM Corp 1981
(,1982)
```

A>

Next to the A> type:

```
BASIC
```

Remember, you can use either upper case or lower case letters. The disk will come on and after a short time you will see:

```
The IBM Personal Computer Basic
Version D1.00 Copyright IBM Corp. 1981
61810 Bytes free
Ok
```

The numbers may be different depending upon which version of BASIC you are using and how much memory you have available, but a similar message should appear. The Ok is the BASIC prompt indicating that the system is ready for you to use. Now type:

```
FILES
```

And you should see:

```
COMMAND .COM BASIC   .COM HELLO    .BAS HELLO2   .BAS
```

Remember, FILES shows the names of the files on the diskette. Now type:

```
NEW
```

This clears the computer's memory. Type:

```
100 REM ***--DATA FILE EXAMPLE--***
120 :
140 :
160 REM **-FILE OUTPUT ROUTINE--**
180 OPEN "ADDRESS.DAT" FOR OUTPUT AS #1
200 PRINT #1,"IBM is a bright computer"
220 CLOSE #1
```

Check your typing carefully. If you make a mistake, you can use the edit keys (the arrow keys and the Ins and Del keys), to correct the mistake, or type the entire line over again. The computer will place the line in the proper sequence. Once your program matches the program above, type:

```
SAVE "EXAMPLE
```

The program is now saved on the diskette under the name EXAMPLE
.BAS. Type:

    FILES

And you now see:

    COMMAND . COM BASIC   . COM HELLO   . BAS HELLO2   . BAS
    EXAMPLE . BAS

Next type:

    LIST

just to see that the program is still in the computer's memory. Then
type:

    RUN

The disk drive comes on but little happens on the screen. Once again,
type:

    FILES

This time you get:

    COMMAND . COM BASIC   . COM HELLO   . BAS HELLO2 . BAS
    EXAMPLE . BAS ADDRESS . DAT

You have created a data file! Even though you did not actually see the
data file being written to the diskette, that is exactly what happened
immediately after you typed RUN and pressed the ENTER key. The
reason you did not see anything on the screen is that your BASIC program told the computer to print your information to the disk rather
than to the screen.

We will look at this program to see what each line does and what
the correct syntax for each should be. Line 100 provides a name for
this program. It is a good practice to make the name of the program
similar to the file name under which the program is saved on disk.
The one problem is that *the file name cannot be more than eight characters long*, while there is no limit to the length the program name can
be. REM is a BASIC reserved word meaning remark, indicating that
what follows is only a comment by the programmer and will not be
executed by the computer. The characters and words ***--DATA
FILE EXAMPLE--** are the actual comment. Lines 120 and 140 contain colons that can be used to help separate sections of programs.
Line 160 names the routine to follow. Again, it is a good idea to identify with a REM statement what it is that you are about to do. The
remark in this case indicates that we are creating a routine to write
information to the disk. Line 180 tells the computer that we are going
to use the disk to open a file called "ADDRESS.DAT". If the file

already exists, the computer prepares to use the file. If no such file exists, the computer first creates such a file and gives it the name of "ADDRESS.DAT". Notice the quotation marks around the words ADDRESS.DAT. These quotation marks must be included in the program statements. That is how the computer understands where the specific file name begins and ends. Next, we tell the computer how we are going to be using that file: FOR OUTPUT. At this point, if the file already exists, the computer destroys the contents of the file and prepares to write new information to the file. If the file has just been created, the computer knows that we want to add information to the file rather than to read information from the file. Finally, we assign a number to the file so that we will need only refer to that number when we want to access the file. Unless manually changed, the maximum number of files that can be opened at one time is three. Therefore, the number in this location will usually be either a 1, 2, or 3.

Next, we tell the computer that we are going to be adding information to the file with the PRINT #1 statement. Line 200 also tells the computer what information to put on the data file. Anything between the quotation marks will be written to the data file on the disk. The PRINT statement in this line does not print the string (the information between the quotation marks) on the screen when the program is RUN, as would normally be expected. This PRINT statement contains the file number telling the computer to print to the disk rather than to the screen. Line 220 contains the computer instruction to CLOSE the file numbered 1. This time, the file number is optional since a CLOSE, without a file number, will close *all* data files that are open. If there is only one file open, that file will be closed with this simplified CLOSE statement. For clarity's sake, it is a better programming habit to include the specific file number with the CLOSE command.

We have now put information onto a diskette. The next task is to be able to read back from the diskette what we wrote. There are a number of different ways that we can read back the information, but, for now, we will use the single program approach and add more lines to the program that wrote the information to the disk. Type:

```
LIST
```

The program should still be in the computer's memory. Add the following lines carefully:

```
240 :
260 :
280 REM **--FILE INPUT ROUTINE--**
300 OPEN "ADDRESS.DAT" FOR INPUT AS #1
320 INPUT #1,LINES$
```

```
340  CLOSE  #1
360  :
380  :
400  REM  **--DISPLAY  ROUTINE--**
420  CLS
440  LOCATE  5,1
460  PRINT  LINES$
480  END
```

Check your typing. Then type:

```
SAVE  "EXAMPLE
```

This replaces the previous and shorter version of our program. Finally, type:

```
RUN
```

No file name is necessary since the program, besides being on the diskette, is also still in the computer's memory. This time the disk drive will come on for a brief time, then the screen will go blank, and the words "IBM is a bright computer" will be printed five lines from the top of the screen.

Let's examine each line of the additional program lines. Lines 240 and 260 provide a separation between the FILE OUTPUT ROUTINE and the FILE INPUT ROUTINE. Line 280 names the next routine. Line 300 informs the computer that we want to open the file called "ADDRESS.DAT" in order to be able to read the contents of that file. We need to reopen the file in order to start at the beginning of the file in order to read from the file what we have just written. We also want the computer to identify that file as our number 1 file. We can use the number 1 since we closed the original number 1 after we finished writing our information to it. Line 320 then tells the computer to bring in from that number 1 file (INPUT #1), a copy of the first (and, in this case, the only) piece of information in the file and store that information in the string variable memory location we have labeled LINES$. A string variable is identified in BASIC by a letter or letters followed by the dollar sign, $. Variables are names assigned to locations in the computer's memory. String variables can contain just about any value; i.e., numbers, letters, punctuation, and so forth. They are referred to as "variables" because their values may vary within a program; i.e., they are not constant. An example of a string variable might be NAMES$ where the first value of NAMES$ is "ANDY", the second value is "MARY", the third value is "PAUL", and the fourth value is "JANE". Therefore, we are storing the contents of the first and only piece of information in the ADDRESS.DAT file in the computer's memory location labeled LINES$. Line 340 is the same as line 220. We close the file before proceeding to the display routine. Lines 360 and 380 again provide the separation between the various parts of the program, while line 400 names the next portion of the program. Line 420 instructs the computer to clear the screen (CLS), and line 440 positions the cursor five lines from the top of the screen and in the first column of that fifth line (LOCATE 5,1). Finally, line 460 provides the instructions necessary to display the contents of the string variable LINES$. Line 460 prints the value contained in memory location LINES$ on the screen 5 lines from the top. The computer prints this information on the screen because we have not told it that we want the information to go anywhere else. The screen is the "default" for PRINT statements. Default, in this sense, means that a certain value, the screen, has been predetermined, and unless the value is specifically changed, the predetermined value is taken as the desired value. Since we have closed our DATA file and not used a file number in the PRINT statement, the computer understands that we want the information printed on the screen.

This program is merely to give a brief explanation of the main file commands used with either sequential or random access data files. It is not intended to be a meaningful or useful program in any other sense. Such programs will begin in the next chapter. Please review this chapter and the program example, with explanation, until you are confident you fully understand what each of the BASIC data file commands, OPEN— CLOSE, INPUT #, and PRINT #— does.

Finally, let's "clean up" our diskette so that we can put some serious programs on it in the next chapter. By following the instructions given below, you will gain practice in the use of two other BASIC file commands and learn about the two modes in which the computer can operate. If you do not wish to erase these programs, you can skip what follows and start the next chapter with a fresh diskette, providing you first remember to format the new diskette and transfer a copy of the BASIC language. (Refer to Chapters 1 and 2, if necessary). Type:

```
FILES
```

The list shows:

```
COMMAND . COM BASIC    . COM HELLO    . BAS HELLO2 . BAS
EXAMPLE . BAS ADDRESS . DAT
```

Now carefully type the following:

```
KILL  "ADDRESS. DAT"
```

Then type FILES again. ADDRESS.DAT should be gone! Next type:

```
KILL  "HELLO. BAS"
NAME  "HELLO2. BAS"  AS  "HELLO. BAS"
```

You have erased one more file and changed the name of another one. As the last step, type:

```
LOAD  "HELLO
KILL  "HELLO.BAS"
SAVE  "HELLO
```

This step puts HELLO back as the first file on the diskette after the two necessary files of COMMAND.COM and BASIC.COM. If you have followed these instructions carefully, the list of files would show just four files:

```
COMMAND .COM BASIC    .COM HELLO   .BAS EXAMPLE .BAS
```

All of the steps you have just taken have been done in what is called the "immediate mode," in which what you type is acted upon immediately after the ENTER key is pressed. The immediate mode, sometimes called the direct mode, can be very helpful in determining what errors exist in your programs. Most of the work we will be doing, however, will be in what is called the "deferred mode." In the deferred mode, sometimes called the indirect mode, the computer does not follow the program instructions immediately, but waits until it is told to RUN the program. It defers action until it is specifically told to act. This is the reason for the line numbers in programs. Line numbers tell the computer the exact sequence by which the computer is to follow the program instructions. In the next chapter, we will create our first useful program.

QUESTIONS

1. Name the type of file that usually contains lists of information, rather than computer instructions.

2. Give the two kinds of data files.

3. Which kind of data file is similar to a cassette tape?

4. How many characters may a file name contain?

5. *True or False*: You can RUN a data file just as you RUN a BASIC program.

6. Give the number of modes in which the computer can operate, and name them.

7. Name the four operations usually used with data files.

8. What does REM stand for?

9. Explain what the BASIC reserved word CLS does.

10. Explain what the BASIC reserved word INPUT, without a file number, does.

11. What symbol is used to designate string variables?

12. What are variables?

ANSWERS

1. DATA files

2. Sequential access, random access

3. Sequential access

4. 8 characters and up to 3 characters for the extension

5. False

6. 2 ; immediate and deferred

7. OPEN, CLOSE, some method of writing to the file (PRINT # or PUT #), and some method of reading from the file (INPUT # or GET #)

8. REMARK

9. Clears the screen, places the cursor in the upper left corner of the screen

10. Brings information into the computer from the KEYBOARD

11. $

12. Names of locations in the computer's memory where values can be stored

EXAMPLE

```
100 REM ***--DATA FILE EXAMPLE--***
120 :
140 :
160 REM **--FILE OUTPUT ROUTINE--**
180 OPEN "ADDRESS.DAT" FOR OUTPUT AS #1
200 PRINT #1,"IBM is a bright computer"
220 CLOSE #1
240 :
260 :
280 REM **--FILE INPUT ROUTINE--**
300 OPEN "ADDRESS.DAT" FOR INPUT AS #1
320 INPUT #1,LINES$
360 :
380 :
400 REM **--DISPLAY ROUTINE--**
420 CLS
440 LOCATE 5 1
460 PRINT LINES$
480 END
```

4
Creating Sequential Files

We begin to get into the heart of our study with the first part of our examination of sequential data files. First, let's briefly review. We have seen that there are different types of files: BASIC program files, FORTRAN or COBOL (or any other language) program files, and data files. You should now understand that program files are files that contain specific instructions for the computer. Data files usually contain only lists or data, not computer instructions. We have also seen that there are two kinds of data files: sequential data files and random access data files. The difference between these two kinds of data files lies in the way the information within them is accessed: sequential files require accessing each record, one after the other, until the desired record is found; and random access allows any record to be reached directly and immediately. In the last chapter, you were introduced to a new set of BASIC file commands common to both sequential and random data files. Now, we are ready to put some of this knowledge to work and create some useful programs.

We will begin by taking a closer look at the program given in the last chapter and modifying it to make it more useful:

```
100 REM ***--DATA FILE EXAMPLE--***
120 :
140 :
160 REM **--FILE OUTPUT ROUTINE--**
180 OPEN "ADDRESS.DAT" FOR OUTPUT AS #1
200 PRINT #1,"IBM is a bright computer"
220 CLOSE #1
240 :
260 :
```

```
280 REM **--FILE INPUT ROUTINE--**
300 OPEN "ADDRESS.DAT" FOR INPUT AS #1
320 INPUT #1,LINES$
340 CLOSE #1
360 :
380 :
400 REM **--DISPLAY ROUTINE--**
420 CLS
440 LOCATE 5,1
460 PRINT LINES$
480 END
```

This is the same program from the last chapter. Take the diskette that you have been using and place it in the disk drive. Start the computer (boot the system) in one of the ways mentioned in the previous chapters. When the cursor appears, bring BASIC up and type the following to see the program instructions:

```
LOAD "EXAMPLE
LIST
```

Type:

```
RUN
```

Again, you should see the screen clear, and five lines from the top the the following will appear:

```
IBM is a bright computer
```

Type:

```
FILES
```

and you should see that ADDRESS.DAT is back! Then change line 200 to:

```
200 PRINT #1,"IBM is ok"
LIST
```

to make sure the change was made. Then type:

```
RUN
```

Yes, again! You should see:

```
IBM is ok
```

That is everything the ADDRESS.DAT file now contains. Reopening a sequential data file for output destroys the original contents of the file. In some cases, this may be exactly what you want, but in other situations, you may not want to destroy the original contents; instead, you might want to add to the file. BASIC provides a word for just such additions to sequential files: APPEND. We will soon use APPEND, but let's go back and make a useful address file program. We need to delete the ADDRESS.DAT file first, so type:

```
KILL "ADDRESS.DAT"
```

Now we can begin on the programs for the MAILING LIST SYSTEM.

MAILING LIST SYSTEM

I am not going to get involved in the discussion over flow-charting or structured programming, but as in building anything, you should have a plan. In this MAILING LIST SYSTEM, we will need several programs. The first program should create the file, and should probably have at least three different parts: an input routine, a correction routine, and a file creation routine. With this minimum plan, let's begin. We start with what might be called the housekeeping statements. Type:

```
NEW
AUTO 100
```

At this point, do not worry about making mistakes in your typing. We will go back and make corrections later. AUTO will automatically number (by 10's) the BASIC program lines for you. We have instructed the computer to begin numbering the program with line 100 and increase each number by a count of 10. If you want to end this automatic numbering, you need only press the CTRL key and the BREAK key at the same time. Type the following:

```
100 REM **--CREATE MAILING LIST--**
110 :
120 :
130 DIM LINES$(20)
140 K = 1: REM LINE COUNTER
150 :
160 :
```

Line 100 simply gives a name to the program. Line 130 uses the DIM (dimension) statement to reserve space in the computer's memory for 20 lines of up to 255 characters per line. This number of lines will be more than enough for a starter program. Line 140 uses a counter, "K", to keep track of the lines used. Type the following:

```
170 REM **--KEYBOARD INPUT ROUTINE--**
180 CLS: LOCATE 5,1: REM Clear screen, cursor 5
    lines down
```

```
190 PRINT "Type name and address as if addressing
    an envelope. "
200 PRINT: PRINT "TYPE 'END' when finished. "
```

The words LOCATE and PRINT can be typed by pressing down on the ALT key and typing the L and P keys, respectively. Upper case is achieved by either the shift key or the CAPS LOCK key. Line 170 labels the routine, and line 180 uses the BASIC reserved word CLS to clear the screen and place the cursor in the upper left-hand corner. LOCATE 5,1 provides for spacing five lines down from the top of the screen and positioning the cursor in the first column of that line. Lines 190–200 provide instructions to the person entering information: in this case, names, addresses, and phone numbers. All of these lines are optional, but I have included them because they help the user enter the information correctly. And, of course, the instructions themselves can be reworded to your own preference. BASIC commands and statements can be typed as lower case letters since the computer automatically converts them to upper case.

Now type the following:

```
210 PRINT: PRINT "Type in line ";K
220 LINE INPUT LINES$(K)
230 IF LINES$(K) = "END" OR LINES$(K) = "end"
    THEN 290
240 IF LINES$(K) = "End" THEN 290
250 IF LINES$(K) = "" THEN PRINT "We need some
    info. ":
    GOTO 190
260 K = K + 1
270 GOTO 210: REM Go back for another line
280 :
```

These lines are the heart of the keyboard input routine. Line 210 instructs the user which line is being typed in. The first PRINT prints a blank line. Next, the phrase "Type in line" is displayed. The semicolon instructs the computer to print the value of the variable K immediately following the quotation mark. Line 220 (LINE INPUT) accepts whatever is typed in and stores it in the reserved memory, depending upon the value of K. Remember that we told the computer to reserve space for 20 possible lines of LINES$. (Reserving multiple space for a variable creates an ARRAY for that variable.) We use the LINE INPUT statement so that the user can type in a comma or other punctuation if needed. The regular INPUT statement does not allow certain punctuation to be entered. Line 230 checks what was typed in to see if it equals the word "END" or "end". Since the user could type in either upper case or lower case, we should check for both. If it does equal either form of the word, the computer is instructed to jump ahead immediately to line 290. If it does not equal either an upper or lower case form of the word "END", this line is ignored and the computer goes to the next instruction in line 240. Line 240 checks for another logical form of the word "end"; i.e., "End". Again, if an exact match occurs, the computer is instructed to jump ahead to line 290. If the response does not equal this form of the word "end", this instruction is ignored, and the computer proceeds to the next line. Line 250 checks for a response that contains no information. Since all the keys on the IBM are auto repeat, it is possible for a new user to accidentally press the ENTER key for more than a fraction of a second. Without the check in line 250, such a mistake would result in a number of blank information-lines. Once more, if the condition is not met, this instruction is ignored and control passes to the next instruction. Line 260 is a method of increasing the line count. The first time through, K will equal 1, so the formula really is: K = 1 + 1, or 2. Once we have increased our line count, we want to go back and get another line, which is exactly what line 270 does.

Next, type the following:

```
290 LINES$(K)  = "*": REM Separator for phone number
300 K = K + 1
310 PRINT "Phone: ";:PRINT "Press 'ENTER' if none."
320 LINE INPUT LINES$(K)
330 K = K + 1
340 LINES$(K) = "!": REM Separator between sets of
    information
350 :
360 :
```

These may be the most confusing lines to understand. In order to easily separate the name and address from the phone number, I have included a separator, "*", on a line by itself. The reason for separating the phone number from the rest of the information is that now we can use the first part of our information to produce mailing labels. I have also included a separator, "!", to easily differentiate between the name, address, and phone number of one person and the name, address, and phone number of the next person. Therefore, line 290 sets the Kth line of LINES$ equal to "*". At this point, if the first line contains the name; the second line the address; and the third line the city, state and zip code; then the fourth line will contain the word "END", and K will be equal to 4. By making the fourth line equal to "*", we have actually accomplished two tasks: eliminating the word "END" and establishing a one character separator before the phone number. We could have required the user to type the "*" when he/she finished entering the name and address, but I prefer to have the user type something natural within the context. Line 300 increases the line count by one for the phone number. Line 310 gives instructions about typing in the phone number. Line 320 accepts whatever format the individual uses to type in the phone number and stores the information in the string reserved memory. Line 330 again increases the count by one, this time for the separator between sets of information. Line 340 makes the Kth line of LINES$ equal to "!". If the fourth line of LINES$ is "*" and the fifth line is the phone number, then K would be 6 and the sixth line would equal "!". This concludes the input routine.

The correction routine is next. Type:

```
370 REM **--CORRECTION ROUTINE--**
380 CLS: LOCATE 5,1
390 PRINT "Do not change the line with the '*'"
400 PRINT "This symbol is used as a separator."
410 PRINT
```

These lines explain what the routine is, set the format for the correction routine, and give instructions to the user about the separator, "*". Line 370 labels the routine. Line 380 clears the screen and places the curser in the upper left-hand corner five lines from the top. Lines 390 and 400 print the instructions for the user, and line 410 prints a blank line after the instructions. Now type:

```
420 FOR I = 1 TO K - 1
430 PRINT I;" ";LINES$(I)
440 NEXT I
```

Lines 420–440 make a loop that is used to get the information stored in the string reserved memory and to print that information on the screen. Line 420 is the first line of a FOR-NEXT loop. It uses a counter (I) that starts with the value of 1 and counts to the value of K − 1. In our example above, the sixth line was the last line and so was set equal to "!". Since that line should not be changed, there is no reason to display the line. Therefore, the counter only goes to K − 1, or 5. Line 430 prints the current value of the counter, a blank space, and then prints the information contained in LINES$(I) that is stored in the computer's memory. Line 440 increases the counter by one until the counter equals the value of K − 1. The instructions between the FOR instruction and the NEXT instruction are executed the number of times specified in the FOR instruction.

To conclude the correction routine, type:

```
450 PRINT
460 INPUT "Change any line? Type 'Y' or 'N' ";YES$
470 IF YES$ = "Y" OR YES$ = "y" THEN 540
480 IF YES$ = "N" OR YES$ = "n" OR YES$ = "" THEN
    520
490 PRINT: PRINT "INCORRECT CHOICE! PLEASE TRY
    AGAIN. "
500 GOTO 450: REM Ask again
510 :
520 GOTO 3000: REM Go to File Creation Routine
530 :
540 INPUT "Change which line? ";LN
550 IF LN > K - 1 THEN PRINT "Number too large":
    GOTO 540
560 IF LINES$(LN) = "*" THEN PRINT "Line";LN;"is
    the *": GOTO 540
570 PRINT "Old line = ";LINES$(LN)
580 LINE INPUT "Correct line = ";LINES$(LN)
590 GOTO 370: REM Check again
600 :
610 :
```

These lines are fairly standard correction routine lines. Line 450 prints a blank line before the question in 460. Line 460 asks the necessary question and provides instructions for answering it. The user's response is stored in the string variable YES$. Line 470 checks the answer stored in YES$ to see if it equals "Y" or "y". If it does, the computer is instructed to jump to line 540 and proceed. If it does not equal "Y" or "y", the computer goes to the next instruction in line 480. Line 480 checks for the negative responses of "N", "n", or " " (the ENTER key). If the value stored in YES$ matches one of those, control is passed to the instruction in line 520. If it does not match one of those negative responses, the computer ignores this instruction-line and proceeds to the following instruction-line. If the computer ever reaches this next line, line 490, we know that the individual typing has typed something other than either a "Y", "y", "N", "n", or " " (the ENTER key). Anything but one of these responses, in this situation, can be viewed as an incorrect response. Therefore, the instruction in line 490 tells the user that he/she has typed something wrong. Line 500 sends the computer back to line 450 to ask the original question again.

With a negative response, the computer is instructed to go to line 520. Since a negative response indicates that the typist believes all the information-lines are correct, the instruction in line 520 directs the computer to the File Creation Routine. A positive response to the question in line 460 indicates that at least one of the information-lines needs changing. Therefore, the computer is instructed to jump to the instruction in line 540 which asks the user to indicate which information-line needs changing.

Line 540 asks the number of the line that needs changing and stores that value in the variable "LN". (Notice that there is no dollar sign following LN. This indicates that this variable is a numeric variable rather than a string variable. Numeric variables can contain only numbers.) Line 550 checks to see if the user has typed a number larger than the total number of lines displayed. If that is the case, a message is printed and the computer returns to line 540 to ask again for the number of the information-line to be changed. Line 560 makes certain that the typist does not change the line with the "*". Line 570 prints the originally typed line, and line 580 waits for the user to type in the correct information. Finally, line 590 returns to line 370 to begin the correction process over again. The correction process will be repeated until the user answers the question in line 460 with an "N", "n", or " " (the ENTER key). There are a number of other lines or checks that could have been included, but these lines are sufficient for our present needs. Press the CTRL and BREAK keys. This will end the AUTO mode. Then type:

    AUTO 3000

(or press the ALT and A keys for the word AUTO) to begin automatically numbering at line 3000.

The last routine is the file creation routine. Type:

```
3000 REM **--FILE CREATION ROUTINE--**
3010 OPEN "ADDPTR.DAT" FOR OUTPUT AS #1
3020 OPEN "ADDRESS.DAT" FOR OUTPUT AS #2
3030 PRINT #1,K
3040 FOR I = 1 TO K
3050 PRINT #2,LINES$(I)
3060 NEXT I
3070 CLOSE #1,#2
3080 END
```

To quit, press the:

    CTRL and BREAK keys

We are finally down to the actual file handling routine. As you can see, the routine is quite short. The key to filing system programs is often in proper planning. If you have tried to anticipate and provide for all possible requirements, present and future, your data files can become very powerful and useful. If you are not careful in your planning, however, you may find that some of the information you thought you had in the file has been overwritten, lost, or made practically unavailable. This is the reason for including the two single character separators and the reason for lines 3010 and 3030 in this routine. Line 3010 opens a file called "ADDPTR.DAT" and readies the file to receive information. This file is also identified as #1 since we will be writing information to two separate files. This first data file will be used to keep track of the number of information-lines we have in the second data file. That is the reason for the name of this data file: ADDPTR.DAT. This data file provides a pointer value for the ADDRESS.DAT data file. Line 3030 prints the current value of K which, in our example, should be a "6". This is done to keep track of the total number of information-lines that will be kept in ADDRESS.DAT so that we know how many lines to read back into the computer with other programs. There are other ways to keep track of this number, but with sequential files, this is one of the easiest and clearest. Line 3020 opens the second data file and readies it to receive our information. Lines 3040 through 3060 are essentially the same loop as lines 420 to 440, except the information is printed to the disk instead of just the screen. This time we do want to print the separator "!", so the counter goes from 1 to the value of K. Finally, we close the files in line 3070 and end the program (3080).

One additional comment needs to be made. Lines 3030 and 3050 print information to the disk rather than to the screen because the word PRINT is followed by the # symbol, a number, a comma, and then the information that is to be written to the specific file. This is the method the computer uses to distinguish between information that is to be sent to the disk instead of the screen and, therefore, is absolutely necessary. If a file name has not been previously identified with the number, an error will occur. If an incorrect number is specified, information can be sent to the wrong file or be lost. It is very important to keep the numbers consistent with the file names.

If you have been following along and typing in the program, you can edit and make corrections to the program by using the arrow keys on the numeric keys to the right of the keyboard. Once a correction has been made, pressing the ENTER key saves the corrected version in the computer's memory. When all corrections have been made, you should save this program on disk by giving it a name such as CREATE. Remember that to save a program, you type the word "SAVE" and the program file name. Like this:

SAVE "CREATE

Or, press the F4 key on the left of the keyboard, and then type the word CREATE. Now type the word "FILES" and see if the file name is listed. It should be listed like this:

    CREATE   . BAS

At this point, you can run the program and enter your own name, address, and phone number if you wish. If you do not get the results given below, you will need to check over the program listing to see that what you have typed is entered exactly as given in this chapter. This checking process is often referred to as debugging a program; i.e., finding the mistakes that have somehow found their way into the program. The mistakes often result from unfamiliarity with the particular keyboard. The more you use the keyboard, the fewer the number of mistakes you will make. Persistence and careful checking will eventually result in a program which operates correctly. The exhilaration of finally getting a program to work is well worth the frustration *all* programmers encounter in creating programs.

When you type the word "RUN", or press the F2 key, the screen will clear and the message from lines 190–210 will appear five lines down. Type in a name and press the "ENTER" key. You will then be told to type in line number 2. If you want to type in a title for the name in the first line, you can. If no title is needed, then type in the street address, and press "ENTER". This process should continue until you type in the word "END" ("end", "End"). When you do type some form of the word "END", you will be asked for the phone number and told that if there is no phone number, you should just press "ENTER".

After the phone number has been typed, you are shown a list of the lines you have typed and asked if you wish to change any of those lines. If you do want to change a line, you must answer the question with a "Y" (or a "y"). If you do not, either type an "N" and the "ENTER" key or just the "ENTER" key. If you need to make changes and have a typed a "Y" (or "y"), you will then be asked which line number you want to change. Respond with one of the numbers on the screen. You will then be shown the originally-typed line and asked for the correct information for this line. After typing in the new line and pressing "ENTER", you will be shown the list of lines again, this time with the new line in place of the old line. You can make as many changes as you wish. When you are satisfied and do not wish to make any more changes, a response of "N" (or just the "ENTER" key) to the question about changes will instruct the computer to write the information out to the disk. The disk drive will come on for a few seconds, and then the Ok prompt will reappear. Now if you type "FILES", in addition to the previously created files, you should see:

ADDPTR   . DAT ADDRESS . DAT

Two additional files have been created with this one program. ADDPTR.DAT has been created to store the number of information-lines now in ADDRESS.DAT. In other words, the first file keeps track of the amount of information in the second file.

Two questions arise at this point. How do you add more names to this file, and how do you actually see what is in the file? As you may have realized by now, there are a number of possible answers. One answer would be to add more lines to this program so that the program reads back what it just wrote to disk. Another answer is to write a separate program, and possibly a program menu, that would be able to switch easily between programs that write information and programs that read the information. In the next chapter, we will explore a number of these possibilities and see a little of what can be done with the information once it is safely and correctly on disk.

To conclude this chapter, I am going to show you a quick way to see what is in data files. Make sure you have saved your program, and then type the following:

SYSTEM

Now type:

TYPE ADDPTR. DAT

The number 6 (or the number of information-lines you had) should appear on the screen. Next type:

TYPE ADDRESS. DAT

The information you provided should be displayed on the screen. The TYPE command is a DOS (Disk Operating System) command telling the computer to display the contents of disk files. It is one of a number of DOS commands that is useful and flexible. Although the emphasis of this book is on the instruction in the use of IBM BASIC file commands, I will include some information on certain DOS commands. (This book is by no means a comprehensive instruction manual on *all* DOS commands.) To conclude this chapter, type:

DIR

and note the different information provided under DOS as opposed to the information given under BASIC with the FILES command.

QUESTIONS

1. *True or False:* Information in a sequential access file can be overwritten by additional information.
2. What BASIC reserved word is used to initiate a sequential data file?
3. Name the three main parts (or routines) in the CREATE program.
4. What does reserving multiple space for a variable create?
5. What symbol did we use to separate sets of information?
6. What does DIM stand for?
7. "FOR I = 1 TO K" is the first line in what kind of loop?
8. The program user's response is tested by what kind of BASIC statement?
9. What DOS command allows us to see the contents of a data file?

ANSWERS

1. False; opening a sequential file for OUTPUT erases the entire contents of any file with the same name.

2. OPEN

3. INPUT, CORRECTION, and FILE routines

4. An ARRAY

5. !

6. Dimension

7. FOR-NEXT loop

8. An IF ... THEN statement; check lines 230, 240, 250, 470, 480, 550, and 560.

9. TYPE

CREATE

```
100 REM ***--CREATE MAILING LIST--***
110 :
120 :
130 DIM LINES$(20)
140 K = 1: REM LINE COUNTER
150 :
160 :
170 REM **--KEYBOARD INPUT ROUTINE--**
180 CLS: LOCATE 5,1: REM Clear screen, cursor 5 lines down
190 PRINT "Type name and address as if addressing an envel
    ope."
200 PRINT : PRINT "Type `END' when finished."
210 PRINT : PRINT "Type in line ";K
220 LINE INPUT LINES$(K)
230 IF LINES$(K) = "END" OR LINES$(K) = "end" THEN 290
240 IF LINES$(K) = "End" THEN 290
250 IF LINES$(K) = "" THEN PRINT "We need some info.":
    GOTO 190
260 K = K + 1
270 GOTO 210: REM Go back for another line
280 :
290 LINES$(K) = "*": REM Separator for phone number
300 K = K + 1
310 PRINT "Phone: ";: PRINT "Press `ENTER' if none."
320 LINE INPUT LINES$(K)
330 K = K + 1
340 LINES$(K) = "|": REM Separator between sets of informa
    tion
350 :
360 :
370 REM **--CORRECTION ROUTINE--**
380 CLS: LOCATE 5,1
390 PRINT "Do not change the line with the `*'"
400 PRINT "This symbol is used as a separator."
410 PRINT
420 FOR I = 1 TO K - 1
430 PRINT I;" ";LINES$(I)
440 NEXT I
450 PRINT
460 INPUT "Change any line? Type `Y' or `N' ";YES$
470 IF YES$ = "Y" OR YES$ = "y" THEN 540
480 IF YES$ = "N" OR YES$ = "n" OR YES$ = "" THEN 520
490 PRINT: PRINT "INCORRECT CHOICE! PLEASE TRY AGAIN."
500 GOTO 450: REM Ask again
510 :
520 GOTO 3000: REM Go to File Creation Routine
530 :
540 INPUT "Change which line ";LN
550 IF LN > K - 1 THEN PRINT "Number too large": GOTO 540
```

```
560 IF LINES$(LN) = "*" THEN PRINT "Line";LN;"is the *":
    GOTO 540
570 PRINT "Old line = ";LINES$(LN)
580 LINE INPUT "Correct line = ";LINES$(LN)
590 GOTO 370: REM Check again
600 :
610 :
3000 REM **--FILE CREATION ROUTINE--**
3010 OPEN "ADDPTR.DAT" FOR OUTPUT AS #1
3020 OPEN "ADDRESS.DAT" FOR OUTPUT AS #2
3030 PRINT #1,K
3040 FOR I = 1 TO K
3050 PRINT #2,LINES$(I)
3060 NEXT I
3070 CLOSE #1,#2
3080 END
```

5
Appending Sequential Files

Now the fun begins. We have created a file, but as you will soon see, the creation is one of the easiest parts of file manipulation. There are two things we would like to do immediately with this file: add to the file, and read what is in the file. Both tasks are easy to do, but because the job of reading is simpler to explain, and more rewarding, we will go over a short program to read the file first. Type the following:

```
100 REM **--MAILING LIST READER1--**
120 :
140 :
160 REM **--FILE INPUT ROUTINE--**
180 OPEN "ADDPTR.DAT" FOR INPUT AS #1
200 OPEN "ADDRESS.DAT" FOR INPUT AS #2
220 INPUT #1,K: REM Get number of records
240 CLOSE #1
260 DIM LINES$(K)
280 FOR I = 1 TO K
300 LINE INPUT #2,LINES$(I)
320 NEXT I
340 CLOSE #2
360 :
380 :
```

By now, lines 100 and 160 should be clear. They name the program and the first routine. Line 180 tells the computer that we want to use the disk and that we want to open the ADDPTR.DAT file as file #1 in order to bring in the number of information-lines stored in our main data file. Line 200 opens that main data file called ADDRESS.DAT as our second file. This instruction-line also opens the file in such a way

(FOR INPUT) that information can only be read from the file, not written to the file. Line 220 brings in the value for the number of lines we wrote to the disk in our file creation program from file #1. If you are not clear on this, check back to the explanation of lines 3010 and 3030 in the previous chapter. We are simply reading back the number written in those lines. Line 260 reserves space in the computer for the information we will be bringing in from the disk. Since we are not sure of the exact number of lines, and the number will change every time we add information, we should use the variable "K", which will always equal the number of lines that have been written. Now, we can bring in a copy of the information contained in the file. Lines 280, 300, and 320 bring in that data. Line 280 establishes the boundaries for the loop. We want the count to go from the first line to the last line, represented by the variable K. Because we have identified the file by its number, the computer understands that the LINE INPUT statement in line 300 refers to the disk and not the keyboard. This instruction-line tells the computer to go to the disk and obtain a copy of the information contained in the information-line specified by the variable I. The operation works on the same principle as the logic of lines 3040 to 3060 in our file creation program, but this time, we are bringing information into the computer from the disk instead of transferring information from the computer to the disk. Now, the information physically exists in two locations. One location is in the computer's memory, and the other location is still out on the disk. By bringing the information into the computer, we have not erased the information on the disk. Merely reading a file does not disturb the contents of that file. Finally, line 340 closes the file. If you run this program, you are not likely to see anything happen except the appearance of the word "OK". We need a routine that will display the information, and, in the next chapter, we will become deeply involved in different ways of displaying our information. For now, the following routine will get the job done. Type:

```
400 REM **--DISPLAY ROUTINE--**
420 CLS: LOCATE 5,1
440 FOR I = 1 TO K
460 PRINT LINES$(I)
480 NEXT I
500 END
```

Our input routine can be used in a number of different programs to bring in all the information from the file, but our display routine will not be functional in very many situations. We will alter this routine later to make it more useable (see Chapter 6). Save this program as READER1, then type FILES to see the list of files now on the disk.

Type:

```
SAVE  "READER1
FILES
```

and you should see:

```
COMMAND . COM BASIC   . COM HELLO     . BAS EXAMPLE . BAS
CREATE    . BAS ADDPTR . DAT ADDRESS . DAT READER1 . BAS
```

Finally, type:

```
RUN
```

or press the F2 key. The information you provided when you used the CREATE program should be displayed on the screen. If it is not, you need to check back over your programs to see that they are entered exactly as given in this book.

In the last chapter, you created a file, ADDRESS.DAT, and wrote the first group of lines containing information to that file. Now, you have read that information back and displayed it. Next, you need to be able to add more information to the file. If you run the file creation program again and use a different set of information-lines, what will happen? Will the new information be added to the file? Will the old information be replaced? If you do not know for certain what will happen, look at the explanation on page 28 concerning reopening a sequential data file for output. Every time this program is RUN, the computer is instructed to erase or delete ADDRESS.DAT before writing any new information. What happens to the first set of information-lines already on the disk if you try to use this program to add a second set of information-lines? That first set is erased, so you need a third program to add more lines of information to your ADDRESS.DAT file. (For those of you itching to put all these programs into one large program, have patience. I will eventually explain how these programs can be tied together without actually existing as one large program.) This third program is really just a modification of the file creation program. But the modification needs to be done, or, as we have seen, the results will be worthless. The modification is relatively simple if you closely follow the instructions given below.

Down to line 610 of the CREATE program (see the complete listing at the end of Chapter 4), the new program can be the same with one minor change. First, load the CREATE program, and then list it to see a complete listing of the instructions in this program. Type:

```
LOAD  "CREATE
LIST
```

Pressing the F3 key displays the word LOAD with the quotation mark so that the file name is the only thing that needs to be typed. All of the program will not fit on the screen at one time. The first instructions disappear from view off the top of the screen. In BASIC, you can list to a certain instruction-line number, or from a certain instruction-line number to the end of the program, or from one line number to another, like this:

```
LIST - 200
LIST 350-
LIST 100-800
```

The F1 key displays the word LIST when pressed. Line 100 should be changed to read:

```
100 REM ***--MAILING LIST ADDER1--**
```

Except for that one change, the CREATE program works fine down to line 610 for our new ADDER1 program, so be certain to make that change before continuing.

The logic for the placement of these next two routines will become clear a little later. For now, add these lines:

```
2000 REM **--REPEAT ROUTINE--**
2010 CLS : LOCATE 5,1
2020 PRINT "Do you want to add more information?"
2030 INPUT "Type 'Y' or 'N' ";YES$
2040 IF YES$ = "Y" OR YES$ = "y" THEN RUN
2050 RUN "MAILMENU
2060 :
2070 :
```

Line 2000 names the routine. Line 2010, as we have seen, clears the screen and spaces down five lines. Line 2020 prints the question about additional information, and line 2030 uses the INPUT statement to wait for a response from the user. The computer knows to wait for the response from the keyboard, because we have not identified a file number with the INPUT statement. Line 2040 checks the response. If the response equals "Y" or "y", then the computer is instructed to "RUN" the program again. If the response is anything else, the computer goes to the next line for its instruction. Line 2050 tells the computer to end this program and to RUN the program called "MAIL-MENU". (MAILMENU, which will be discussed in detail in the next chapter, will be our means of simulating a large program with a number of options.) Neither the choice to add more information nor the choice to run the MAILMENU program writes anything to the disk. Therefore, we need another routine, the File Addition Routine. Rather than modifying the File Creation Routine, it is probably best to delete the old routine and then type in the new instructions. Type:

```
DELETE 3000-3080
```

This new routine will do three things: (1) check to see how many infor-mation-lines are currently in the ADDRESS.DAT file, (2) add the number of information-lines in the file to the number of new informa-tion-lines for a revised information-line total, and (3) actually append the new information-lines to the ADDRESS.DAT file. Type:

```
3000  REM  **--FILE ADDITION ROUTINE--**
3010  OPEN "ADDPTR.DAT" FOR INPUT AS #1
3020  INPUT #1,REC: REM Get number of records
3030  CLOSE #1
3040  :
```

This part of the routine should look somewhat familiar. It is almost exactly the same as the first few lines in our program to read the file (READER1). Line 3000 again names the routine. Line 3010 opens the pointer file for input as the first file. Line 3020 tells the computer we want to read the number one file (ADDPTR.DAT) and input the same number as line 220 in the READER1 program. This time, however, we want to store its value in the variable REC (for record). We cannot use the variable K because we are already using it in the first part of our program and want to continue using it. Once again, this number represents the number of lines of information already in the file. Line 3030 then closes the file.

Next type:

```
3050 REC = REC + K
3060 OPEN "ADDPTR.DAT" FOR OUTPUT AS #1
3070 PRINT #1,REC
3080 CLOSE #1
3090 :
```

These lines add up the number of lines already on the disk to the number of new lines we have just typed into the computer. This new total is then written back out to the disk over the previous total. Line 3050 provides the method for totaling the previous line count with the additional number of new lines. The logic for this line is the same as for our now standard "K = K + 1" lines. If you are not clear about this logic, it is best to just accept that this is one way the com-puter totals things. The other lines should be clear. Line 3060 opens the file and prepares to write to the file; line 3070 actually writes the new total of the line count to the disk, and line 3080 closes the file. It is necessary to open the file again, this time for output, in order to write the new line count total to the pointer file.

The following is the actual part of the routine that adds new information-lines to the existing ADDRESS.DAT file. Type:

```
3100 OPEN "ADDRESS.DAT" FOR APPEND AS #2
3110 FOR I = 1 TO K
3120 PRINT #2,LINES$(I)
3130 NEXT I
3140 CLOSE #2
3150 :
3160 GOTO 2000: REM Go to Repeat Routine
```

Line 3100 uses a new BASIC file commend, APPEND, to do just what it says. It appends, or adds, to the file rather than overwriting any of the information already in the file. This line tells the computer to open the ADDRESS.DAT file as the number two file and prepare to add to it. From line 3110 on, the routine is the same as the routine in the CREATE program (lines 3040 to 3060). Line 3110 sets up the loop; line 3120 prints the information in line "I" to the disk after the information already on the disk. Line 3130 goes back for another line of information, and line 3140 closes the file. Line 3160 directs the computer to jump back up to the instruction in line 2000, which is the start of the routine that asks if the user wants to add more information. Thus, we have finished the program to add more information to our ADDRESS.DAT file. You should now save this new program to the disk as ADDER1.

```
SAVE "ADDER1
```

You can check your typing by going over the complete listing of the program given at the end of this chapter. Please remember that it is very important to follow along by typing the necessary lines on your IBM.

We now have three complete programs: CREATE, READER1, and ADDER1. The combination of these programs will create a file, add information to the file, and read information back from that file. The three programs adequately demonstrate the procedures used to accomplish these tasks, but the programs are not really very useful or practical as they now exist. For instance, every time you run the READER1 program, you will read the entire file and display the entire file. This happens even if you want only one name and address. After just a few names and addresses are added to the file, the list will begin to disappear off the top of the screen during display. It is quite obvious that more modification needs to be done in order to make these programs useful. If you are already a good programmer in BASIC, you probably have some ideas about "features", or additional options, you would like to see in one or more of these programs. If you have little experience in programming, you will soon become much more experienced.

I am going to add a few features to these programs and fully explain each additional step. If you would like to include these options and become more experienced at programming, especially with file information data, closely follow the different programming lines and explanations given. If you don't need these features, or if you want to create your own, you might want to skip ahead to Chapter 8 on advanced sequential data file manipulation. Or, if you have had enough of sequential data files, you might want to jump immediately to Chapter 10 on random access data files. We will be using some of these same routines in the chapters on random access, but I will not go into the same explanatory detail then as in these present chapters. Let's begin adding features to our three programs and making them more useful.

ADDER2

We will begin by modifying the ADDER1 program. If you have used this program to enter a number of names and addresses, you will have noticed that the disk operates every time you have accepted a set of information-lines as correct. This disk operation may not bother you if you are somewhat slow in typing or are in no hurry to enter a large number of names and addresses, but there is no reason that the disk needs to operate after every name. Why not write the information out to disk only after we have finished entering all of our information-lines? Such a change is clearly a preference feature that proponents and opponents often argue about. In this situation, I prefer to enter all of my information before writing any of it to the disk. In another situation, I may want to print a mailing label of the information I have just entered before typing in a second set of information-lines. This is obviously a preference feature, and it will do you no good if you do not have a printer. If you do not have a printer, the routine may still be of interest because you will be formatting your display in a new way.

The first two additional routines will be to the ADDER1 program. The first will consist of adding lines of computer instructions to allow the user to print out, in a mailing label, the information the user just entered. The second includes the computer instructions necessary so that the information will be written to the disk after all information for the current session has been entered and corrected. The additional computer instructions necessary to include both of these features are fairly small in number.

PRINT LABEL ROUTINE

First, we will begin with the PRINT LABEL ROUTINE. Add the following lines to the ADDER1 program: (Remember that if the ADDER1 program is not already in memory, you must load it into the computer's memory from the diskette.)

```
1000 REM **--PRINT LABEL ROUTINE--**
1010 CLS: LOCATE 5,1
1020 PRINT "You may now print a mailing label.
     Please make"
1030 PRINT "sure the Printer is on and ready to
     use."
1040 PRINT
1050 ON ERROR GOTO 0: REM Reset the error flag
```

Line 1000 gives the title of the routine. Line 1010 clears the screen and places the cursor five lines from the top. Lines 1020 and 1030 print (display on the screen) instructions for the user. Line 1040 prints a blank line so that any user instruction that follows will not come immediately below the last line. Line 1050 is the real puzzle in this section of code. Rather than explain the ON ERROR GOTO statement at this time, I will wait until the actual error-trapping line appears in the next section of code.

The label routine is next. Type:

```
1060 PRINT "Do you want to print a label now?"
1070 INPUT "Type 'Y' or 'N' ";YES$
1080 IF YES$ = "Y" OR YES$ = "y" THEN GOTO 1110
1090 GOTO 2000: REM If no label, then go to Repeat
     Routine
1100 :
1110 ON ERROR GOTO 1200: REM Go to Printer Error
     Routine
1120 FOR I = 1 TO K
1130 IF LINES$(I) = "*" THEN I = I + 1: GOTO 1160
1140 IF LINES$(I) = "!" THEN 1160
1150 LPRINT LINES$(I)
1160 NEXT I
1170 ON ERROR GOTO 0: REM Reset error flag
1180 GOTO 2000: REM Go to Repeat Routine
1190 :
1200 REM **--PRINTER ERROR ROUTINE--**
1210 PRINT
1220 PRINT "Either you do not have a printer or it
     is not on."
```

```
1230 PRINT
1240 RESUME 1020: REM Ask again
1250 :
1260 :
```

Change line 520 to:

```
520 GOTO 1000: REM Go to Print Label Routine
```

With these few additional instructions, we can now print a mailing label of the information just entered. Line 1060 prints the question while line 1070 waits for the response from the keyboard, and line 1080 checks the response. If the response is positive, which indicates that a printed label is desired, the computer is instructed to jump over the next line and go on to the rest of the routine. Line 1090 is only reached if the response is something other than "Y" or "y". In other words, the computer will treat everything but a "Y" or "y" as a negative response, indicating that the user does not want a printed label. If the user presses the ENTER key instead of either the "Y" or "N" keys, the computer will view that as a negative response. Negative responses end the routine and transfer the computer to the instruction at line 2000 for the REPEAT ROUTINE.

Line 1110 checks for an error condition that may occur during execution of the next instructions. If the system does not have a printer or if the printer is not turned on, the computer will report an error when it tries to follow the instruction in line 1150; i.e., LPRINT LINES$(I). Without this ON ERROR GOTO instruction, the computer would halt operation after reporting the error statement. (Usually, the message "Device timeout" will be displayed.) With this instruction in line 1110, however, the computer is told to go to a Printer Error Routine instead of halting operation. Then, in the Printer Error Routine, the user is informed that either they do not have a printer or it is not on (line 1220). The next instruction (line 1240) tells the computer to resume normal operation at instruction-line 1020, where the user is again asked if he/she wants to print a label.

The instruction in line 1120 is the now-familiar beginning of the loop. Lines 1130 and 1140 are different from anything you have had so far. Line 1130 checks the contents of each LINES$ string for the "*" symbol. If, and only if, it locates that symbol, it instructs the computer to add 1 to the value of the variable I and then to proceed to the instruction at line 1160. The reason for this is simple but hard to explain. When the computer comes to an asterisk, we do not want that asterisk printed, nor do we want the phone number printed in a mailing label. So, we skip printing the asterisk and the phone number by adding 1 to the counter (I) and jumping to the end of the loop, line 1160. Line 1160 increases the counter by one more, so we have skipped two lines in the file: the lines that contained the separator symbol "*" and the phone number. I think this will become clear, if not already so, when you type in and try the routine. Line 1140 does much the same thing. It tells the computer to jump over the LPRINT statement and go to the instruction that increases the counter. Thus, we are "skipping over" the "!" separator symbol and not printing it either. Line 1150 does the printing. It prints to the printer the contents of every string in LINES$ that is not either a "*", "!", or phone number, unless the phone number has been typed in before the "*" symbol. The information is sent to the printer instead of the screen because we have used the BASIC statement LPRINT instead of PRINT. In the next chapter, we will see how we can send information to either the printer or the screen with just one line of code, but for this routine, the LPRINT statement is sufficient. Line 1110, as I have said, increases the counter. When the loop is finished, when all lines of information have either been printed or skipped and the I counter has reached the value of K, then the computer can go on to the next instruction "outside" the loop. Line 1170 is the first instruction outside the loop, and because we are finished printing, we need to "turn off the error flag" or "reset the error flag" to its normal condition. We can do this now because the computer has obviously reached this point without encountering a printer error. If other, non-printer errors should occur, we would not want the computer to return to the Printer Error Routine. That is why the error flag is turned off at the beginning of the routine. Without line 1050, it would be possible for the error flag to be activated, the user then to change his/her mind and depart the PRINT LABEL ROUTINE, thus leaving the error flag still set. The ON ERROR GOTO and RESUME statements must be used with extreme care or some very undesirable results may occur. Line 1180 simply transfers control to the REPEAT ROUTINE. We are now finished with the PRINT LABEL ROUTINE.

REPEAT ROUTINE

The new REPEAT ROUTINE is even shorter and easier than the PRINT LABEL ROUTINE. Add the following to line 130:

```
, TOTAL. LINES$ (100)
```

Line 130 now reads:

```
130 DIM LINES$ (20) , TOTAL. LINES$ (100)
```

Add the following lines:

```
2012 FOR I = 1 TO K
2014 TOTAL.LINES$(TK + I) = LINES$(I)
2016 NEXT I
2018 TK = TK + K
```

Change line 2040 to read:

```
2040 IF YES$ = "Y" OR YES$ = "y" THEN GOTO 140
```

Change the following lines to:

```
2050 REM If no more info, go to File Addition
     Routine
3050 REC = REC + TK
3110 FOR I = 1 TO TK
3120 PRINT #2, TOTAL.LINES$(I)
3160 RUN "MAILMENU
```

They look like such small changes, but when viewed by the computer, the changed and added instructions make quite a difference in the way the program works. The program now becomes more practical. First, we have added another string variable, and, therefore, we must have the computer reserve memory for the contents of this new variable. That is what the added code does in line 130. We have DIMensioned the string variable, TOTAL.LINES$, so that we can now add 100 lines of information before we need to write the information to the disk. You can make this number smaller or larger. The number 100 was a completely arbitrary choice. You must be careful about the choice of variable names though. You cannot use a dash or almost any other punctuation to separate the words TOTAL and LINES. Variables that contain (or are) reserved words must be used with caution. For instance, LINE$ cannot be used, but LINES$ is acceptable. Check your selection of variable names very carefully.

Next, we have added four lines of code: 2012, 2014, 2016, 2018. The choice of these line numbers was also arbitrary. They could just as easily have been any combination between 2011 and 2019. Line 2012 is the start of a loop. Line 2014 is the real reason for the loop, and the instruction that allows us to continue entering information without the necessity of writing each set of information to the disk separately. Again, the logic is fairly easy. We are going to keep the contents of the string variable LINES$ in the string variable TOTAL.LINES$ also. Then, since we have the information stored in two locations in the computer, we can use the LINES$ string variable over again. In other words, we have moved the information from one memory location to another memory location. We have moved it from

LINES$(1) TO TOTAL.LINES$(1), and from LINES$(2) to TOTAL.LINES$(2), etc. The instruction at line 2018 helps us keep track of all the lines that are typed in. TK (which may stand for Total K) is a cumulative total of all the lines of information typed in during one session. For the first set of information-lines, the value of TK is a zero since we have not previously given TK any value. After the first set of information-lines, TK becomes the value of K, or the number of lines of information in the first set of information. In the loop, we have moved the contents of the second LINES$(1) to TOTAL.LINES$(TK + 1), LINES$(2) to TOTAL.LINES$(TK + 2), etc. This process can continue until we have accumulated 100 lines of information (or more if you have dimensioned TOTAL.LINES$ to more than 100). If you are adding more lines of information, line 2040 must direct the computer to begin again by resetting the counter K to 1 and then proceeding with the Keyboard Input Routine. Finally, line 3120 is changed to write the information contained in the string variable TOTAL.LINES$ instead of the contents of LINES$. This last change is a very important one and will mess up the file badly if it is not made. In the next chapter, we will add some features to our display program and combine all our programs so that they can operate together. When you have made the necessary changes, be sure to save this new version. There are several ways of saving a new version of the same program. But for now, type the following:

    SAVE "ADDER2

Then type FILES and you should see:

```
COMMAND  . COM BASIC   . COM HELLO    . BAS EXAMPLE  . BAS
CREATE   . BAS ADDPTR  . DAT ADDRESS  . DAT READER1  . BAS
ADDER1   . BAS ADDER2  . BAS
```

QUESTIONS

1. *True or False:* Running the CREATE program a second time with new information does no harm to the first information stored in the ADDRESS.DAT file.

2. Give the name of the BASIC command that erases program lines from the computer's memory.

3. To what does line 3120 in the ADDER1 program print the information?

4. What is the BASIC word used to tell the computer to jump to a certain line number?

5. Give the purpose of the first four function keys while in BASIC.

6. What BASIC command allows us to add information to an existing sequential data file?

ANSWERS

1. False

2. DELETE

3. Disk or diskette

4. GOTO

5. F1 = LIST
   F2 = RUN and the equivalent of pressing the ENTER key
   F3 = LOAD with the necessary "
   F4 = SAVE with the necessary "

6. APPEND, opening a sequential file with the APPEND command

READER1A

```
100 REM **--MAILING LIST READER1--**
120 :
140 :
160 REM **--FILE INPUT ROUTINE--**
180 OPEN "ADDPTR.DAT" FOR INPUT AS #1
200 OPEN "ADDRESS.DAT" FOR INPUT AS #2
220 INPUT #1,K: REM Get number of records
240 CLOSE #1
260 DIM LINES$(K)
280 FOR I = 1 TO K
300 LINE INPUT #2,LINES$(I)
320 NEXT I
340 CLOSE #2
360 :
380 :
400 REM **--DISPLAY ROUTINE--**
420 CLS: LOCATE 5,1
440 FOR I = 1 TO K
460 PRINT LINES$(I)
480 NEXT I
500 END
```

ADDER1

```
100 REM ***--MAILING LIST ADDER1--***
110 :
120 :
130 DIM LINES$(20)
140 K = 1: REM LINE COUNTER
150 :
160 :
170 REM **--KEYBOARD INPUT ROUTINE--**
180 CLS: LOCATE 5,1: REM Clear screen, cursor 5 lines down
190 PRINT "Type name and address as if addressing an envel
    ope."
200 PRINT : PRINT "Type `END' when finished."
210 PRINT : PRINT "Type in line ";K
220 LINE INPUT LINES$(K)
230 IF LINES$(K) = "END" OR LINES$(K) = "end" THEN 290
240 IF LINES$(K) = "End" THEN 290
250 IF LINES$(K) = "" THEN PRINT "We need some info.": GO
    TO 190
260 K = K + 1
270 GOTO 210: REM Go back for another line
280 :
290 LINES$(K) = "*": REM Separator for phone number
300 K = K + 1
310 PRINT "Phone: ";: PRINT "Press `ENTER' if none."
320 LINE INPUT LINES$(K)
330 K = K + 1
340 LINES$(K) = "|": REM Separator between sets of informa
    tion
350 :
360 :
370 REM **--CORRECTION ROUTINE--**
380 CLS: LOCATE 5,1
390 PRINT "Do not change the line with the `*'"
400 PRINT "This symbol is used as a separator."
410 PRINT
420 FOR I = 1 TO K - 1
430 PRINT I;" ";LINES$(I)
440 NEXT I
450 PRINT
460 INPUT "Change any line? Type `Y' or `N' ";YES$
470 IF YES$ = "Y" OR YES$ = "y" THEN 540
480 IF YES$ = "N" OR YES$ = "n" OR YES$ = "" THEN 520
490 PRINT: PRINT "INCORRECT CHOICE! PLEASE TRY AGAIN."
500 GOTO 450: REM Ask again
510 :
520 GOTO 3000: REM Go to File Addition Routine
530 :
540 INPUT "Change which line ";LN
550 IF LN > K - 1 THEN PRINT "Number too large": GOTO 540
```

```
560 IF LINES$(LN) = "*" THEN PRINT "Line";LN;"is the *":
    GOTO 540
570 PRINT "Old line = ";LINES$(LN)
580 LINE INPUT "Correct line = ";LINES$(LN)
590 GOTO 370: REM Check again
600 :
610 :
2000 REM **--REPEAT ROUTINE--**
2010 CLS: LOCATE 5,1
2020 PRINT "Do you want to add more information?"
2030 INPUT "Type `Y' or `N' ";YES$
2040 IF YES$ = "Y" OR YES$ = "y" THEN RUN
2050 RUN "MAILMENU
2060 :
2070 :
3000 REM **--FILE ADDITION ROUTINE--**
3010 OPEN "ADDPTR.DAT" FOR INPUT AS #1
3020 INPUT #1,REC: REM Get number of records
3030 CLOSE #1
3040 :
3050 REC = REC + K
3060 OPEN "ADDPTR.DAT" FOR OUTPUT AS #1
3070 PRINT #1,REC
3080 CLOSE #1
3090 :
3100 OPEN "ADDRESS.DAT" FOR APPEND AS #2
3110 FOR I = 1 TO K
3120 PRINT #2,LINES$(I)
3130 NEXT I
3140 CLOSE #2
3150 :
3160 GOTO 2000: REM Repeat Routine
```

ADDER2

```
100 REM ***--MAILING LIST ADDER2--***
110 :
120 :
130 DIM LINES$(20),TOTAL.LINES$(100)
140 K = 1: REM LINE COUNTER
150 :
160 :
170 REM **--KEYBOARD INPUT ROUTINE--**
180 CLS: LOCATE 5,1: REM Clear screen, cursor 5 lines down
190 PRINT "Type name and address as if addressing an envel
    ope."
200 PRINT : PRINT "Type `END' when finished."
210 PRINT : PRINT "Type in line ";K
220 LINE INPUT LINES$(K)
230 IF LINES$(K) = "END" OR LINES$(K) = "end" THEN 290
240 IF LINES$(K) = "End" THEN 290
250 IF LINES$(K) = "" THEN PRINT "We need some info.": GO
    TO 190
260 K = K + 1
270 GOTO 210: REM Go back for another line
280 :
290 LINES$(K) = "*": REM Separator for phone number
300 K = K + 1
310 PRINT "Phone: ";: PRINT "Press `ENTER' if none."
320 LINE INPUT LINES$(K)
330 K = K + 1
340 LINES$(K) = "|": REM Separator between sets of informa
    tion
350 :
360 :
370 REM **--CORRECTION ROUTINE--**
380 CLS: LOCATE 5,1
390 PRINT "Do not change the line with the `*'"
400 PRINT "This symbol is used as a separator."
410 PRINT
420 FOR I = 1 TO K - 1
430 PRINT I;" ";LINES$(I)
440 NEXT I
450 PRINT
460 INPUT "Change any line? Type `Y' or `N' ";YES$
470 IF YES$ = "Y" OR YES$ = "y" THEN 540
480 IF YES$ = "N" OR YES$ = "n" OR YES$ = "" THEN 520
490 PRINT: PRINT "INCORRECT CHOICE! PLEASE TRY AGAIN."
500 GOTO 450: REM Ask again
510 :
520 GOTO 1000: REM Go to Print Label Routine
530 :
540 INPUT "Change which line ";LN
550 IF LN > K - 1 THEN PRINT "Number too large": GOTO 540
```

```
560 IF LINES$(LN) = "*" THEN PRINT "Line";LN;"is the *":
    GOTO 540
570 PRINT "Old line = ";LINES$(LN)
580 LINE INPUT "Correct line = ";LINES$(LN)
590 GOTO 370: REM Check again
600 :
610 :
1000 REM **--PRINT LABEL ROUTINE--**
1010 CLS: LOCATE 5,1
1020 PRINT "You may now print a mailing label. Please make"
1030 PRINT "sure the printer is on and ready to use."
1040 PRINT
1050 ON ERROR GOTO 0: REM Reset error flag
1060 PRINT "Do you want to print a label now?"
1070 INPUT "Type a `Y' or `N' ";YES$
1080 IF YES$ = "Y" OR YES$ = "y" THEN GOTO 1110
1090 GOTO 2000: REM If no label, then go to Repeat Routine
1100 :
1110 ON ERROR GOTO 1200: REM Go to Printer Error Routine
1120 FOR I = 1 TO K
1130 IF LINES$(I) = "*" THEN I = I + 1: GOTO 1160
1140 IF LINES$(I) = "|" THEN 1160
1150 LPRINT LINES$(I)
1160 NEXT I
1170 ON ERROR GOTO 0: REM Reset error flag
1180 GOTO 2000: REM Go to Repeat Routine
1190 :
1200 REM **--PRINTER ERROR ROUTINE--**
1210 PRINT
1220 PRINT "Either you do not have a printer or it is not
    on."
1230 PRINT
1240 RESUME 1020: REM Ask again
1250 :
1260 :
2000 REM **--REPEAT ROUTINE--**
2010 CLS: LOCATE 5,1
2012 FOR I = 1 TO K
2014 TOTAL.LINES$(TK + I) = LINES$(I)
2016 NEXT I
2018 TK = TK + K
2020 PRINT "Do you want to add more information?"
2030 INPUT "Type `Y' or `N' ";YES$
2040 IF YES$ = "Y" OR YES$ = "y" THEN GOTO 140
2050 REM If no more info, go to File Addition Routine
2060 :
2070 :
3000 REM **--FILE ADDITION ROUTINE--**
3010 OPEN "ADDPTR.DAT" FOR INPUT AS #1
3020 INPUT #1,REC: REM Get number of records
3030 CLOSE #1
3040 :
3050 REC = REC + TK
```

```
3060 OPEN "ADDPTR.DAT" FOR OUTPUT AS #1
3070 PRINT #1,REC
3080 CLOSE #1
3090 :
3100 OPEN "ADDRESS.DAT" FOR APPEND AS #2
3110 FOR I = 1 TO TK
3120 PRINT #2,TOTAL.LINES$(I)
3130 NEXT I
3140 CLOSE #2
3150 :
3160 RUN "MAILMENU
```

6
Displaying Sequential Files

In this chapter, we will begin to put together a *system* of programs and improve our display program. When you want to use the READER1 program, you must type: RUN "READER1. When you are ready to add to the file, you need to type: RUN "ADDER2 (or "1" depending upon your preference). For occasional use, that amount of typing is not a problem, but if you are going to use the program quite often, the necessity of typing RUN and the file name can become bothersome. Besides, the computer can help eliminate the need to type that, so why not let it do so? All that is needed is another program. You will still have to type RUN and the name of this new program. The difference is that when properly set up, you may need to do the typing only once, and then you will be able to switch back and forth between programs by typing little more than a number. You will then have a *system* of programs that work together and are controlled by one *master* program.

Let's see how this can work. Make sure any program currently in memory is saved on disk, and then type the following:

```
NEW
100    REM **--MAILING LIST PROGRAM MENU--**
110    :
120    :
130    KEY OFF
140    :
150    :
160    REM **--MENU ROUTINE--**
170    CLS: LOCATE 5,24: PRINT "PROGRAM MENU"
180    LOCATE  7,20: PRINT "1. FILE CREATION PROGRAM"
```

```
190  LOCATE   9,20: PRINT "2. FILE ADDITION PROGRAM"
200  LOCATE  11,20: PRINT "3. FILE DISPLAY PROGRAM"
210  LOCATE  13,20: PRINT "4. FILE CORRECTION PROGRAM"
220  LOCATE  15,20: PRINT "5. LIST OF FILES"
230  LOCATE  17,20: PRINT "6. END"
240  LOCATE  19,20: INPUT "Which Program Number?
     ";NUMBER
250  IF NUMBER < 1 OR NUMBER > 6 THEN 340
260  IF NUMBER = 1 THEN 1000
270  IF NUMBER = 2 THEN 2000
280  IF NUMBER = 3 THEN RUN "READER2"
290  IF NUMBER = 4 THEN RUN "CORRECT"
300  IF NUMBER = 5 THEN 5000
310  IF NUMBER = 6 KEY ON: END
320  :
330  :
340  REM **--INCORRECT NUMBER ROUTINE--**
350  LOCATE 21,20
360  PRINT "INCORRECT NUMBER! PLEASE TRY AGAIN."
370  GOTO 240: REM Ask again
380  :
390  :
1000 REM **--FILE CREATION PROGRAM--**
1010 CLS: LOCATE 5,1
1020 PRINT "If the Address File already exists,
     do not RUN this program!"
1030 PRINT : PRINT "Do you want the File Creation
     Program?"
1040 PRINT : INPUT "Type 'YES' if you do: ";YES$
1050 IF YES$ = "YES" OR YES$ = "yes" THEN RUN
     "CREATE"
1060 GOTO 160: REM MENU ROUTINE
1070 :
1080 :
2000 REM **--FILE ADDITION PROGRAM--**
2010 CLS: LOCATE 5,1
2020 PRINT "You want to add to the existing Address
     File. Is this correct?"
2030 PRINT : INPUT "Type 'YES' if it is: ";YES$
2040 IF YES$ = "YES" OR YES$ = "yes" THEN RUN
     "ADDER2"
2050 GOTO 160: REM MENU ROUTINE
2060 :
```

```
2070 :
5000 REM **--LIST OF FILES ROUTINE--**
5010 CLS: LOCATE 5,1
5020 FILES
5030 PRINT : PRINT
5040 INPUT "Press 'ENTER' to go to the MENU ";L$
5050 GOTO 160: REM Menu Routine
```

When you have all the program lines typed in, save it to disk as MAILMENU. Type:

SAVE "MAILMENU

Now, all that is needed to run any of your programs is: RUN "MAIL-MENU. Then choose a number and let the computer do the rest. Please notice that I have included a choice for a program that we do not yet have; i.e., FILE CORRECTION PROGRAM (lines 210 and 290) and an update to the READER1 program called READER2 (line 280). Line 100 is the name of the program (a name we have shortened for the actual file name). Line 130 provides the opportunity to turn off the display of the function keys at the bottom of the screen. Turning the display off does not deactivate the function keys. We turn the display back on when we end the program and exit the MAILING LIST SYS-TEM. Line 170 clears the screen and places the cursor 5 lines down and 24 spaces from the left side of the screen and then prints the words "PROGRAM MENU". We tab over 24 spaces to place the words we want printed in line with the names of the choices. (Throughout the book, I will format the displays for an 80 character line. If you are using a display device such as a television, that requires less than an 80 character line, you will need to modify the program instructions for the various display screens.) Lines 180 through 230 set up the actual menu of choices with a blank line between each choice (because the first numbers in the LOCATE statements are not consecutive). Line 240 requests which program to run. The number typed is stored in the numeric variable "NUMBER". This value is first checked (line 250) to see that it is really within the range of actual possibili-ties. If the number is either less than 1 or greater than 6, the com-puter is instructed to go to the INCORRECT NUMBER ROUTINE beginning with line 340. This routine first displays the message from line 360, then returns the user to the instruction in line 240 and requests another number. Therefore, if the computer reaches the instruction at line 260, we know that we have a number somewhere between (or including) 1 and 6. Instructions 260 to 310 are checking which number is contained in the numeric variable NUMBER. If, for instance, the value is "3", indicating that the user wants to read the

ADDRESS.DAT file, we simply instruct the computer to go to the disk and RUN the appropriate program. Control is then transferred to the program READER2, and the computer receives and follows the instructions contained in that program. Such transfer of control erases the MAILMENU program from the computer's memory, replacing those instructions with the instructions in the selected program. That is why it is important to SAVE this MAILMENU to disk before RUNning it. It is also the reason why, when you are finished adding information, for example, and the information has been written out to the disk, the program returns you to the PROGRAM MENU. That is the reason we must include the instructions to RUN "MAILMENU in each of our previous programs (line 3080 in CREATE, line 500 in READER1, line 2050 in ADDER1, and line 3160 in ADDER2). We can add the necessary lines to the CREATE and READER1 programs by loading the respective programs into the computer's memory, listing the appropriate line number, changing the instruction to read RUN "MAILMENU, and saving each program back to the diskette under its same name. Type

```
LOAD "CREATE
LIST 3080
```

Change 3080 to:

```
3080 RUN "MAILMENU
```

Then type:

```
SAVE "CREATE
```

Then,

```
LOAD "READER1
LIST 500
```

Change 500 to:

```
500 RUN "MAILMENU
```

and type:

```
SAVE "READER1
```

We now have a *system* of programs that work together and are controlled by one *master* program. There is no need to go through all the antics that are sometimes involved in building one large program. In addition, it is much easier to make changes to individual programs than to change something in a large program that might have an unnoticed effect. This borders somewhat on programmer preference, but I have found this method to be easy.

We now have a system that will create a file, add to that file, and, in a primitive way, read the file. Two main tasks are left: improving the display features of the READER1 program, and creating a program that will change and delete information in the file. One other feature that we will add within our display program is the reformatting of our data and possible creation of a new file for this reformatted data. We will begin with the program to increase our display options.

READER2

Our present program displays every line in the ADDRESS.DAT file, including the two separator symbols. You don't really want to see those symbols, so eliminating them should be one of the first tasks in creating a new display program. What else would be nice or useful to have in this display program? The computer could display a list of just the names of the individuals in the file. How about a list of the names and addresses without the phone numbers? Can we get a display of a single name, address, and phone number? How about a single name and address, without a phone number? What about an alphabetical list? Can we have a range of names and addresses displayed rather than just the entire list or a single individual? The answer to all these questions is "yes", we can do these things and others also. With all these possibilities, the obvious solution would be to have a menu for these choices.

If you LOAD "READER1 and LIST it, the lines should go from 100 to 500 and are numbered by 20's. IBM BASIC provides a very convenient method of renumbering programs, the RENUM command. We can use many of these same instruction lines, but for long programs it may be more convenient if most of the program is numbered by 10's rather than 20's. Use the RENUM command to renumber the READER1 program like this:

```
RENUM 100
```

After you press the ENTER key, the computer responds with the OK prompt. Now, if you list this program, the line numbers go from 100 to 300 and are numbered by 10's. Used properly, the RENUM command can be a very handy tool in program development.

We can keep lines 100 through 240 of our newly renumbered READER1 program pretty much the same. Line 180 must have some additional variables dimensioned, so line 180 should read:

```
180 DIM LINES$ (K), ND$ (K), L (K), R (K), AD$ (K)
```

Delete lines 250 through 300:

```
DELETE 250-300
```

and add the following lines:

```
250 REM **--MENU ROUTINE--**
260 CLS
270 LOCATE  2,24: PRINT "DISPLAY MENU"
280 LOCATE  4,20: PRINT "1. DISPLAY INFORMATION --
    ORIGINAL ORDER"
290 LOCATE  6,20: PRINT "2 DISPLAY NAMES ONLY"
300 LOCATE  8,20: PRINT "3. DISPLAY INFORMATION --
    NO PHONE"
310 LOCATE 10,20: PRINT "4. DISPLAY SPECIFIC NAME"
320 LOCATE 12,20: PRINT "5. DISPLAY SPECIFIC NAME
    -- NO PHONE"
330 LOCATE 14,20: PRINT "6. DISPLAY INFORMATION --
    RANGE"
340 LOCATE 16,20: PRINT "7. DISPLAY INFORMATION --
    ALPHABETICAL"
350 LOCATE 18,20: PRINT "8. RETURN TO PROGRAM MENU"
360 LOCATE 20,20: INPUT "Which number please ";
    NUMBER
370 IF NUMBER < 1 OR NUMBER > 8 THEN GOSUB 9000
```

If you have been following along with our programs, these lines of code should now be easy to understand. We are doing the same sequence of programming we did when we created the MAILMENU program. We format the menu display, request a number, and check to see that the number is within the actual possibilities. (See the program listing at the end of the chapter for the INCORRECT NUMBER ROUTINE, lines 9000 to 9100.) The next series of program lines is familiar also.

```
380 IF NUMBER = 1 THEN 1000
390 IF NUMBER = 2 THEN 2000
400 IF NUMBER = 3 THEN 3000
410 IF NUMBER = 4 THEN 4000
420 IF NUMBER = 5 THEN 5000
430 IF NUMBER = 6 THEN 6000
440 IF NUMBER = 7 THEN 7000
450 IF NUMBER = 8 THEN RUN "MAILMENU"
460 GOTO 270: REM Ask again
470 :
480 :
```

Now, you have the basic structure for the rest of the program. All that is necessary is to fill in the code for each routine. The routines get progressively more difficult to follow. It is not the intent of this book to teach the concepts behind routines such as sorting and searching, but it is within its scope to present examples of such routines so that readers can make use of these routines in their own file manipulation programs.

ORIGINAL ORDER ROUTINE

```
1000 REM **--ORIGINAL ORDER ROUTINE--**
1010 GOSUB 10000: REM Printer Routine
1020 CLS: LOCATE 5,1
1030 FOR I = 1 TO K
1040 IF LINES$(I) = "*" THEN
     1070
1050 IF LINES$(I) = "!" THEN PRINT #3,"": GOTO
     1070
1060 PRINT #3, LINES$(I)
1070 NEXT I
1080 GOTO 20000: REM Return to Menu Routine
1090 :
1100 :
```

If you look closely, this routine is very similar to the original READER1 Display Routine (lines 250 to 290). All this routine does is display every information line in the file in the order it was entered. There are a few differences. In lines 1040 and 1050, we have eliminated the display of the separator symbols "*" and "!". There are two new lines: lines 1010 and 1080, which direct the computer to separate routines used by each of the main routines. Line 1010, as indicated by the REM statement, will be the code that asks if the user wants the information printed on a printer. This instruction uses a GOSUB statement which directs the computer to go to the instructions that begin at line 10000 and follow those instructions until the computer encounters a RETURN statement. At that point, the computer returns to the instruction following the GOSUB instruction. Line 1080 is the instruction that directs the computer to the routine that returns the user to the DISPLAY MENU when the user is ready.

NAME ONLY ROUTINE

```
2000  REM **--NAME ONLY ROUTINE--**
2010  GOSUB 10000: REM Printer Routine
```

```
2020   CLS: LOCATE 5,1
2030   FOR I = 1 TO (K - 1)
2040   IF LINES$(I) = LINES$(1) THEN PRINT
       #3,I;LINES$(I)
2050   IF LINES$(I) = "!" THEN PRINT #3,I + 1;
       LINES$(I + 1)
2060   NEXT I
2070   GOTO 20000: REM Return to Menu Routine
2080   :
2090   :
```

This routine should not be very difficult to understand. We want to print only those lines that follow the "!" separator. We print those lines because those are the lines that should contain the names of the individuals. We need the instruction at line 2040 because there was no separator for the first name. We use K − 1 because we do not want to get to the last "!" separator since there is no name to follow it yet.

NO PHONE ROUTINE

```
3000   REM **--NO PHONE ROUTINE--**
3010   GOSUB 10000: REM Printer Routine
3020   CLS: LOCATE 5,1
3030   FOR I = 1 TO K
3040   IF LINES$(I) = "*" THEN I = I + 1: GOTO 3070
3050   IF LINES$(I) = "!" THEN PRINT #3,"": GOTO
       3070
3060   PRINT #3,LINES$(I)
3070   NEXT I
3080   GOTO 20000: REM Return to Menu Routine
3090   :
3100   :
```

This routine should look completely familiar. It is practically the same routine we used to print a label in ADDER2 (lines 1120 to 1160 in that program). The effect is the same here also. We can print a mailing label for every person in our file with this routine. Because just about every type of printer works differently, you will probably need additional code to get the labels to space properly. One method of spacing would be to find out the number of lines on the label and the number of lines between the labels. Then, adjust the routine to advance exactly that number of lines, regardless of the number of lines to be printed. That method would always start the printer at the top of the label and not center the material on the label, but it is probably the easiest method to develop.

SEARCH ROUTINE

```
4000 REM **--SEARCH ROUTINE--**
4010 GOSUB 10000: REM Printer Routine
4020 CLS: LOCATE 5,1
4030 PRINT "Type 'END' when finished."
4040 INPUT "Name to find? ";FIND$
4050 IF FIND$ = "END" OR FIND$ = "end" THEN 4220
4060 PRINT
4070 FOR I = 1 TO K
4080 IF LINES$(I) = FIND$ THEN 4100
4090 GOTO 4190
4100 IF LINES$(I) = "*" THEN 4190
4110 IF LINES$(I) = "!" THEN 4190
4120 PRINT #3,LINES$(I)
4130 PRINT #3,LINES$(I + 1)
4140 PRINT #3,LINES$(I + 2)
4150 IF LINES$(I + 3) < > "*" THEN PRINT #3,LINES$
     (I + 3)
4160 IF LINES$(I + 4)   =  "*" THEN 4180
4170 PRINT #3,LINES$(I + 4): GOTO 4190
4180 PRINT #3,LINES$(I + 5)
4190 NEXT I
4200 PRINT
4210 GOTO 4030: REM Repeat the Routine until done
4220 GOTO 20000: REM Return to Menu Routine
4230 :
4240 :
```

The routines now begin to get more difficult. Up to this point, we have not made any assumptions about the number of lines of information in each set. With this routine, however, we make the assumption that there are a maximum of five lines containing information in any set. If you want a greater maximum, then additional code will have to be added to print out those other lines. The additional code would follow the pattern of lines 4150 to 4180. We begin in the same way with lines 4000, 4010, and 4020 (our routine name, GOSUB printer routine, and clear screen lines). Line 4030 gives instructions to the user to type the word "END" when the user is finished looking for a specific name.

Line 4040 requests the name from the user and stores that name in the string variable "FIND$". Line 4050 checks the contents of "FIND$" to see if it contains the word "END" or "end". If it does, the computer is directed to go to line 4220 which further directs the computer to go to the "RETURN TO MENU ROUTINE". One might logically ask why 4050 does not instruct the computer to go directly to the "RETURN TO MENU ROUTINE". The reason lies in the necessity of structuring the various routines in the same way so that any programmer can easily locate the exit point of the routine. There are a number of GOTO statements in this routine, but all of them direct the computer (and any programmer) to various lines within this routine. In following the logic of this routine (and all the other routines also), you never need to look outside the routine, except for the print routine and exit routine, which are common to all other routines. The idea is to keep the flow of logic in one place as much as possible. You enter at the top of the routine and exit at the base of the routine. This is the case for all the routines.

Lines 4070 to 4190 are the heart of this routine. They are also the boundaries of the loop used to find and print the information associated with a specific name. Line 4080 checks the contents of LINES$(I) to see if it equals the contents of FIND$. If it does, the computer is instructed to jump over the next instruction. If it does not, the next instruction is executed. Line 4090 is reached only if the contents of LINES$(I) and FIND$ do not match, and 4100 is reached only if they do match. Lines 4100 and 4110 check for the separators and skip them when they are found. At this point in the routine, we have found the name we are looking for and now want to print out the information associated with this name. We assume that the first three lines will not contain a separator and, therefore, we will automatically print those lines. Lines 4120, 4130, and 4140 accomplish this task. Lines 4150 through 4180 are lines of code that require some thought. If the fourth information-line does not contain the separator "*", then we want to print this line (4150) also, but if it does contain the separator, we do not want the fourth information-line printed. Rather, we know that the fifth information-line contains something to be printed (the line following the "*" will have the phone number if there is a phone number). Line 4170 prints this fifth information-line. Line 4160 first checks the fifth information-line to see if it contains the asterisk separator. If it does contain the separator, then we need to jump over line 4170 (the instruction that prints that fifth information-line) and instead, print the sixth information-line (4180). Go back through the explanation if you are not certain you understand. We use this same routine, combined with the previous one, for our next routine.

SEARCH ROUTINE—NO PHONE

```
5000 REM **--SEARCH ROUTINE NO PHONE--**
5010 GOSUB 10000: REM Printer Routine
5020 CLS: LOCATE 5,1
5030 PRINT "Type 'END' when finished."
5040 INPUT "Name to find ";FIND$
5050 IF FIND$ = "END" OR FIND$ = "end"  THEN 5230
5060 PRINT
5070 FOR I = 1 TO K
5080 IF LINES$(I) = FIND$ THEN 5100
5090 GOTO 5200
5100 IF LINES$(I) = "*" THEN I = I + 1: GOTO 5200
5110 IF LINES$(I) = "!" THEN PRINT #3,"": GO TO
     5200
5120 PRINT #3,LINES$(I)
5130 PRINT #3,LINES$(I + 1)
5140 PRINT #3,LINES$(I + 2)
5150 IF LINES$(I + 3) < > "*" THEN PRINT #3,LINES$
     (I + 3)
5160 IF LINES$(I + 3)  =  "*" THEN I = I + 1: GOTO
     5200
5170 IF LINES$(I + 4)  =  "*" THEN I = I + 1: GOTO
     5200
5180 PRINT #3,LINES$(I + 4): GOTO 5200
5190 PRINT #3,LINES$(I + 5)
5200 NEXT I
5210 PRINT
5220 GOTO 5030: REM Repeat the Routine until done
5230 GOTO 20000: REM Return to Menu Routine
5240 :
5250 :
```

I included this routine for a number of reasons. First, it is a very useful routine because, with a printer, one can print out a specific mailing label. Second, it shows how two routines can be combined into a third routine. This latter point is the most important reason. Very few programs will do everything anyone could ever want of them, but if a person understands these separate routines, then combining two or more to form others should be possible. There are quite a number of combinations that are possible and might be useful to some people. As you can see, this routine is exactly the same as the previous one down to the instruction at 5100. The only difference is that when we find the

"*" separator, we add one to I, thus skipping the phone number. Lines 5110 through 5150 are the same instructions as lines 4110 through 4150. The instructions at lines 5160 and 5170 are the only different instructions. Both of those instructions simply check to see which information line contains the separator symbol and then advance the counter by one. The end of the routine is the same as the end of the previous routine.

With the routines at lines 4000 and 5000, you have the ability to search for a specific name and display that name, either with the phone number or without the phone number. But both of these routines require that you know and type in the exact spelling of the name, including spaces. That presents a reason for the next routine, the range routine. With this routine, you will only need to know the starting and ending information-line numbers to be able to display the information you want. You can obtain those numbers from the DISPLAY NAMES ONLY routine. I will present the range routine only, but you might want to combine this routine with the DISPLAY NAMES ONLY routine and possibly some others also.

RANGE ROUTINE

```
6000 REM **--RANGE ROUTINE--**
6010 GOSUB 10000: REM Printer Routine
6020 CLS: LOCATE 5,1
6030 INPUT "Type beginning line number ";BL
6040 PRINT
6050 IF BL < 1 THEN PRINT "Number too small": GOTO
     6030
6060 INPUT "Type ending line number ";EL
6070 PRINT
6080 IF EL > K THEN PRINT "Number too large": GOTO
     6060
6090 FOR I = BL TO EL
6100 IF LINES$(I) = "*" THEN I = I + 1: GOTO 6130
6110 IF LINES$(I) = "!" THEN PRINT #3,"": GOTO 6130
6120 PRINT #3,LINES$(I)
6130 NEXT I
6140 GOTO 20000: REM Return to Menu Routine
6150 :
6160 :
```

Line 6030 asks for the beginning information-line number. Remember that you can check the numbers first by using the

DISPLAY NAMES ONLY routine or by actually including that routine at the beginning of this one. Line 6050 checks the number typed to see if it is less than 1, the number of the first information-line. If it is too small, a message is printed and the user is again asked for a beginning number. Line 6060 requests the ending information-line number and goes through the same checking process, this time for a number larger than the maximum number of information-lines. The loop follows on lines 6090 to 6130. I have included the code for printing the information without the phone number (line 6100), thus providing a routine that can print out a selected range of mailing labels.

I have tried to show how you can take various routines and combine them in just about any way you might want. With the addition of each new routine, the number of possible combinations of routines increases so much that no single programmer could include all possibilities within one program, but, with a minimum of understanding, everyone can create combinations of routines to meet their needs.

ALPHABETICAL ORDER ROUTINE

We come now to the most complex of our routines. I will not even attempt to explain the logic involved in all parts of this alphabetizing routine since complete books have been written on various sorting techniques. The sort method I am including is sometimes called the *Quicksort* technique. There are a number of other public domain sorting routines that I could have used, such as the bubble sort or the Shell-Metzner sort, but I decided on the Quicksort because it is very efficient and somewhat less publicized. I modified the sort to enable it to work with string variables. Otherwise, the sort subroutine is a standard routine that can be used in a number of different ways to order lists composed of numbers or letters. For example, if you want to display the information in the ADDRESS.DAT file in zip code order, you need to access the zip codes first and then use the Quicksort subroutine to arrange the zip codes and their associated information-lines in either ascending or descending order. The creation of such a routine would require that you completely understand another feature of this routine: the flexibility possible with string variables and the manner of utilizing that flexibility. Again, I will not try to fully explain the logic or programming power behind the BASIC statements of LEFT$, MID$, or RIGHT$. I strongly encourage you to learn as much as possible about these BASIC statements and how they can be used to take string variables apart and put them back together in just about any way you want.

This alphabetizing routine will be presented in two sections. The first section makes use of this string variable flexibility to access the last section of characters in that first information-line; reverse the order of that information-line placing the last section of characters first; and then combine all other information-lines associated with this first line into one, long string variable, AD$(I). The second section alphabetizes the list now stored in the string variable ND$(J).

```
7000 REM **--ALPHABETICAL ORDER ROUTINE--**
7020 CLS: LOCATE 5,1
7040 PRINT "WORKING--PLEASE DON'T TOUCH!!"
7060 :
7080 :
7100 REM Get first information-line
7120 FOR I = 1 TO K - 1
7140 IF LINES$(I) = LINES$(1) THEN 7240
7160 IF LINES$(I) = "!" THEN I = I + 1: GOTO 7240
7180 GOTO 7460: REM Next I
7200 :
7220 :
7240 REM Reverse order
7260 LN = LEN (LINES$(I))
7280 FOR J1 = 1 TO LN: IF MID$( LINES$(I),J1,1) =
     " " THEN J2 = J1
7300 NEXT J1
7320 IF J2 = 0 OR J2 > LN THEN AD$(I) = LINES$(I):
     GOTO 7360
7340 AD$(I) = MID$ (LINES$(I),J2 + 1,LN - J2) + "
     " + LEFT$ (LINES$(I),J2)
7360 AD$(I) = AD$(I) + "**" + LINES$(I + 1) + "**"
     + LINES$(I + 2)
7380 IF LINES$(I + 3) < > "*" THEN AD$(I) = AD$(I)
     + "**" + LINES$(I + 3)
7400 IF LINES$(I + 4) = "*" THEN 7440
7420 AD$(I) = AD$(I) + "**" + LINES$(I + 4)": GOTO
     7460
7440 AD$(I) = AD$(I) + "**" + LINES(I + 5)
7460 NEXT I
7480 :
7500 :
7520 REM Renumber for sort
7540 J = 1
```

```
7560 FOR I = 1 TO K
7580 IF LEN (AD$(I)) > 0 THEN ND$(J) = AD$(I):
     J = J + 1
7600 NEXT I
7620 N = J - 1
7640 :
7660 :
```

As I said, the routines get more complex. If you do not understand the LEFT$, MID$, and RIGHT$ statements, the best thing to do is to get a clear definition of them from a book devoted to teaching BASIC and then practice their uses. They essentially perform the functions for which they are named. The LEFT$ statement will retrieve a specified number of characters beginning at the left side of a string variable. Left$(A$,4) gets the first four characters of the string variable A$. The RIGHT$ statement retrieves a specified number of characters from the right-most character of a string variable. RIGHT$(B$,3) gets the last three characters in the string variable B$. The MID$ statement retrieves a specified number of characters from a specified position within a string variable. MID$(C$,2,6) gets the next six characters beginning at the second character in the string variable C$. Therefore, the instructions in lines 7120 to 7180 identify the first information-line in each set of data. Lines 7260 through 7460 reverse the order of the first information-line and then combine all the other information-lines associated with it. Finally, lines 7540 to 7600 are the instructions that renumber the sets of information in such a way that the sort subroutine can function.

```
7680 REM ***--QUICKSORT--***
7700 S1 = 1
7720 PRINT "WORKING--PLEASE DON'T TOUCH!!"
7740 L(1) = 1
7760 R(1) = N
7780 L1 = L(S1)
7800 R1 = R(S1)
7820 S1 = S1 - 1
7840 L2 = L1
7860 R2 = R1
7880 X$ = ND$(INT((L1 + R1)/2))
7900 C = C + 1
7920 IF ND$(L2) = X$ OR ND$(L2) > X$ THEN 7980
7940 L2 = L2 + 1
7960 GOTO 7900
7980 C = C1
```

```
8000 IF X$ = ND$(R2)  OR X$ > ND$(R2)  THEN 8060
8020 R2 = R2 - 1
8040 GOTO 7980
8060 IF L2 > R2 THEN 8200
8080 S = S + 1
8100 T$ = ND$(L2)
8120 ND$(L2) = ND$(R2)
8140 ND$(R2) = T$
8160 L2 = L2 + 1
8180 R2 = R2 - 1
8200 IF L2 = R2 OR L2 < R2 THEN 7900
8220 IF L2 = R1 or L2 > R1 THEN 8300
8240 S1 = S1 + 1
8260 L(S1) = L2
8280 R(S1) = R1
8300 R1 = R2
8320 IF L1 < R1 THEN 7840
8340 IF S1 > 0 THEN 7780
8360 REM Sort Completed!
8380 :
8400 :
```

Now you have access to a sorting method. The only code necessary, outside this subroutine, to transfer it to another program is to set:

1. The DIM of L() and R() to the number of things to be sorted.

2. The numeric variable "N" = to the number of things to be sorted.

If you have a different sort method that you like or understand better and want to include it instead, the code for your sort should replace the code between lines 7680 and 8360.

We still need to display the results after sorting. I am going to present the code to display the results in their most elementary way. I will leave it to those of you who want to, or who are able to use the flexibility in string variables, to format the display in any way you desire.

```
8420 REM **--Display--**
8440 GOSUB 10000: REM Printer Routine
8460 FOR I = 1 TO N
8480 PRINT #3, ND$(I)
8500 PRINT #3, " "
8520 NEXT I
8540 GOTO 20000: REM Return to Menu Routine
8560 :
8580 :
```

We now have an opportunity to create a sequential access file in a way that may be more powerful than in our MAILING LIST SYSTEM. The usefulness of the new file creation method depends on the programmer's knowledge of, and willingness to work with, string variables; i.e., LEFT\$, MID\$, RIGHT\$, INSTR, LEN, STR\$, VAL, and DIM. All of the associated information with LINES\$(1)—that is the address, city, state, zip code, and phone number—are all stored in the string variable ND\$(1). Everything for the next name is stored in ND\$(2), and so on. If you want to locate the zip code, all you need to do is use the MID\$ function to determine where in the string the zip code is located. You could use the same MID\$ function with our present file set up, but it might be more difficult to locate the zip code precisely. (For instance, some people might put the zip code on a separate line, while others would put it on the same line as the city and state. If everything is combined into one string variable, it might be easier to locate for all possible situations.) I have used a lot of conditional statements because there are many possibilities, and the correct choice often depends upon a number of factors: the programmer's experience and preference, the value of the file being established, the necessity of backup, the amount of use the file will get, and so forth. The code necessary to establish a separate file for our now-alphabetized information should be easy to develop.

To finish, we need two brief subroutines used by each of our main routines: the printer subroutine and the return-to-menu subroutine.

```
10000 REM **--PRINTER ROUTINE--**
10020 CLS: LOCATE 5,1
10040 PRINT "Do you want a paper print out?"
10060 PRINT : INPUT "Type 'Y' or 'N' ";YES$
10080 IF YES$ = "Y" OR YES$ = "y" THEN DISPLAY$ =
      "LPT1:" : GOTO 10200
10100 IF YES$ = "N" OR YES$ = "n" THEN DISPLAY$ =
      "SCRN:" : GOTO 10200
10120 PRINT "INCORRECT CHOICE. PLEASE CHOOSE AGAIN!"
10140 FOR I = 1 TO 1000: NEXT I
10160 GOTO 10000
10180 :
10200 OPEN DISPLAY$ FOR OUTPUT AS #3
10220 RETURN
10240 :
10260 :
20000 REM **--RETURN TO MENU ROUTINE--**
20020 CLOSE #3: REM Reset printer option
```

```
20040  INPUT "Press 'ENTER' to go to Display Menu
       ";L$
20060  GOTO 250 : REM Menu
```

The only new code in both these routines is in the Printer Routine. Lines 10080 and 10100 determine which mode of display the user wants. If the user wants a paper print out, then the string variable DISPLAY$ is set equal to "LPT1:" (for line printer 1). If the user does not want a paper print out, then the string variable DISPLAY$ is set equal to "SCRN:" (for screen). In either case, once the value of DISPLAY$ is set, control is transferred to the instruction at line 10200. Line 10200 treats DISPLAY$ as a file, instructing the computer to open the value of DISPLAY$ for output and identify it as the number 3 file. This procedure thus opens whichever device the user wants for the display; i.e., either the screen or the printer. Finally, control is RETURNed to the instruction following the GOSUB by the RETURN statement in line 10220. The Return To Menu Routine, which acts as the exit routine for all of the main routines, closes file number 3 so that the user can decide differently on every part of the program. Line 20060 returns the user to the menu.

At the end of the chapter, I have also included the program listing that uses the LPRINT statement instead of the method given above. By reading through the additional listing, I think you will see why I prefer the file device method. Have you saved this new READER program? If not, be certain that the program is still in memory and then type the following:

```
SAVE "READER2
```

By using a different name from our original display program, the number 2 instead of the number 1, we have not written over that original program. Now the list of files should show:

```
COMMAND  . COM BASIC   . BAS HELLO    . BAS EXAMPLE . BAS
CREATE   . BAS ADDPTR  . DAT ADDRESS  . DAT READER1  . BAS
ADDER1   . BAS ADDER2  . BAS READER2  . BAS
```

In the next chapter, we will examine ways of correcting, changing, or deleting information from our file.

QUESTIONS

1. *True or False*: BASIC allows you to RUN a program from within another program.

2. What IBM BASIC word allows you to position text on the screen?

3. Which BASIC word is used to instruct the computer to go to a subroutine?

4. Which BASIC word is used to instruct the computer to return from a subroutine?

5. *True or False*: In programming, it is a good idea to have just one main entrance and exit point in every routine.

6. Name three public domain sorting routines.

7. What are the three main BASIC words that provide a great deal of power in working with strings?

8. What BASIC word retrieves a specified number of characters from a specified position within a string variable?

9. Name four other BASIC words that can be used in some way with string variables.

10. *True or False*: When you save a file with the same name as a file already on the disk, the first file is replaced by the second file.

ANSWERS

1. True
2. LOCATE
3. GOSUB
4. RETURN
5. True
6. bubble, Quicksort, Shell-Metzner
7. LEFT$, RIGHT$, MID$
8. MID$
9. LEN, STR$, VAL, INSTR
10. True

MAILMENU

```
100 REM ***--MAILING LIST MENU--***
110 :
120 :
130 KEY OFF
140 :
150 :
160 REM **--MENU ROUTINE--**
170 CLS: LOCATE 5,24: PRINT "PROGRAM MENU"
180 LOCATE  7,20: PRINT "1.  FILE CREATION PROGRAM"
190 LOCATE  9,20: PRINT "2.  FILE ADDITION PROGRAM"
200 LOCATE 11,20: PRINT "3.  FILE DISPLAY PROGRAM"
210 LOCATE 13,20: PRINT "4.  FILE CORRECTION PROGRAM"
220 LOCATE 15,20: PRINT "5.  LIST OF FILES"
230 LOCATE 17,20: PRINT "6.  END"
240 LOCATE 19,20: INPUT "Which Program Number ";NUMBER
250 IF NUMBER < 1 OR NUMBER > 6 THEN 340
260 IF NUMBER = 1 THEN 1000
270 IF NUMBER = 2 THEN 2000
280 IF NUMBER = 3 THEN RUN "READER2"
290 IF NUMBER = 4 THEN RUN "CORRECT"
300 IF NUMBER = 5 THEN 5000
310 IF NUMBER = 6 THEN KEY ON: END
320 :
330 :
340 REM **--INCORRECT NUMBER ROUTINE--**
350 LOCATE 21,20
360 PRINT "INCORRECT NUMBER! PLEASE TRY AGAIN."
370 GOTO 240: REM Ask again
380 :
390 :
1000 REM **--FILE CREATION PROGRAM--**
1010 CLS: LOCATE 5,1
1020 PRINT "If the Address File already exists, do not RUN
     this program!"
1030 PRINT : PRINT "Do you want the File Creation Program?"
1040 PRINT : INPUT "Type `YES' if you do: ";YES$
1050 IF YES$ = "YES" OR YES$ = "yes" THEN RUN "CREATE"
1060 GOTO 160: REM Menu Routine
1070 :
1080 :
2000 REM **--FILE ADDITION PROGRAM--**
2010 CLS: LOCATE 5,1
2020 PRINT "You want to add to the existing Address File.
     Is this correct?"
2030 PRINT : INPUT "Type `YES' if it is: ";YES$
2040 IF YES$ = "YES" OR YES$ = "yes" THEN RUN "ADDER2"
2050 GOTO 160: REM Menu Routine
2060 :
2070 :
```

```
5000 REM **--LIST OF FILES ROUTINE--**
5010 CLS: LOCATE 5,1
5020 FILES
5030 PRINT: PRINT
5040 INPUT "Press `ENTER' to go to the MENU ";L$
5050 GOTO 160: REM Menu Routine
```

READER1B

```
100 REM **--MAILING LIST READER1--**
110 :
120 :
130 REM **--FILE INPUT ROUTINE--**
140 OPEN "ADDPTR.DAT" FOR INPUT AS #1
150 OPEN "ADDRESS.DAT" FOR INPUT AS #2
160 INPUT #1,K: REM Get number of records
170 CLOSE #1
180 DIM LINES$(K)
190 FOR I = 1 TO K
200 LINE INPUT #2,LINES$(I)
210 NEXT I
220 CLOSE #2
230 :
240 :
250 REM **--DISPLAY ROUTINE--**
260 CLS: LOCATE 5,1
270 FOR I = 1 TO K
280 PRINT LINES$(I)
290 NEXT I
300 RUN "MAILMENU
```

READER2

```
100 REM   ***--MAILING LIST READER2--***
110 :
120 :
130 REM **--FILE INPUT ROUTINE--**
140 OPEN "ADDPTR.DAT" FOR INPUT AS #1
150 OPEN "ADDRESS.DAT" FOR INPUT AS #2
160 INPUT #1,K: REM Get number of records
170 CLOSE #1
180 DIM LINES$(K),ND$(K),L(K),R(K),AD$(K)
190 FOR I = 1 TO K
200 LINE INPUT #2,LINES$(I)
210 NEXT I
220 CLOSE #2
230 :
240 :
250 REM **--MENU ROUTINE--**
260 CLS
270 LOCATE   2,24: PRINT "DISPLAY MENU"
280 LOCATE   4,20: PRINT "1.   DISPLAY INFORMATION--ORIGINAL
    ORDER"
290 LOCATE   6,20: PRINT "2.   DISPLAY NAMES ONLY"
300 LOCATE   8,20: PRINT "3.   DISPLAY INFORMATION--NO PHONE"
310 LOCATE  10,20: PRINT "4.   DISPLAY SPECIFIC NAME"
320 LOCATE  12,20: PRINT "5.   DISPLAY SPECIFIC NAME--NO PHON
    E"
330 LOCATE  14,20: PRINT "6.   DISPLAY INFORMATION--RANGE"
340 LOCATE  16,20: PRINT "7.   DISPLAY INFORMATION--ALPHABETI
    CAL"
350 LOCATE  18,20: PRINT "8.   RETURN TO PROGRAM MENU"
360 LOCATE  20,20: INPUT "Which number please ";NUMBER
370 IF NUMBER < 1 OR NUMBER > 8 THEN GOSUB 9000
380 IF NUMBER = 1 THEN 1000
390 IF NUMBER = 2 THEN 2000
400 IF NUMBER = 3 THEN 3000
410 IF NUMBER = 4 THEN 4000
420 IF NUMBER = 5 THEN 5000
430 IF NUMBER = 6 THEN 6000
440 IF NUMBER = 7 THEN 7000
450 IF NUMBER = 8 THEN RUN "MAILMENU"
460 GOTO 270
470 :
480 :
1000 REM **--ORIGINAL ORDER ROUTINE--**
1010 GOSUB 10000: REM Printer Routine
1020 CLS: LOCATE 5,1
1030 FOR I = 1 TO K
1040 IF LINES$(I) = "*" THEN 1070
1050 IF LINES$(I) = "¦" THEN PRINT #3,"": GOTO 1070
1060 PRINT #3, LINES$(I)
1070 NEXT I
```

```
1080 GOTO 20000: REM Return to Menu Routine
1090 :
1100 :
2000 REM **--NAME ONLY ROUTINE--**
2010 GOSUB 10000: REM Printer Routine
2020 CLS: LOCATE 5,1
2030 FOR I = 1 TO (K - 1)
2040 IF LINES$(I) = LINES$(1) THEN PRINT #3,I;LINES$(I)
2050 IF LINES$(I) = "|" THEN PRINT #3,I + 1;LINES$(I + 1)
2060 NEXT I
2070 GOTO 20000: REM Return to Menu Routine
2080 :
2090 :
3000 REM **--NO PHONE ROUTINE--**
3010 GOSUB 10000: REM Printer Routine
3020 CLS: LOCATE 5,1
3030 FOR I = 1 TO K
3040 IF LINES$(I) = "*" THEN I = I + 1: GOTO 3070
3050 IF LINES$(I) = "|" THEN PRINT #3,"": GOTO 3070
3060 PRINT #3,LINES$(I)
3070 NEXT I
3080 GOTO 20000: REM Return to Menu Routine
3090 :
3100 :
4000 REM **--SEARCH ROUTINE--**
4010 GOSUB 10000: REM Printer Routine
4020 CLS: LOCATE 5,1
4030 PRINT "Type `END' when finished."
4040 INPUT "Name to find ";FIND$
4050 IF FIND$ =  "END" OR FIND$ = "end" THEN 4220
4060 PRINT
4070 FOR I = 1 TO K
4080 IF LINES$(I) = FIND$ THEN 4100
4090 GOTO 4190
4100 IF LINES$(I) = "*" THEN 4190
4110 IF LINES$(I) = "|" THEN 4190
4120 PRINT #3,LINES$(I)
4130 PRINT #3,LINES$(I + 1)
4140 PRINT #3,LINES$(I + 2)
4150 IF LINES$(I + 3) < > "*" THEN PRINT #3,LINES$(I + 3)
4160 IF LINES$(I + 4) = "*" THEN 4180
4170 PRINT #3,LINES$(I + 4): GOTO 4190
4180 PRINT #3,LINES$(I + 5)
4190 NEXT I
4200 PRINT
4210 GOTO 4030: REM Repeat the routine until done
4220 GOTO 20000: REM Return to Menu Routine
4230 :
4240 :
5000 REM **--SEARCH ROUTINE NO PHONE--**
5010 GOSUB 10000: REM Printer Routine
5020 CLS: LOCATE 5,1
5030 PRINT "Type `END' when finished."
5040 INPUT "Name to find ";FIND$
```

```
5050 IF FIND$ =  "END" OR FIND$ = "end" THEN 5230
5060 PRINT
5070 FOR I = 1 TO K
5080 IF LINES$(I) = FIND$ THEN 5100
5090 GOTO 5200
5100 IF LINES$(I) = "*" THEN I = I + 1: GOTO 5200
5110 IF LINES$(I) = "|" THEN PRINT #3,"": GOTO 5200
5120 PRINT #3,LINES$(I)
5130 PRINT #3,LINES$(I + 1)
5140 PRINT #3,LINES$(I + 2)
5150 IF LINES$(I + 3) < > "*" THEN PRINT #3,LINES$(I + 3)
5160 IF LINES$(I + 3) = "*" THEN I = I + 1: GOTO 5200
5170 IF LINES$(I + 4) = "*" THEN I = I + 1: GOTO 5200
5180 PRINT #3,LINES$(I + 4): GOTO 5200
5190 PRINT #3,LINES$(I + 5)
5200 NEXT I
5210 PRINT
5220 GOTO 5030: REM Repeat the routine until done
5230 GOTO 20000: REM Return to Menu Routine
5240 :
5250 :
6000 REM **--RANGE ROUTINE--**
6010 GOSUB 10000: REM Printer Routine
6020 CLS: LOCATE 5,1
6030 INPUT "Type beginning line number please ";BL
6040 PRINT
6050 IF BL < 1 THEN PRINT "Number too small": GOTO 6030
6060 INPUT "Type ending line number please ";EL
6070 PRINT
6080 IF EL > K THEN PRINT "Number too large": GOTO 6060
6090 FOR I = BL TO EL
6100 IF LINES$(I) = "*" THEN I = I + 1: GOTO 6130
6110 IF LINES$(I) = "|" THEN PRINT #3,"": GOTO 6130
6120 PRINT #3,LINES$(I)
6130 NEXT I
6140 GOTO 20000: REM Return to Menu Routine
6150 :
6160 :
7000 REM **--ALPHABETICAL ORDER ROUTINE--**
7020 CLS: LOCATE 5,1
7040 PRINT "WORKING--PLEASE DON'T TOUCH!!"
7060 :
7080 :
7100 REM Get first information-line
7120 FOR I = 1 TO K - 1
7140 IF LINES$(I) = LINES$(1) THEN 7240
7160 IF LINES$(I) = "|" THEN I = I + 1: GOTO 7240
7180 GOTO 7460: REM Next I
7200 :
7220 :
7240 REM Reverse order
7260 LN = LEN (LINES$(I))
7280 FOR J1 = 1 TO LN: IF MID$ (LINES$(I),J1,1) = " "
     THEN J2 = J1
```

```
7300 NEXT J1
7320 IF J2 = 0 OR J2 > LN THEN AD$(I) = LINES$(I): GOTO
     7360
7340 AD$(I) = MID$ (LINES$(I),J2 + 1,LN - J2) +   "  " +
     LEFT$ (LINES$(I),J2)
7360 AD$(I) = AD$(I) + "**" + LINES$(I + 1) + "**" + LIN
     ES$(I + 2)
7380 IF LINES$(I + 3) < > "*" THEN AD$(I) = AD$(I) + "**"
     + LINES$(I + 3)
7400 IF LINES$(I + 4) = "*" THEN 7440
7420 AD$(I) = AD$(I) + "**" + LINES$(I + 4): GOTO 7460
7440 AD$(I) = AD$(I) + "**" + LINES$(I + 5)
7460 NEXT I
7480 :
7500 :
7520 REM Renumber for sort
7540 J = 1
7560 FOR I = 1 TO K
7580 IF LEN (AD$(I)) > 0 THEN ND$(J) = AD$(I): J = J + 1
7600 NEXT I
7620 N = J - 1
7640 :
7660 :
7680 REM   ***--QUICKSORT--***
7700 S1 = 1
7720 PRINT "WORKING--PLEASE DON'T TOUCH!!"
7740 L(1) = 1
7760 R(1) = N
7780 L1 = L(S1)
7800 R1 = R(S1)
7820 S1 = S1 -1
7840 L2 = L1
7860 R2 = R1
7880 X$ = ND$(INT((L1 + R1)/2))
7900 C = C + 1
7920 IF ND$(L2) = X$ OR ND$(L2) > X$ THEN 7980
7940 L2 = L2 + 1
7960 GOTO 7900
7980 C = C1
8000 IF X$ = ND$(R2) OR X$ > ND$(R2) THEN 8060
8020 R2 = R2 -1
8040 GOTO 7980
8060 IF L2 > R2 THEN 8200
8080 S = S + 1
8100 T$ = ND$(L2)
8120 ND$(L2) = ND$(R2)
8140 ND$(R2) = T$
8160 L2 = L2 + 1
8180 R2 = R2 - 1
8200 IF L2 = R2 OR L2 < R2 THEN 7900
8220 IF L2 = R1 OR L2 > R1 THEN 8300
8240 S1 = S1 + 1
8260 L(S1) = L2
8280 R(S1) = R1
```

```
8300 R1 = R2
8320 IF L1 < R1 THEN 7840
8340 IF S1 > 0 THEN 7780
8360 REM Sort Completed!
8380 :
8400 :
8420 REM **--Display--**
8440 GOSUB 10000: REM Printer Routine
8460 FOR I = 1 TO N
8480 PRINT #3,ND$(I)
8500 PRINT #3,""
8520 NEXT I
8540 GOTO 20000: REM Return to Menu Routine
8560 :
8580 :
9000 REM **--INCORRECT NUMBER ROUTINE--**
9020 LOCATE 22,20
9040 PRINT "INCORRECT NUMBER. PLEASE CHOOSE AGAIN."
9060 RETURN
9080 :
9100 :
10000 REM **--PRINTER ROUTINE--**
10020 CLS: LOCATE 5,1
10040 PRINT "Do you want a paper print out?"
10060 PRINT : INPUT "Type `Y' or `N' ";YES$
10080 IF YES$ = "Y" OR YES$ ="y" THEN DISPLAY$ = "LPT1:":
      GOTO 10200
10100 IF YES$ = "N" OR YES$ = "n" THEN DISPLAY$ = "SCRN:":
      GOTO 10200
10120 PRINT "INCORRECT CHOICE. PLEASE CHOOSE AGAIN!"
10140 FOR I = 1 TO 1000: NEXT I
10160 GOTO 10000
10180 :
10200 OPEN DISPLAY$ FOR OUTPUT AS #3
10220 RETURN
10240 :
10260 :
20000 REM **--RETURN TO MENU ROUTINE--**
20020 CLOSE #3: REM Reset printer option
20040 INPUT "Press `ENTER' to go to Display Menu ";L$
20060 GOTO 250
```

READER2B

```
100 REM   ***--MAILING LIST READER2--***
120 :
140 :
160 REM **--FILE INPUT ROUTINE--**
180 OPEN "ADDPTR.DAT" FOR INPUT AS #1
200 OPEN "ADDRESS.DAT" FOR INPUT AS #2
220 INPUT #1,K: REM Get number of records
240 CLOSE #1
260 DIM LINES$(K),ND$(K),L(K),R(K),AD$(K)
280 FOR I = 1 TO K
300 LINE INPUT #2,LINES$(I)
320 NEXT I
340 CLOSE #2
360 :
380 :
400 REM **--MENU ROUTINE--**
420 CLS
440 LOCATE   2,24: PRINT "DISPLAY MENU"
460 LOCATE   4,20: PRINT "1.   DISPLAY INFORMATION--ORIGIN
    AL ORDER"
480 LOCATE   6,20: PRINT "2.   DISPLAY NAMES ONLY"
500 LOCATE   8,20: PRINT "3.   DISPLAY INFORMATION--NO PHO
    NE"
520 LOCATE 10,20: PRINT "4.   DISPLAY SPECIFIC NAME"
540 LOCATE 12,20: PRINT "5.   DISPLAY SPECIFIC NAME--NO P
    HONE"
560 LOCATE 14,20: PRINT "6.   DISPLAY INFORMATION--RANGE"
580 LOCATE 16,20: PRINT "7.   DISPLAY INFORMATION--ALPHAB
    ETICAL"
600 LOCATE 18,20: PRINT "8.   RETURN TO PROGRAM MENU"
620 LOCATE 20,20: INPUT "Which number please ";NUMBER
640 IF NUMBER < 1 OR NUMBER > 8 THEN GOSUB 9000
660 IF NUMBER = 1 THEN 1000
680 IF NUMBER = 2 THEN 2000
700 IF NUMBER = 3 THEN 3000
720 IF NUMBER = 4 THEN 4000
740 IF NUMBER = 5 THEN 5000
760 IF NUMBER = 6 THEN 6000
780 IF NUMBER = 7 THEN 7000
800 IF NUMBER = 8 THEN RUN "MAILMENU"
820 GOTO 440
840 :
860 :
1000 REM **--ORIGINAL ORDER ROUTINE--**
1020 GOSUB 10000: REM Printer Routine
1040 CLS: LOCATE 5,1
1060 FOR I = 1 TO K
1080 IF LINES$(I) = "*" THEN 1160
1100 IF LINES$(I) = "!" AND PRINTER$ = "NO" THEN PRINT:G
     OTO 1160
```

```
1120 IF LINES$(I) = "⌐" AND PRINTER$ = "YES" THEN LPRINT
     :GOTO 1160
1140 IF PRINTER$ = "NO" THEN PRINT LINES$(I) ELSE LPRINT
     LINES$(I)
1160 NEXT I
1180 GOTO 20000: REM Return to Menu Routine
1200 :
1220 :
2000 REM **--NAME ONLY ROUTINE--**
2020 GOSUB 10000: REM Printer Routine
2040 CLS: LOCATE 5,1
2060 FOR I = 1 TO (K - 1)
2080 IF LINES$(I) = LINES$(1) AND PRINTER$ = "NO" THEN P
     RINT I;LINES$(I)
2100 IF LINES$(I) = LINES$(1) AND PRINTER$ = "YES" THEN
     LPRINT I;LINES$(I)
2120 IF LINES$(I) = "⌐" AND PRINTER$ = "NO" THEN PRINT I
     + 1;LINES$(I + 1)
2140 IF LINES$(I) = "⌐" AND PRINTER$ = "YES" THEN LPRINT
     I + 1;LINES$(I + 1)
2160 NEXT I
2180 GOTO 20000: REM Return to Menu Routine
2200 :
2220 :
3000 REM **--NO PHONE ROUTINE--**
3020 GOSUB 10000: REM Printer Routine
3040 CLS: LOCATE 5,1
3060 FOR I = 1 TO K
3080 IF LINES$(I) = "*" THEN I = I + 1: GOTO 3160
3100 IF LINES$(I) = "⌐" AND PRINTER$ = "NO" THEN PRINT:
     GOTO 3160
3120 IF LINES$(I) = "⌐" AND PRINTER$ = "YES" THEN LPRINT
     : GOTO 3160
3140 IF PRINTER$ = "NO" THEN PRINT LINES$(I) ELSE LPRINT
     LINES$(I)
3160 NEXT I
3180 GOTO 20000: REM Return to Menu Routine
3200 :
3220 :
4000 REM **--SEARCH ROUTINE--**
4020 GOSUB 10000: REM Printer Routine
4040 CLS: LOCATE 5,1
4060 PRINT "Type `END' when finished."
4080 INPUT "Name to find ";FIND$
4100 IF FIND$ =  "END" OR FIND$ = "end" THEN 4480
4120 PRINT
4140 FOR I = 1 TO K
4160 IF LINES$(I) = FIND$ THEN 4200
4180 GOTO 4420
4200 IF LINES$(I) = "*" THEN 4420
4220 IF LINES$(I) = "⌐" THEN 4420
4240 IF PRINTER$ = "NO" THEN PRINT LINES$(I) ELSE LPRINT
     LINES$(I)
```

```
4260 IF PRINTER$ = "NO" THEN PRINT LINES$(I + 1) ELSE LP
     RINT LINES$(I + 1)
4280 IF PRINTER$ = "NO" THEN PRINT LINES$(I + 2) ELSE LP
     RINT LINES$(I + 2)
4300 IF LINES$(I + 3) < > "*" AND PRINTER$ = "NO" THEN P
     RINT LINES$(I + 3)
4320 IF LINES$(I + 3) < > "*" AND PRINTER$ = "YES" THEN
     LPRINT LINES$(I + 3)
4340 IF LINES$(I + 4) = "*" THEN 4400
4360 IF PRINTER$ = "NO" THEN PRINT LINES$(I + 4): GOTO 4
     420
4380 IF PRINTER$ = "YES" THEN LPRINT LINES$(I + 4): GOTO
     4420
4400 IF PRINTER$ = "NO" THEN PRINT LINES$(I + 5) ELSE LP
     RINT LINES$(I + 5)
4420 NEXT I
4440 PRINT
4460 GOTO 4060: REM Repeat the routine until done
4480 GOTO 20000: REM Return to Menu Routine
5000 REM **--SEARCH ROUTINE NO PHONE--**
5020 GOSUB 10000: REM Printer Routine
5040 CLS: LOCATE 5,1
5060 PRINT "Type 'END' when finished."
5080 INPUT "Name to find ";FIND$
5100 IF FIND$ =  "END" OR FIND$ = "end" THEN 5520
5120 PRINT
5140 FOR I = 1 TO K
5160 IF LINES$(I) = FIND$ THEN 5200
5180 GOTO 5460
5200 IF LINES$(I) = "*" THEN I = I + 1: GOTO 5460
5220 IF LINES$(I) = "1" AND PRINTER$ = "NO" THEN PRINT :
     GOTO 5460
5240 IF LINES$(I) = "1" AND PRINTER$ = "YES" THEN LPRINT
     : GOTO 5460
5260 IF PRINTER$ = "NO" THEN PRINT LINES$(I) ELSE LPRINT
     LINES$(I)
5280 IF PRINTER$ = "NO" THEN PRINT LINES$(I + 1) ELSE LP
     RINT LINES$(I + 1)
5300 IF PRINTER$ = "NO" THEN PRINT LINES$(I + 2) ELSE LP
     RINT LINES$(I + 2)
5320 IF LINES$(I + 3) < > "*" AND PRINTER$ = "NO" THEN P
     RINT LINES$(I + 3)
5340 IF LINES$(I + 3) < > "*" AND PRINTER$ = "YES" THEN
     LPRINT LINES$(I + 3)
5360 IF LINES$(I + 3) = "*" THEN I = I + 1: GOTO 5460
5380 IF LINES$(I + 4) = "*" THEN I = I + 1: GOTO 5460
5400 IF PRINTER$ = "NO" THEN PRINT LINES$(I + 4): GOTO 5
     460
5420 IF PRINTER$ = "YES" THEN LPRINT LINES$(I + 4): GOTO
     5460
5440 IF PRINTER$ = "NO" THEN PRINT LINES$(I + 5) ELSE LP
     RINT LINES$(I + 5)
5460 NEXT I
5480 PRINT
```

```
5500 GOTO 5060: REM Repeat the routine until done
5520 GOTO 20000: REM Return to Menu Routine
5540 :
5560 :
6000 REM **--RANGE ROUTINE--**
6020 GOSUB 10000: REM Printer Routine
6040 CLS: LOCATE 5,1
6060 INPUT "Type beginning line number please ";BL
6080 PRINT
6100 IF BL < 1 THEN PRINT "Number too small": GOTO 6060
6120 INPUT "Type ending line number please ";EL
6140 PRINT
6160 IF EL > K THEN PRINT "Number too large": GOTO 6120
6180 FOR I = BL TO EL
6200 IF LINES$(I) = "*" THEN I = I + 1: GOTO 6280
6220 IF LINES$(I) = "|" AND PRINTER$ = "NO" THEN PRINT:
GOTO 6280
6240 IF LINES$(I) = "|" AND PRINTER$ = "YES" THEN LPRINT
     : GOTO 6280
6260 IF PRINTER$ = "NO" THEN PRINT LINES$(I) ELSE LPRINT
     LINES$(I)
6280 NEXT I
6300 GOTO 20000: REM Return to Menu Routine
6320 :
6340 :
7000 REM **--ALPHABETICAL ORDER ROUTINE--**
7020 CLS: LOCATE 5,1
7040 PRINT "WORKING--PLEASE DON'T TOUCH!!"
7060 :
7080 :
7100 REM Get first information-line
7120 FOR I = 1 TO K - 1
7140 IF LINES$(I) = LINES$(1) THEN 7240
7160 IF LINES$(I) = "|" THEN I = I + 1: GOTO 7240
7180 GOTO 7460
7200 :
7220 :
7240 REM Reverse order
7260 LN = LEN (LINES$(I))
7280 FOR J1 = 1 TO LN: IF MID$ (LINES$(I),J1,1) = " " TH
     EN J2 = J1
7300 NEXT J1
7320 IF J2 = 0 OR J2 > LN THEN AD$(I) = LINES$(I): GOTO
     7360
7340 AD$(I) = MID$ (LINES$(I),J2 + 1,LN - J2) +    "  " +
     LEFT$ (LINES$(I),J2)
7360 AD$(I) = AD$(I) + "**" + LINES$(I + 1) + "**" + LIN
     ES$(I + 2)
7380 IF LINES$(I + 3) < > "*" THEN AD$(I) = AD$(I) + "**
     " + LINES$(I + 3)
7400 IF LINES$(I + 4) = "*" THEN 7440
7420 AD$(I) = AD$(I) + "**" + LINES$(I + 4): GOTO 7460
7440 AD$(I) = AD$(I) + "**" + LINES$(I + 5)
7460 NEXT I
```

```
7480 :
7500 :
7520 REM Renumber for sort
7540 J = 1
7560 FOR I = 1 TO K
7580 IF LEN (AD$(I)) > Ø THEN ND$(J) = AD$(I): J = J + 1
7600 NEXT I
7620 N = J - 1
7640 :
7660 :
7680 REM  ***--QUICKSORT--***
7700 S1 = 1
7720 PRINT "WORKING--PLEASE DON'T TOUCH!!"
7740 L(1) = 1
7760 R(1) = N
7780 L1 = L(S1)
7800 R1 = R(S1)
7820 S1 = S1 -1
7840 L2 = L1
7860 R2 = R1
7880 X$ = ND$(INT((L1 + R1)/2))
7900 C = C + 1
7920 IF ND$(L2) = X$ OR ND$(L2) > X$ THEN 7980
7940 L2 = L2 + 1
7960 GOTO 7900
7980 C = C1
8000 IF X$ = ND$(R2) OR X$ > ND$(R2) THEN 8060
8020 R2 = R2 -1
8040 GOTO 7980
8060 IF L2 > R2 THEN 8200
8080 S = S + 1
8100 T$ = ND$(L2)
8120 ND$(L2) = ND$(R2)
8140 ND$(R2) = T$
8160 L2 = L2 + 1
8180 R2 = R2 - 1
8200 IF L2 = R2 OR L2 < R2 THEN 7900
8220 IF L2 = R1 OR L2 > R1 THEN 8300
8240 S1 = S1 + 1
8260 L(S1) = L2
8280 R(S1) = R1
8300 R1 = R2
8320 IF L1 < R1 THEN 7840
8340 IF S1 > Ø THEN 7780
8360 REM Sort Completed!
8380 :
8400 :
8420 REM **--Display--**
8440 GOSUB 10000: REM Printer Routine
8460 FOR I = 1 TO N
8480 PRINT ND$(I)
8500 PRINT
8520 NEXT I
8540 GOTO 20000: REM Return to Menu Routine
```

```
8560 :
8580 :
9000 REM **--INCORRECT NUMBER ROUTINE--**
9020 LOCATE 22,20
9040 PRINT "INCORRECT NUMBER. PLEASE CHOOSE AGAIN."
9060 RETURN
9080 :
9100 :
10000 REM **--PRINTER ROUTINE--**
10020 CLS: LOCATE 5,1
10040 PRINT "Do you want a paper print out?"
10060 PRINT : INPUT "Type `Y' or `N' ";YES$
10080 IF YES$ = "Y" OR YES$ ="y" THEN 10220
10100 IF YES$ = "N" OR YES$ = "n" THEN 10180
10120 PRINT "INCORRECT CHOICE. PLEASE CHOOSE AGAIN!"
10140 FOR I = 1 TO 1000: NEXT I
10160 GOTO 10000
10180 PRINTER$ = "NO"
10200 RETURN
10220 PRINTER$ = "YES"
10240 RETURN
10260 :
10280 :
20000 REM **--RETURN TO MENU ROUTINE--**
20020 PRINTER$ = "NO"
20040 INPUT "Press `ENTER' to go to Display Menu ";L$
20060 GOTO 400
```

7
Correcting Sequential Files

We can use the same beginning for our CORRECT program as we have for both of our READER programs. The one exception is line 100, which should be changed to reflect the proper name for this program. Once again, we need a menu, so our routine beginning at line 400 will be much the same also.

```
400 REM **--MENU ROUTINE--**
420 CLS: LOCATE 5,24: PRINT "CORRECTOR MENU"
440 LOCATE  7,20: PRINT "1. CHANGE OR CORRECT
    INFORMATION"
460 LOCATE  9,20: PRINT "2. DELETE INFORMATION"
480 LOCATE 11,20: PRINT "3. WRITE REVISED FILE"
500 LOCATE 13,20: PRINT "4. RETURN TO PROGRAM MENU"
520 LOCATE 15,20: INPUT "Which number ";NB
540 IF NB < 1 OR NB > 4 THEN 520
560 IF NB = 1 THEN 1000
580 IF NB = 2 THEN 2000
600 IF NB = 3 THEN 3000
620 IF NB = 4 THEN RUN "MAILMENU"
```

By now, these statements should be familiar enough that no further explanation need be given. We are simply going to display a menu of a number of choices on the screen. Line 540 checks to see if the user has typed a valid number. If not, control is returned to the instruction (line 520) which again asks for a number.

The following correction and deletion routines show only one method out of many possible ones for accomplishing the same task. Some may object to rewriting the entire file for a single correction, but, for now, the method we will use is to bring the entire file into memory, make our necessary corrections or deletions, and then write the file back out to disk again.

CORRECTION ROUTINE

```
1000 REM **--CORRECTION ROUTINE--**
1020 CLS: LOCATE 5,1
1040 PRINT "Type '0' when finished"
1060 INPUT "Display which line ";NUMBER
1080 IF NUMBER = 0 THEN 400
1100 PRINT
1120 PRINT NUMBER;"   ";LINES$(NUMBER)
1140 PRINT
1160 PRINT "Is this correct? ";
1180 INPUT "Type 'Y' OR 'N' ";YES$
1200 IF YES$ = "Y" OR YES$ = "y" THEN 1000
1220 PRINT
1240 PRINT "Type in the correct information"
1260 PRINT
1280 PRINT NUMBER;"   ";:INPUT CN$
1300 PRINT: LINES$(NUMBER) = CN$
1320 PRINT NUMBER;"   ";LINES$(NUMBER)
1340 PRINT
1360 GOTO 1160: REM Ask again
1990 :
1995 :
```

We ask for the line number the user believes to contain incorrect information. The line of information is displayed. If it is not correct, the individual is given an opportunity to type in the correct information. The amount of new information or corrected information is not limited except by the normal 255-character string limitation. This feature is one big advantage over other correction methods, which may require that the corrected information be exactly the same number of characters as the original information. Finally, the corrected information is displayed and the correct information question is repeated. Line 1200 checks for a positive response to the question about correct information. If the information is correct, the user is taken back to the original request concerning the line number to be displayed. Line 1080 checks for a "0" which indicates that the user wishes to return to the menu. Line 1300 is the instruction that actually exchanges the corrected information for the old information. You will notice that nothing is written to disk at this time. This may cause problems for some individuals. Under this system, it is possible to make a number of changes before the file is rewritten to the disk. It is also possible, therefore, to forget to write the corrected file back to disk. Such a system may be impractical in certain situations ... for example, when a somewhat forgetful person is making the changes. For our purposes, however, we want to make all corrections and deletions before rewriting the file.

DELETION ROUTINE

The deletion routine is more complicated than the correction routine.

```
2000 REM **--DELETE ROUTINE--**
2020 CLS: LOCATE 5,1
2040 PRINT "Type '0' when finished"
2060 INPUT "Delete which line ";LN
2080 IF LN = 0 THEN 400
2100 PRINT
2120 PRINT LN;"   ";LINES$(LN)
2140 PRINT
2160 PRINT "ARE YOU SURE? TYPE 'YES' IF SURE";
2180 INPUT YES$
2200 IF YES$ = "YES" OR YES$ = "yes" THEN 2260
2220 GOTO 2000: REM Begin again
2240 :
2260 J = LN
2280 IF LINES$(J) = "!" THEN 2320
2300 J = J + 1: GOTO 2280
2320 FOR I = LN TO J
2340 PRINT I;"   ";LINES$(I)
2360 LINES$(I) = "DELETED": D = D + 1
2380 NEXT I
2400 PRINT
2420 PRINT "DELETING THIS INFORMATION"
2440 Q = 1
2460 FOR I = 1 TO K
2480 IF LINES$(I) = "DELETED" THEN 2540
2500 LINES$(Q) = LINES$(I)
2520 Q = Q + 1
```

```
2540 NEXT I
2560 :
2580 K = K - D: REM Subtract # of lines deleted
     for new total.
2600 D = 0: J = 0
2620 PRINT : INPUT "Press 'ENTER' to return to the
     MENU. "; L$
2640 GOTO 400: REM Return to Menu
2990 :
2995 :
```

There are other ways of doing the same thing we did in this routine. Some of the other ways might be shorter, but this way is understandable. Several things need to be done in this deletion routine. First, the information to be deleted must be identified (lines 2000 to 2220). Second, the information following the deleted material must be renumbered (instruction-lines 2260 to 2540) so that there are no empty information-lines; otherwise, an ERROR will occur when these information-lines are encountered. Finally, the number of deleted information-lines must be subtracted (line 2580) from the original total number of lines.

Down to line 2220, there is nothing new. It is essentially the same beginning as the correction routine. At 2260, we set a counter (J) equal to the line number of the name of the individual to be deleted. Next, we increase the counter by one until we have found the information-line for the end of the information associated with the individual to be deleted; i.e., the separator symbol "!". Now we know which information-lines to delete: the lines beginning with LN and going through J. We can use a loop (lines 2320–2380) to delete our information, and we use another loop (lines 2460–2540) to do the resequencing of the remaining information. We use two additional counters: Q to keep track of the new information line-numbers, and D to keep track of the number of deleted lines. Q is set to 1 for the beginning of the file, but it could be set to LN, the start of the deleted material. Line 2480 is the key to the resequencing. If LINES$(I) equals the word "DELETED", then the counter Q is not increased while the counter I is increased. Remember that Q is keeping track of the new line numbers while I is the old line number. Line 2500 resequences the LINES$ string array. Line 2580 subtracts the number of deleted lines from the original number of lines (K). Line 2600 is necessary in case more information is to be deleted during this session.

```
3000 REM **--FILE OUTPUT ROUTINE--**
3020 OPEN "ADDRESS.BAK" FOR OUTPUT AS #1
3040 CLOSE #1
```

```
3060 KILL "ADDRESS.BAK"
3080 NAME "ADDRESS.DAT" AS "ADDRESS.BAK"
3100 :
3120 OPEN "ADDPTR.DAT" FOR OUTPUT AS #2
3140 OPEN "ADDRESS.DAT" FOR OUTPUT AS #3
3160 PRINT #2,K: REM New pointer value
3180 FOR I = 1 TO K
3200 PRINT #3,LINES$(I): REM Changed information
3220 NEXT I
3240 CLOSE #2,#3
3260 :
3280 RUN "MAILMENU
```

There is something different with this file routine. Where did
ADDRESS.BAK come from? What is NAME? The DOS command
OPEN will create a file by that name if the file does not already exist.
Therefore, if the file, ADDRESS.BAK, does not already exist, the command, OPEN "ADDRESS.BAK", will create a file by that name. Next,
we delete that file since it must either be an empty file or a now
unnecessary backup copy. (The first time this program is used, there
will not be an ADDRESS.BAK file.) Line 3080 renames the file
ADDRESS.DAT (which now contains our uncorrected information) so
that it becomes ADDRESS.BAK. Finally, we open a new
ADDRESS.DAT file and write out our corrected information to it
(lines 3120−3240). Line 3280 returns to the MAILMENU program. At
this point, if you have not already done so, you should save this program to the diskette that contains all the other MAILING LIST SYS-
TEM programs. Type:

SAVE "CORRECT

Typing FILES now should show:

```
COMMAND .COM BASIC  .BAS HELLO   .BAS EXAMPLE .BAS
CREATE  .BAS ADDPTR .DAT ADDRESS .DAT READER1 .BAS
ADDER1  .BAS ADDER2 .BAS READER2 .BAS CORRECT .BAS
```

It is not necessary to make changes in the MAILMENU program in
order to include this CORRECTor program. Remember that additional
code was added in anticipation of this program. The MAILING LIST
SYSTEM should now be complete.

This general method of correcting or deleting information has the
added benefit of providing us with a backup copy of our precorrected
ADDRESS.DAT file. A very useful routine is the sequence of opening
and deleting a backup file, renaming the uncorrected file as the new
backup, and writing out the corrected information to a new file under
the original file name. If you have two disk drives, you can put the

backup in one drive and the new master in the other drive and have the computer switch between the two drives. The more drives you have, the greater your flexibility in manipulating files in this manner.

Even without two drives, the ADDRESS.DAT file and the ADDRESS.BAK file can be put on two different diskettes. Some method of making the computer pause after line 3080 would be necessary in order to allow the user to swap diskettes. Two possibilities would be: a loop of a certain duration, or an input statement informing the user that it is time to switch diskettes.

In the next chapter, we will take a look at some more techniques for accessing sequential data files.

QUESTIONS

1. *True or False:* Under the correction method presented in this chapter, corrected information is immediately written to the disk.

2. What happens to the original ADDRESS.DAT file once information in it has been changed?

3. What is the BASIC command used to remove unwanted files?

4. What is the BASIC command used to change the name of files?

5. *True or False:* Two disk drives are necessary in order to back up a data file.

ANSWERS

1. False
2. It becomes ADDRESS.BAK.
3. KILL
4. NAME
5. False

CORRECT

```
100 REM   ***--MAILING LIST CORRECTOR--***
120 :
140 :
160 REM **--FILE INPUT ROUTINE--**
180 OPEN "ADDPTR.DAT" FOR INPUT AS #1
200 OPEN "ADDRESS.DAT" FOR INPUT AS #2
220 INPUT #1,K: REM Get number of records
240 CLOSE #1
260 DIM LINES$(K)
280 FOR I = 1 TO K
300 LINE INPUT #2,LINES$(I)
320 NEXT I
340 CLOSE #2
360 :
380 :
400 REM **--MENU ROUTINE--**
420 CLS: LOCATE 5,24: PRINT "CORRECTOR MENU"
440 LOCATE  7,20: PRINT "1.   CHANGE OR CORRECT INFORMATION"
460 LOCATE  9,20: PRINT "2.   DELETE INFORMATION"
480 LOCATE 11,20: PRINT "3.   WRITE REVISED FILE"
500 LOCATE 13,20: PRINT "4.   RETURN TO PROGRAM MENU"
520 LOCATE 15,20: INPUT "Which number ";NB
540 IF NB < 1 OR NB > 4 THEN 520
560 IF NB = 1 THEN 1000
580 IF NB = 2 THEN 2000
600 IF NB = 3 THEN 3000
620 IF NB = 4 THEN RUN"MAILMENU"
640 :
660 :
1000 REM **--CORRECTION ROUTINE--**
1020 CLS: LOCATE 5,1
1040 PRINT "Type `0' when finished."
1060 INPUT "Display which line ";NUMBER
1080 IF NUMBER = 0 THEN 400
1100 PRINT
1120 PRINT NUMBER;" ";LINES$(NUMBER)
1140 PRINT
1160 PRINT "Is this correct?"
1180 INPUT "Type `Y ' or `N' ";YES$
1200 IF YES$ = "Y" OR YES$ = "y" THEN 1000
1220 PRINT
1240 PRINT "Type in the correct information"
1260 PRINT
1280 PRINT NUMBER;" ";:INPUT CN$
1300 PRINT : LINES$(NUMBER) = CN$
1320 PRINT NUMBER;" ";LINES$(NUMBER)
1340 PRINT
1360 GOTO 1160: REM Ask again
1990 :
1995 :
```

```
2000 REM **--DELETION ROUTINE--**
2020 CLS: LOCATE 5,1
2040 PRINT "Type `0' when finished."
2060 INPUT "Delete which line ";LN
2080 IF LN = 0 THEN 400
2100 PRINT
2120 PRINT LN;" ";LINES$(LN)
2140 PRINT
2160 PRINT "ARE YOU SURE? TYPE `YES' IF SURE";
2180 INPUT YES$
2200 IF YES$ = "YES" OR YES$ = "yes" THEN 2260
2220 GOTO 2000: REM Begin again
2240 :
2260 J = LN
2280 IF LINES$(J) = "|" THEN 2320
2300 J = J + 1: GOTO 2280
2320 FOR I = LN TO J
2340 PRINT I;" ";LINES$(I)
2360 LINES$(I) = "DELETED": D = D + 1
2380 NEXT I
2400 PRINT
2420 PRINT "DELETING THIS INFORMATION"
2440 Q = 1
2460 FOR I = 1 TO K
2480 IF LINES$(I) = "DELETED" THEN 2540
2500 LINES$(Q) = LINES$(I)
2520 Q = Q + 1
2540 NEXT I
2560 :
2580 K = K - D: REM Subtract # of lines deleted for new
     total.
2600 D = 0: J = 0
2620 PRINT : INPUT "Press `ENTER' to return to the MENU.
     ";L$
2640 GOTO 400: REM Return to Menu
2990 :
2995 :
3000 REM **--FILE OUTPUT ROUTINE--**
3020 OPEN "ADDRESS.BAK" FOR OUTPUT AS #1
3040 CLOSE #1
3060 KILL "ADDRESS.BAK"
3080 NAME "ADDRESS.DAT" AS "ADDRESS.BAK"
3100 :
3120 OPEN "ADDPTR.DAT" FOR OUTPUT AS #2
3140 OPEN "ADDRESS.DAT" FOR OUTPUT AS #3
3160 PRINT #2,K: REM New pointer value
3180 FOR I = 1 TO K
3200 PRINT #3,LINES$(I): REM Changed information
3220 NEXT I
3240 CLOSE #2,#3
3260 :
3280 RUN "MAILMENU
```

8

Additional
Sequential File Techniques

We are going to explore some other ways to work with sequential files and look at additional techniques for file handling. In this chapter, I am going to concentrate on the file routines of the various programs presented and not discuss the rest of the programming. The listings for the complete programs are included at the end of this chapter along with an explanation of the new commands used in these programs.

We will begin with a series of programs that allows an individual to practice math and keep a record of the scores achieved. These programs are essentially drill and practice and may not be the best educational use of the computer, but for the purpose of demonstrating how files can be used in a variety of ways, these drill and practice programs will be sufficient.

We again start with careful thought and preparation. We need a separate program for each mathematical operation, along with a program for the scores. This means that another program menu would be convenient. The essential difference between the operation programs is the sign of the operation—"+" for addition, "×" for multiplication, etc. With the exception of division, the numbers can be displayed in basically the same way. Therefore, the program presented for addition can also be used for subtraction and multiplication with changes made to only five lines: 100, 360, 380, 710, and 720. In all of those lines, the references to addition should be changed to the desired operation. Type:

```
LOAD ADD
LIST 100
```

Line 100 is:

```
100 REM ***--ADDITION--***
```

Line 100 should be:

```
100 REM ***--SUBTRACTION--***
```

or, for multiplication:

```
100 REM ***--MULTIPLICATION--***
```

Lines 710 and 720 are the most important to change. They are:

```
710 C = B + A
720 S$ = "+"
```

and should be changed to:

```
710 C = B - A
720 S$ = "-"
```

or, for multiplication:

```
710 C = B * A
720 S$ = "X"
```

Once all the changes have been made, SAVE the new program by typing:

```
SAVE "SUBTRACT
```

or, for multiplication:

```
SAVE "MULTIPLY
```

The program for division requires additional code because the numbers must be formatted differently, and provision has been made so that all problems come out even. This last provision slows the generation of problems. The process speeds up considerably when the number being divided contains at least two more digits than the divisor.

All these programs can be included in one large program, but the flow of logic in the program would not be as easy to follow as it is with separate programs. Little would be gained by forcing everything into one program since BASIC allows us to switch from one program to another.

We must carefully consider what information we want to save in our data file for scores. There are several pieces of information that might be important to save, but a good rule is to save only what is absolutely necessary—what it would be hard or impossible to calculate from existing information. For example, we could save the total number of problems, the number correct, the number wrong, the percentage, the name of the individual, the kind of mathematical operation, the number of digits chosen, etc. If the programs were slightly altered, we could also save the actual problems missed, the number of tries on a particular problem, and the last question the person tried. Obviously, all of this information is not necessary, although certain individuals might value and save information others would not want.

The first step is to decide what information to save. In this example, we will save four things: the type of operation, the number of digits in the operation, the number of correct answers, and the number of wrong answers. Once we decide what to save, we need only save the assigned variables for these pieces of information. The code to do this is given below.

```
3000 REM **--FILE OUTPUT ROUTINE--**
3010 OPEN NAMES$ + ".DAT" FOR APPEND AS #1
3020 PRINT #1,S$: REM SIGN
3030 PRINT #1,DT: REM # OF DIGITS
3040 PRINT #1,CR: REM # CORRECT
3050 PRINT #1,WR: REM # WRONG
3060 CLOSE #1
3070 RUN "MATHMENU
3080:
3090:
```

Some of this should be familiar. But the sequence and a few commands may appear different.

Remember that in our MAILING LIST SYSTEM programs we used one program to create the ADDRESS.DAT file and another program to add to it. Such a sequence is usually necessary when creating a file that will later be added to. The use of the OPEN ... FOR OUTPUT command sequence places the file pointer at the very beginning of the file and destroys any information already in the file. That is the reason for the APPEND command. By OPENing the file FOR APPEND, the need for two separate programs is eliminated.

Now we have the following sequence. The first time the program is run, the computer will attempt to APPEND the information into a file that does not yet exist. When it finds that no such file exists, it first creates the file and then APPENDs the first set of information into the file. Thus, the file is created and the first set of information written into the file. The second time (and succeeding times) the program is run, the computer simply APPENDs information into the file because it finds that such a file does exist. We have accomplished in one routine what would normally have taken two routines to do.

You should also notice that we are using a variable for the file name. In our MAILING LIST SYSTEM programs, we always used the constant "ADDRESS.DAT" for our file name. But in this situation, and in many file routines, it is more convenient to assign a variable as the file name. Every time an individual uses any of these programs, the information is kept in a file under that person's name. By using a variable for the file name, we eliminate the need for separate programs for each person that uses any of the math operation programs.

You must be careful to type your name the same way every time you use the programs. For example, if I answer that my name is DAVID the first time I use these programs, the file will be created under the name of DAVID. If I come back later and answer that my name is DAVE, a new and separate file will be created for DAVE. As with most things, there are advantages to the use of a variable for the file name, but there are also disadvantages. The user may get tired of being required to type his/her name, but the use of a variable for the file name remains a popular programming technique. The variable must be a string variable since no file name can begin with a number. (The file name can contain a number; it just cannot begin with a number.)

The file routine used in the program SCORES is very similar to the one just discussed, but instead of writing information to the disk, this routine reads information from the disk.

```
100  REM ***--SCORES--***
110  :
120  :
130  DIM S$(100), DT(100), CR(100), WR(100)
140  I = 1
150  CLS: LOCATE 5,1
160  INPUT "Student's Name Please"; NAMES$
170  :
180  :
190  REM **--FILE INPUT ROUTINE--**
200  OPEN NAMES$ + ".DAT" FOR INPUT AS #1
210  IF EOF(1) THEN 280
220  INPUT #1,S$(I): REM SIGN OF OPERATION
230  INPUT #1,DT(I): REM # OF DIGITS
240  INPUT #1,CR(I): REM # CORRECT
250  INPUT #1,WR(I): REM # WRONG
260  I = I + 1
270  GOTO 210
280  CLOSE #1
290  :
300  :
```

Lines 100 to 180 are necessary to set up the file input routine in lines 190 to 280. This time, the EOF (1) function is used to test for the end of file number 1, or the end of the data. If the EOF function is not included, we have no way of telling how much information or how many records exist in the file. We did not keep track of that information by writing out a counter to the file like we did in the MAILING LIST SYSTEM. Without the EOF function, we would get an END OF DATA error message and the program would halt. With that EOF function, the computer is instructed to go to the instruction at line 280 and proceed from there. At this point, we close the file since we are now certain that we have all the information the file contains. The use of the EOF function saves both programming and disk space.

You should notice one other major difference in this routine. In most of our programs, we have used FOR ... NEXT loops. But this time, we do not know how many items the file contains and, therefore, we do not know how large the counter eventually needs to become. It is true that we could pick an arbitrary number, but a better method is the one used in this routine. This method is still a loop since the computer is instructed to follow the instructions down to line 270 and then go back to the instruction at line 210 and do everything over again. What gets us out of this loop? The EOF function does when it executes as the end of the file is encountered. When this loop is finished, we should have the values we want from the file and can proceed to the display routine.

These math programs provide additional file handling techniques, as well as a set of useful drill and practice programs. The menu program used the same method we have been using to display a set of choices and then run the appropriate program. Apart from file handling, the math programs also have some programming techniques that might prove interesting.

To conclude this chapter, I have added three other programs that make use of file handling and fit our purpose of demonstrating filing techniques. The programs are presented in a rough form. Individuals may wish (and, in fact, are encouraged) to add parts to these programs or modify the format. A random access recipe file would probably provide a better method for this particular application. To make this recipe program useful, recipes should probably be grouped; i.e. desserts, appetizers, main dish, etc., with a separate file for each grouping (change recipe name to appetizer name, dessert name, etc). The final programs present an elementary method of drill and practice on any subject.

In the final chapter on sequential access files, we will take a brief look at the possibility of a standard method for storing data so that the data can be used by a variety of commercial programs.

QUESTIONS

1. A good rule to follow in deciding what information to save is to save: (a) everything possible, (b) as little as possible, (c) only what is absolutely necessary.

2. *True or False*: APPEND can open a file.

3. *True or False*: It is never possible to use a variable as a file name.

4. What type of variable can be used as a file name?

5. Which BASIC statement retrieves only the integer portion of a number?

6. Which BASIC statement converts a number into a string?

7. Which BASIC statement converts a string into a number?

8. Which BASIC statement can be used to test for the end of a sequential access file?

ANSWERS

1. c
2. True
3. False
4. String
5. INT
6. STR$
7. VAL
8. EOF ()

NEW COMMANDS OR TERMS
IN THE FOLLOWING PROGRAMS

1. ^: Raise to the power of the number following this symbol.
2. RANDOMIZE: Seed the random number generator with a different number every time the program is run.
3. TIME$: Retrieve the current time.
4. RND: Generate a random number.
5. INT: Take only the integer portion of the number in parentheses.
6. LEN: Find the length of the string in terms of the number of characters in the string.
7. STR$: Convert the specified number into a string value.
8. CHR$(95): Display the underline character.
9. VAL: Give the numeric value of a string.
10. SGN: Returns the signum function.
11. CHR$(34): Display the quotation mark character.
12. CSRLIN: Current screen line.

MATHMENU

```
100 REM ***--MATH MENU--***
110 :
120 :
130 TB = 28: CLS
140 KEY OFF
150 LOCATE 2,TB
160 PRINT "MATH MENU"
170 LOCATE 5,TB
180 PRINT "1.  ADDITION"
190 LOCATE 7,TB
200 PRINT "2.  SUBTRACTION"
210 LOCATE 9,TB
220 PRINT "3.  MULTIPLICATION"
230 LOCATE 11,TB
240 PRINT "4.  DIVISION"
250 LOCATE 13,TB
260 PRINT "5.  SCORES"
270 LOCATE 15,TB
280 PRINT "6.  INFORMATION"
290 LOCATE 17,TB
300 PRINT "7.  END"
310 LOCATE 19,TB
320 INPUT "WHICH PROGRAM NUMBER";NUMBER
330 IF NUMBER < 1 OR NUMBER > 7 THEN GOSUB 9000
340 IF NUMBER = 1 THEN RUN "ADD
350 IF NUMBER = 2 THEN RUN "SUBTRACT
360 IF NUMBER = 3 THEN RUN "MULTIPLY
370 IF NUMBER = 4 THEN RUN "DIVIDE
380 IF NUMBER = 5 THEN RUN "SCORES
390 IF NUMBER = 6 THEN 1000
400 IF NUMBER = 7 THEN KEY ON: END
410 GOTO 310: REM ASK AGAIN
420 :
430 :
1000 REM **--INFORMATION--**
1010 CLS
1020 PRINT "This is a series of math drill and practice
     programs."
1030 PRINT
1040 PRINT "It is designed to allow for as much flexibil
     ity as"
1050 PRINT
1060 PRINT "possible. The question about the number of d
     igits"
1070 PRINT
1080 PRINT "might, at first, seem confusing. The questio
     n simply"
1090 PRINT
1100 PRINT "asks for the greatest number of digits possi
     ble in"
```

```
1110 PRINT
1120 PRINT "either figure. The next two questions furthe
     r allow"
1130 PRINT
1140 PRINT "you to limit the possible problems. For exam
     ple, if"
1150 PRINT
1160 PRINT "you wanted to practice multiplying by `5',
     you could"
1170 PRINT
1180 PRINT "choose three digit numbers and then answer w
     ith a `5'"
1190 PRINT
1200 PRINT "for each of the next two questions. You woul
     d then be"
1210 PRINT
1220 PRINT "given problems like: 345 x 5 or 823 x 5."
1230 PRINT
1240 GOSUB 5000: REM PAUSE ROUTINE
1250 PRINT
1260 PRINT "Another example would be to add two digit nu
     mbers by"
1270 PRINT
1280 PRINT "answering the questions in this way:"
1290 PRINT
1300 PRINT "HOW MANY DIGITS--2"
1310 PRINT
1320 PRINT "LARGEST NUMBER--99"
1330 PRINT
1340 PRINT "SMALLEST NUMBER--1"
1350 PRINT
1360 PRINT "You could then get problems like:"
1370 PRINT
1380 PRINT "58 + 34 or 87 + 9."
1390 PRINT
1400 PRINT "Trying the different possibilities will soon
     indicate"
1410 PRINT
1420 PRINT "the flexibility."
1430 PRINT
1440 GOSUB 5000: REM PAUSE ROUTINE
1450 PRINT
1460 PRINT "The division section will only give problems
     that come"
1470 PRINT
1480 PRINT "out even. You may have to wait a short time
     for the next"
1490 PRINT
1500 PRINT "problem. This is because the numbers generat
     ed must meet"
1510 PRINT
1520 PRINT "certain specifications. The process speeds u
     p when the"
1530 PRINT
```

```
1540 PRINT "number being divided contains at least two m
     ore digits"
1550 PRINT
1560 PRINT "than the divisor."
1570 PRINT
1580 GOSUB 5000: REM PAUSE SUBROUTINE
1590 PRINT
1600 PRINT "This is not a professional program and, ther
     efore, does"
1610 PRINT
1620 PRINT "not do a lot of error checking. You can cras
     h the programs"
1630 PRINT
1640 PRINT "with confusing answers or mistakes in typing
     . Typing a"
1650 PRINT
1660 PRINT "`CTRL C' will end any program. You must then
     start over."
1670 PRINT
1680 PRINT "This series of programs was done mainly to d
     emonstrate,"
1690 PRINT
1700 PRINT "in a useful manner, certain file handling ca
     pabilities."
1710 PRINT
1720 GOSUB 5000: REM PAUSE SUBROUTINE
1730 GOTO 100: RETURN TO MENU
1740 :
1750 :
5000 REM **--PAUSE ROUTINE--**
5010 LOCATE 25,1
5020 INPUT "Press `ENTER' to continue";L$
5030 CLS
5040 RETURN
5050 :
5060 :
9000 REM **--INCORRECT NUMBER ROUTINE--**
9010 LOCATE 22,20
9020 PRINT"INCORRECT NUMBER. PLEASE CHOOSE AGAIN."
9030 RETURN
```

ADD

```
100 REM ***--ADDITION--***
110 :
120 :
130 REM **--VARIABLE LIST--**
140 REM A  =   TOP NUMBER
150 REM B  =   BOTTOM NUMBER
160 REM C  =   CORRECT ANSWER
170 REM D  =   STUDENT'S ANSWER
180 REM Q  =   COUNTER
190 REM W  =   PREVIOUS ANSWER
200 REM Z  =   NUMBER OF TRIES
210 REM CR =   CORRECT ANSWERS
220 REM RD =   RANDOM # SEED
230 REM WR =   WRONG ANSWERS
240 REM DT =   # OF DIGITS
250 REM LA =   # OF DIGITS IN A
260 REM LB =   # OF DIGITS IN B
270 REM LC =   # OF DIGITS IN C
280 REM LM =   # OF DIGITS IN MAX AMOUNT
290 REM OTHER VARIABLES ARE DESCRIPTIVE
300 :
310 :
320 REM **--REQUEST USER INFORMATION--**
330 CLS: LOCATE 5,1
340 INPUT "HOW MANY DIGITS ";DIGIT
350 PRINT
360 INPUT "WHAT IS THE LARGEST FIGURE FOR THE NUMBER YOU
    ARE ADDING BY";MAX
370 PRINT
380 INPUT "WHAT IS THE SMALLEST FIGURE FOR THE NUMBER YOU
    ARE ADDING BY";MN
390 DT = DIGIT: DIGIT = 10 ^ DIGIT
400 PRINT
410 INPUT "What is your name";NAMES$
420 :
430 REM CONVERT TO UPPERCASE
440 CVT$ = NAMES$
450 GOSUB 6000: REM UPPERCASE SUBROUTINE
460 NAMES$ = CVT$
470 :
480 :
490 REM **--CREATE PROBLEM--**
500 REM SEED RND W/SECONDS FROM TIME
510 RD = VAL(RIGHT$(TIME$,2))
520 RANDOMIZE RD
530 :
540 MAX$ = STR$(MAX)
550 LM = LEN (MAX$)
560 LM = LM - 1
570 :
```

```
580 REM WHEN B'S DIGITS < DT
590 IF DT = LM + 1 OR DT < LM + 1 THEN 660
600 LM = 10 ^ LM
610 B = INT(RND(1) * LM)
620 IF B < MN THEN 610
630 IF B > MAX THEN 610
640 GOTO 700: REM GET # FOR `A'
650 :
660 Z = 1
670 B = INT (RND (1) * DIGIT)
680 IF B < MN THEN 670
690 IF B > MAX THEN 670
700 A = INT (RND (1) * DIGIT)
710 C = A + B: REM DETERMINE OPERATION
720 S$ = "+"
730 IF C < 0 THEN 670: REM FOR SUBTRACTION
740 IF C = W THEN 670: REM PREVIOUS ANSWER
750 W = C
760 :
770 :
780 REM **--DISPLAY PROBLEM--**
790 REM DETERMINE LENGTHS
800 A$ = STR$(A)
810 LA = LEN (A$)
820 A$ = RIGHT$(A$,LA - 1): REM STRIP OFF SIGN
830 LA = LEN(A$)
840 B$ = STR$(B)
850 LB = LEN (B$)
860 B$ = RIGHT$(B$,LB - 1): REM STRIP OFF SIGN
870 LB = LEN (B$)
880 C$ = STR$(C)
890 LC = LEN (C$)
900 C$ = RIGHT$(C$,LC - 1): REM STRIP OFF SIGN
910 LC = LEN (C$)
920 :
930 REM FORMAT
940 CLS: LOCATE 5,25
950 PRINT "Type `END' when finished!"
960 LOCATE 10,37 - LA: PRINT A$
970 LOCATE 11,(37 - (LB + 1)): PRINT S$;B$
980 :
990 REM DRAW LINE
1000 Q = 1
1010 IF LA > LB THEN Q = 0
1020 LOCATE 12,37 - (DT + Q)
1030 FOR I = 1 TO (DT + Q)
1040 PRINT "-";
1050 NEXT I
1060 :
1070 :
1080 REM **--GET ANSWER--**
1090 LOCATE 13,(37 - LC)
1100 INPUT "", ANSWER$: REM COMMA ELIMINATES ? MARK
1110 :
```

```
1120 REM CONVERT TO UPPERCASE
1130 CVT$ = ANSWER$
1140 GOSUB 6000: REM UPPERCASE SUBROUTINE
1150 ANSWER$ = CVT$
1160 :
1170 IF ANSWER$ = "END" THEN 2000
1180 D = VAL (ANSWER$)
1190 IF D = C THEN 4000: REM CORRECT ANSWER ROUTINE
1200 IF Z < 3 THEN 5000: REM WRONG ANSWER ROUTINE
1210 :
1220 REM GIVE ANSWER AFTER 3 TRIES
1230 PRINT
1240 PRINT "NO, THE ANSWER IS ";C
1250 PRINT: PRINT A;" ";S$;" ";B;" = ";C
1260 PRINT: Z = 1: WR = WR + 1
1270 INPUT "Press `ENTER' when ready to go on ";L$
1280 GOTO 490: REM ANOTHER PROBLEM
1290 :
1300 :
2000 REM **--TOTAL ROUTINE--**
2010 CLS: LOCATE 5,1
2020 PRINT "You got";CR;"right!"
2030 PRINT
2040 PRINT"You missed";WR
2050 :
2060 :
3000 REM **--FILE OUTPUT ROUTINE--**
3010 OPEN NAMES$ + ".DAT" FOR APPEND AS #1
3020 PRINT #1,S$: REM SIGN
3030 PRINT #1,DT: REM # OF DIGITS
3040 PRINT #1,CR: REM # CORRECT
3050 PRINT #1,WR: REM # WRONG
3060 CLOSE #1
3070 RUN "MATHMENU
3080 :
3090 :
4000 REM **--CORRECT ANSWER ROUTINE--**
4010 LOCATE 20,33
4020 PRINT "GOOD"
4030 FOR I = 1 TO 1000: NEXT I
4040 CR = CR + 1
4050 GOTO 490: REM ANOTHER PROBLEM
4060 :
4070 :
5000 REM **--WRONG ANSWER ROUTINE--**
5010 LOCATE 20,25
5020 PRINT"NO, PLEASE TRY AGAIN."
5030 Z = Z + 1
5040 PRINT
5050 FOR I = 1 TO 1000: NEXT I
5060 GOTO 930: REM DISPLAY AGAIN
5070 :
5080 :
```

```
6000 REM **--CONVERT TO UPPERCASE ROUTINE--**
6010 FOR CV = 1 TO LEN(CVT$)
6020 X = ASC (MID$(CVT$,CV,1))
6030 IF X > 96 AND X < 123 THEN X = X - 32
6040 CVTUP$ = CVTUP$ + CHR$(X)
6050 NEXT CV
6060 CVT$ = CVTUP$
6070 CVTUP$ = ""
6080 RETURN
```

SUBTRACT

```
100 REM ***--SUBTRACTION--***
110 :
120 :
130 REM **--VARIABLE LIST--**
140 REM A  =   TOP NUMBER
150 REM B  =   BOTTOM NUMBER
160 REM C  =   CORRECT ANSWER
170 REM D  =   STUDENT'S ANSWER
180 REM Q  =   COUNTER
190 REM W  =   PREVIOUS ANSWER
200 REM Z  =   NUMBER OF TRIES
210 REM CR =   CORRECT ANSWERS
220 REM RD =   RANDOM # SEED
230 REM WR =   WRONG ANSWERS
240 REM DT =   # OF DIGITS
250 REM LA =   # OF DIGITS IN A
260 REM LB =   # OF DIGITS IN B
270 REM LC =   # OF DIGITS IN C
280 REM LM =   # OF DIGITS IN MAX AMOUNT
290 REM OTHER VARIABLES ARE DESCRIPTIVE
300 :
310 :
320 REM **--REQUEST USER INFORMATION--**
330 CLS: LOCATE 5,1
340 INPUT "HOW MANY DIGITS ";DIGIT
350 PRINT
360 INPUT "WHAT IS THE LARGEST FIGURE FOR THE NUMBER YOU
    ARE SUBTRACTING BY";MAX
370 PRINT
380 INPUT "WHAT IS THE SMALLEST FIGURE FOR THE NUMBER YOU
    ARE SUBTRACTING BY";MN
390 DT = DIGIT: DIGIT = 10 ^ DIGIT
400 PRINT
410 INPUT "What is your name";NAMES$
420 :
430 REM CONVERT TO UPPERCASE
440 CVT$ = NAMES$
450 GOSUB 6000: REM UPPERCASE SUBROUTINE
```

```
460 NAMES$ = CVT$
470 :
480 :
490 REM **--CREATE PROBLEM--**
500 REM SEED RND W/SECONDS FROM TIME
510 RD = VAL(RIGHT$(TIME$,2))
520 RANDOMIZE RD
530 :
540 MAX$ = STR$(MAX)
550 LM = LEN (MAX$)
560 LM = LM - 1
570 :
580 REM WHEN B'S DIGITS < DT
590 IF DT = LM + 1 OR DT < LM + 1 THEN 660
600 LM = 10 ^ LM
610 B = INT(RND(1) * LM)
620 IF B < MN THEN 610
630 IF B > MAX THEN 610
640 GOTO 700: REM GET # FOR `A'
650 :
660 Z = 1
670 B = INT (RND (1) * DIGIT)
680 IF B < MN THEN 670
690 IF B > MAX THEN 670
700 A = INT (RND (1) * DIGIT)
710 C = A - B: REM DETERMINE OPERATION
720 S$ = "-"
730 IF C < 0 THEN 670: REM FOR SUBTRACTION
740 IF C = W THEN 670: REM PREVIOUS ANSWER
750 W = C
760 :
770 :
780 REM **--DISPLAY PROBLEM--**
790 REM DETERMINE LENGTHS
800 A$ = STR$(A)
810 LA = LEN (A$)
820 A$ = RIGHT$(A$,LA - 1): REM STRIP OFF SIGN
830 LA = LEN(A$)
840 B$ = STR$(B)
850 LB = LEN (B$)
860 B$ = RIGHT$(B$,LB - 1): REM STRIP OFF SIGN
870 LB = LEN (B$)
880 C$ = STR$(C)
890 LC = LEN (C$)
900 C$ = RIGHT$(C$,LC - 1): REM STRIP OFF SIGN
910 LC = LEN (C$)
920 :
930 REM FORMAT
940 CLS: LOCATE 5,25
950 PRINT "Type `END' when finished!"
960 LOCATE 10,37 - LA: PRINT A$
970 LOCATE 11,(37 - (LB + 1)): PRINT S$;B$
980 :
```

```
990 REM DRAW LINE
1000 Q = 1
1010 IF LA > LB THEN Q = 0
1020 LOCATE 12,37 - (DT + Q)
1030 FOR I = 1 TO (DT + Q)
1040 PRINT "-";
1050 NEXT I
1060 :
1070 :
1080 REM **--GET ANSWER--**
1090 LOCATE 13,(37  - LC)
1100 INPUT "", ANSWER$: REM COMMA ELIMINATES ? MARK
1110 :
1120 REM CONVERT TO UPPERCASE
1130 CVT$ = ANSWER$
1140 GOSUB 6000: REM UPPERCASE SUBROUTINE
1150 ANSWER$ = CVT$
1160 :
1170 IF ANSWER$ = "END" THEN 2000
1180 D = VAL (ANSWER$)
1190 IF D = C THEN 4000: REM CORRECT ANSWER ROUTINE
1200 IF Z < 3 THEN 5000: REM WRONG ANSWER ROUTINE
1210 :
1220 REM GIVE ANSWER AFTER 3 TRIES
1230 PRINT
1240 PRINT "NO, THE ANSWER IS ";C
1250 PRINT: PRINT A;" ";S$;" ";B;" = ";C
1260 PRINT: Z = 1: WR = WR + 1
1270 INPUT "Press `ENTER' when ready to go on ";L$
1280 GOTO 490: REM ANOTHER PROBLEM
1290 :
1300 :
2000 REM **--TOTAL ROUTINE--**
2010 CLS: LOCATE 5,1
2020 PRINT "You got";CR;"right!"
2030 PRINT
2040 PRINT"You missed";WR
2050 :
2060 :
3000 REM **--FILE OUTPUT ROUTINE--**
3010 OPEN NAMES$ + ".DAT" FOR APPEND AS #1
3020 PRINT #1,S$: REM SIGN
3030 PRINT #1,DT: REM # OF DIGITS
3040 PRINT #1,CR: REM # CORRECT
3050 PRINT #1,WR: REM # WRONG
3060 CLOSE #1
3070 RUN "MATHMENU
3080 :
3090 :
4000 REM **--CORRECT ANSWER ROUTINE--**
4010 LOCATE 20,33
4020 PRINT "GOOD"
4030 FOR I = 1 TO 1000: NEXT I
```

```
4040 CR = CR + 1
4050 GOTO 490: REM ANOTHER PROBLEM
4060 :
4070 :
5000 REM **--WRONG ANSWER ROUTINE--**
5010 LOCATE 20,25
5020 PRINT"NO, PLEASE TRY AGAIN."
5030 Z = Z + 1
5040 PRINT
5050 FOR I = 1 TO 1000: NEXT I
5060 GOTO 930: REM DISPLAY AGAIN
5070 :
5080 :
6000 REM **--CONVERT TO UPPERCASE ROUTINE--**
6010 FOR CV = 1 TO LEN(CVT$)
6020 X = ASC (MID$(CVT$,CV,1))
6030 IF X > 96 AND X < 123 THEN X = X - 32
6040 CVTUP$ = CVTUP$ + CHR$(X)
6050 NEXT CV
6060 CVT$ = CVTUP$
6070 CVTUP$ = ""
6080 RETURN
```

MULTIPLY

```
100 REM ***--MULTIPLICATION--***
110 :
120 :
130 REM **--VARIABLE LIST--**
140 REM A  =   TOP NUMBER
150 REM B  =   BOTTOM NUMBER
160 REM C  =   CORRECT ANSWER
170 REM D  =   STUDENT'S ANSWER
180 REM Q  =   COUNTER
190 REM W  =   PREVIOUS ANSWER
200 REM Z  =   NUMBER OF TRIES
210 REM CR =   CORRECT ANSWERS
220 REM RD =   RANDOM # SEED
230 REM WR =   WRONG ANSWERS
240 REM DT =   # OF DIGITS
250 REM LA =   # OF DIGITS IN A
260 REM LB =   # OF DIGITS IN B
270 REM LC =   # OF DIGITS IN C
280 REM LM =   # OF DIGITS IN MAX AMOUNT
290 REM OTHER VARIABLES ARE DESCRIPTIVE
300 :
310 :
320 REM **--REQUEST USER INFORMATION--**
330 CLS: LOCATE 5,1
340 INPUT "HOW MANY DIGITS ";DIGIT
```

```
350 PRINT
360 INPUT "WHAT IS THE LARGEST FIGURE FOR THE NUMBER YOU
    ARE MULTIPLYING BY";MAX
370 PRINT
380 INPUT "WHAT IS THE SMALLEST FIGURE FOR THE NUMBER YOU
    ARE MULTIPLYING BY";MN
390 DT = DIGIT: DIGIT = 10 ^ DIGIT
400 PRINT
410 INPUT "What is your name";NAMES$
420 :
430 REM CONVERT TO UPPERCASE
440 CVT$ = NAMES$
450 GOSUB 6000: REM UPPERCASE SUBROUTINE
460 NAMES$ = CVT$
470 :
480 :
490 REM **--CREATE PROBLEM--**
500 REM SEED RND W/SECONDS FROM TIME
510 RD = VAL(RIGHT$(TIME$,2))
520 RANDOMIZE RD
530 :
540 MAX$ = STR$(MAX)
550 LM = LEN (MAX$)
560 LM = LM - 1
570 :
580 REM WHEN B'S DIGITS < DT
590 IF DT = LM + 1 OR DT < LM + 1 THEN 660
600 LM = 10 ^ LM
610 B = INT(RND(1) * LM)
620 IF B < MN THEN 610
630 IF B > MAX THEN 610
640 GOTO 700: REM GET # FOR 'A'
650 :
660 Z = 1
670 B = INT (RND (1) * DIGIT)
680 IF B < MN THEN 670
690 IF B > MAX THEN 670
700 A = INT (RND (1) * DIGIT)
710 C = A * B: REM DETERMINE OPERATION
720 S$ = "X"
730 IF C < 0 THEN 670: REM FOR SUBTRACTION
740 IF C = W THEN 670: REM PREVIOUS ANSWER
750 W = C
760 :
770 :
780 REM **--DISPLAY PROBLEM--**
790 REM DETERMINE LENGTHS
800 A$ = STR$(A)
810 LA = LEN (A$)
820 A$ = RIGHT$(A$,LA - 1): REM STRIP OFF SIGN
830 LA = LEN(A$)
840 B$ = STR$(B)
850 LB = LEN (B$)
860 B$ = RIGHT$(B$,LB - 1): REM STRIP OFF SIGN
```

```
870 LB = LEN (B$)
880 C$ = STR$(C)
890 LC = LEN (C$)
900 C$ = RIGHT$(C$,LC - 1): REM STRIP OFF SIGN
910 LC = LEN (C$)
920 :
930 REM FORMAT
940 CLS: LOCATE 5,25
950 PRINT "Type `END' when finished!"
960 LOCATE 10,37 - LA: PRINT A$
970 LOCATE 11,(37 - (LB + 1)): PRINT S$;B$
980 :
990 REM DRAW LINE
1000 Q = 1
1010 IF LA > LB THEN Q = 0
1020 LOCATE 12,37 - (DT + Q)
1030 FOR I = 1 TO (DT + Q)
1040 PRINT "-";
1050 NEXT I
1060 :
1070 :
1080 REM **--GET ANSWER--**
1090 LOCATE 13,(37  - LC)
1100 INPUT "", ANSWER$: REM COMMA ELIMINATES ? MARK
1110 :
1120 REM CONVERT TO UPPERCASE
1130 CVT$ = ANSWER$
1140 GOSUB 6000: REM UPPERCASE SUBROUTINE
1150 ANSWER$ = CVT$
1160 :
1170 IF ANSWER$ = "END" THEN 2000
1180 D = VAL (ANSWER$)
1190 IF D = C THEN 4000: REM CORRECT ANSWER ROUTINE
1200 IF Z < 3 THEN 5000: REM WRONG ANSWER ROUTINE
1210 :
1220 REM GIVE ANSWER AFTER 3 TRIES
1230 PRINT
1240 PRINT "NO, THE ANSWER IS ";C
1250 PRINT: PRINT A;" ";S$;" ";B;" = ";C
1260 PRINT: Z = 1: WR = WR + 1
1270 INPUT "Press `ENTER' when ready to go on ";L$
1280 GOTO 490: REM ANOTHER PROBLEM
1290 :
1300 :
2000 REM **--TOTAL ROUTINE--**
2010 CLS: LOCATE 5,1
2020 PRINT "You got";CR;"right!"
2030 PRINT
2040 PRINT"You missed";WR
2050 :
2060 :
3000 REM **--FILE OUTPUT ROUTINE--**
3010 OPEN NAMES$ + ".DAT" FOR APPEND AS #1
3020 PRINT #1,S$: REM SIGN
```

```
3030 PRINT #1,DT: REM # OF DIGITS
3040 PRINT #1,CR: REM # CORRECT
3050 PRINT #1,WR: REM # WRONG
3060 CLOSE #1
3070 RUN "MATHMENU
3080 :
3090 :
4000 REM **--CORRECT ANSWER ROUTINE--**
4010 LOCATE 20,33
4020 PRINT "GOOD"
4030 FOR I = 1 TO 1000: NEXT I
4040 CR = CR + 1
4050 GOTO 490: REM ANOTHER PROBLEM
4060 :
4070 :
5000 REM **--WRONG ANSWER ROUTINE--**
5010 LOCATE 20,25
5020 PRINT"NO, PLEASE TRY AGAIN."
5030 Z = Z + 1
5040 PRINT
5050 FOR I = 1 TO 1000: NEXT I
5060 GOTO 930: REM DISPLAY AGAIN
5070 :
5080 :
6000 REM **--CONVERT TO UPPERCASE ROUTINE--**
6010 FOR CV = 1 TO LEN(CVT$)
6020 X = ASC (MID$(CVT$,CV,1))
6030 IF X > 96 AND X < 123 THEN X = X - 32
6040 CVTUP$ = CVTUP$ + CHR$(X)
6050 NEXT CV
6060 CVT$ = CVTUP$
6070 CVTUP$ = ""
6080 RETURN
```

DIVIDE

```
100 REM ***--DIVISION--***
110 :
120 :
130 REM **--VARIABLE LIST--**
140 REM A  =  DIVISOR
150 REM B  =  DIVIDEND
160 REM C  =  CORRECT ANSWER
170 REM D  =  STUDENT'S ANSWER
180 REM Q  =  COUNTER
190 REM W  =  PREVIOUS ANSWER
200 REM Z  =  NUMBER OF TRIES
210 REM CR =  CORRECT ANSWERS
220 REM RD =  RANDOM # SEED
230 REM WR =  WRONG ANSWERS
240 REM DT =  # OF DIGITS
250 REM LA =  # OF DIGITS IN A
260 REM LB =  # OF DIGITS IN B
270 REM LC =  # OF DIGITS IN C
280 REM LM =  # OF DIGITS IN MAX AMOUNT
290 REM OTHER VARIABLES ARE DESCRIPTIVE
300 :
310 :
320 REM **--REQUEST USER INFORMATION--**
330 CLS: LOCATE 5,1
340 INPUT "HOW MANY DIGITS ";DIGIT
350 PRINT
360 INPUT "WHAT IS THE LARGEST FIGURE FOR THE NUMBER YOU
    ARE DIVIDING BY";MAX
370 PRINT
380 INPUT "WHAT IS THE SMALLEST FIGURE FOR THE NUMBER YOU
    ARE DIVIDING BY";MN
390 DT = DIGIT: DIGIT = 10 ^ DIGIT
400 PRINT
410 INPUT "What is your name";NAMES$
420 :
430 REM CONVERT TO UPPERCASE
440 CVT$ = NAMES$
450 GOSUB 6000: REM UPPERCASE SUBROUTINE
460 ANSWER$ = CVT$
470 :
480 :
490 REM **--CREATE PROBLEM--**
500 REM SEED RND W/SECONDS FROM TIME
510 RD = VAL(RIGHT$(TIME$,2))
520 RANDOMIZE RD
530 :
540 MAX$ = STR$(MAX)
550 LM = LEN (MAX$)
560 LM = LM - 1
570 LM = 10 ^ LM
```

```
580 Z = 1
590 A = INT (RND (1) * DIGIT)
600 CT = Ø: REM COUNTER FOR RND B
610 PRINT "PATIENCE...I'M THINKING!!"
620 IF A = Ø THEN 590
630 B = 2: GOSUB 7000: IF M = Ø THEN 660
640 B = 3: GOSUB 7000: IF M = Ø THEN 660
650 B = 5: GOSUB 7000: IF M < > Ø THEN 590
660 B = INT (RND (1) * LM)
670 CT = CT + 1: IF CT > 100 THEN 590
680 IF B < MN THEN 660
690 IF B > MAX THEN 660
700 GOSUB 7000: REM REMAINDER ROUTINE
710 IF M < > Ø THEN 660
720 C = INT (A) / (B): REM DETERMINE OPERATION
730 C = INT (C)
740 S$ = "/"
750 IF C < Ø THEN 660
760 :
770 :
780 REM **--DISPLAY PROBLEM--**
790 REM DETERMINE LENGTHS
800 A$ = STR$(A)
810 LA = LEN (A$)
820 A$ = RIGHT$(A$,LA - 1): REM STRIP OFF SIGN
830 LA = LEN(A$)
840 B$ = STR$(B)
850 LB = LEN (B$)
860 B$ = RIGHT$(B$,LB - 1): REM STRIP OFF SIGN
870 LB = LEN (B$)
880 C$ = STR$(C)
890 LC = LEN (C$)
900 C$ = RIGHT$(C$,LC - 1): REM STRIP OFF SIGN
910 LC = LEN (C$)
920 :
930 REM FORMAT
940 CLS: LOCATE 5,25
950 PRINT "Type `END' when finished!"
960 LOCATE 10,37
970 FOR I = 1 TO DT + 1
980 PRINT CHR$ (95);: REM TOP LINE
990 NEXT I
1000 PRINT
1010 LOCATE 11,(37 - LB): PRINT B$;")";A$
1020 :
1030 :
1040 REM **--GET ANSWER--**
1050 LOCATE 10,(37 + LA) - (LC - 1)
1060 INPUT "",ANSWER$: REM COMMA ELIMINATES ? MARK
1070 CT = Ø: REM COUNTER FOR RND B
1080 :
1090 REM CONVERT TO UPPERCASE
1100 CVT$ = ANSWER$
1110 GOSUB 6000: REM UPPERCASE ROUTINE
```

```
1120 ANSWER$ = CVT$
1130 :
1140 IF ANSWER$ = "END" THEN 2000
1150 D = VAL (ANSWER$)
1160 IF D = C THEN 4000: REM CORRECT ANSWER ROUTINE
1170 IF Z < 3 THEN 5000: REM WRONG ANSWER ROUTINE
1180 :
1190 REM GIVE ANSWER AFTER 3 TRIES
1200 PRINT
1210 PRINT "NO, THE ANSWER IS ";C
1220 PRINT: PRINT A;" ";S$;" ";B;" = ";C
1230 PRINT: Z = 1: WR = WR + 1
1240 INPUT "Press `ENTER' when ready to go on ";L$
1250 GOTO 490: REM ANOTHER PROBLEM
1260 :
1270 :
2000 REM **--TOTAL ROUTINE--**
2010 CLS: LOCATE 5,1
2020 PRINT "You got";CR;"right!"
2030 PRINT
2040 PRINT"You missed";WR
2050 :
2060 :
3000 REM **--FILE OUTPUT ROUTINE--**
3010 OPEN NAMES$ + ".DAT" FOR APPEND AS #1
3020 PRINT #1,S$: REM SIGN
3030 PRINT #1,DT: REM # OF DIGITS
3040 PRINT #1,CR: REM # CORRECT
3050 PRINT #1,WR: REM # WRONG
3060 CLOSE #1
3070 RUN "MATHMENU
3080 :
3090 :
4000 REM **--CORRECT ANSWER ROUTINE--**
4010 LOCATE 20,33
4020 PRINT "GOOD"
4030 FOR I = 1 TO 1000: NEXT I
4040 CR = CR + 1
4050 GOTO 490: REM ANOTHER PROBLEM
4060 :
4070 :
5000 REM **--WRONG ANSWER ROUTINE--**
5010 LOCATE 20,25
5020 PRINT "NO, PLEASE TRY AGAIN."
5030 Z = Z + 1
5040 PRINT
5050 FOR I = 1 TO 1000: NEXT I
5060 GOTO 910: REM DISPLAY AGAIN
5070 :
5080 :
6000 REM **--CONVERT TO UPPERCASE ROUTINE--**
6010 FOR CV = 1 TO LEN(CVT$)
6020 X = ASC (MID$(CVT$,CV,1))
6030 IF X > 96 AND X < 123 THEN X = X - 32
```

```
6040 CVTUP$ = CVTUP$ + CHR$(X)
6050 NEXT CV
6060 CVT$ = CVTUP$
6070 CVTUP$ = ""
6080 RETURN
6090 :
6100 :
7000 REM **--REMAINDER ROUTINE--**
7010 M = INT ((A / B - INT(A / B)) * B + .05) * SGN (A /
     B)
7020 RETURN
```

SCORES

```
100 REM ***--SCORES--***
110 :
120 :
130 DIM S$(100),DT(100),CR(100),WR(100)
140 I = 1
150 CLS: LOCATE 5,1
160 INPUT "Student's Name Please";NAMES$
170 :
180 :
190 REM **--FILE INPUT ROUTINE--**
200 OPEN NAMES$ + ".DAT" FOR INPUT AS #1
210 IF EOF(1) THEN 280
220 INPUT #1,S$(I): REM SIGN OF OPERATION
230 INPUT #1,DT(I): REM # OF DIGITS
240 INPUT #1,CR(I): REM # CORRECT
250 INPUT #1,WR(I): REM # WRONG
260 I = I + 1
270 GOTO 210
280 CLOSE #1
290 :
300 :
310 REM **--DISPLAY ROUTINE--**
320 CLS: LOCATE 1,38: PRINT NAMES$
330 LOCATE 3,15: PRINT "SESSION"
340 LOCATE 3,26: PRINT "OPERATION"
350 LOCATE 3,38: PRINT "DIGITS"
360 LOCATE 3,47: PRINT "CORRECT"
370 LOCATE 3,57: PRINT "WRONG"
375 J = 1
380 FOR K = 1 TO I - 1
390 IF S$(K) = "+" THEN S$(K) = "ADD"
400 IF S$(K) = "-" THEN S$(K) = "SUB"
410 IF S$(K) = "X" THEN S$(K) = "MLT"
420 IF S$(K) = "/" THEN S$(K) = "DIV"
430 LOCATE J + 4,17: PRINT K
440 LOCATE J + 4,29: PRINT S$(K)
```

```
450 LOCATE J + 4,39: PRINT DT(K)
460 IF CR(K) > 9 THEN L = - 1
470 LOCATE J + 4,49 + L: PRINT CR(K)
480 L = 0
490 IF WR(K) > 9 THEN L = - 1
500 LOCATE J + 4,58 + L: PRINT WR(K)
510 L = 0
515 J = J + 1
517 IF J > 3 THEN GOSUB 2000: GOSUB 3100
520 NEXT K
530 GOSUB 2000
540 RUN "MATHMENU
2000 LOCATE 20,15
2005 INPUT "PRESS `ENTER' WHEN FINISHED!",L$
2010 J = 1
2020 RETURN
3100 REM **--DISPLAY ROUTINE--**
3200 CLS: LOCATE 1,38: PRINT NAMES$
3300 LOCATE 3,15: PRINT "SESSION"
3400 LOCATE 3,26: PRINT "OPERATION"
3500 LOCATE 3,38: PRINT "DIGITS"
3600 LOCATE 3,47: PRINT "CORRECT"
3700 LOCATE 3,57: PRINT "WRONG"
3750 J = 1
3800 RETURN
```

RECIPES

```
100 REM ***--RECIPES--***
110 :
120 :
130 REM **--VARIABLES LIST--**
140 REM RECNBR        = NUMBER OF RECORDS
150 REM INGNBR        = TOTAL # OF INGRED.
160 REM ING$ & ID$    = INGRED.
170 REM REC$ & RC$    = RECIPES
180 REM IG$           = CURRENT SESS. INGRED.
190 REM RZ$           = RECIPE NAMES ONLY
200 :
210 :
220 REM **--INITIALIZATION--**
230 DIM REC(100),ING$(50),IG$(100,50),RC$(100),RZ$(100),ID$(50)
240 Q$ = CHR$(34): REM Quotation mark
250 KEY OFF
260 TB = 28: REM Tab value
270 GOTO 10000
280 :
290 REM Pointer input routine
300 OPEN "RECPTR.DAT" FOR INPUT AS #1
310 INPUT #1,NUMBER$
320 CLOSE #1
330 LR = LEN (NUMBER$)
340 T = 1
350 IF MID$(NUMBER$,T,1) = "*" THEN 370
360 T = T + 1: GOTO 350
370 RECNBR = VAL (LEFT$(NUMBER$,T - 1))
380 INGNBR = VAL (MID$(NUMBER$,T + 1,LR - T))
390 :
400 :
410 REM **--RECIPE MENU--**
420 CLS
430 LOCATE 5,TB + 4
440 PRINT "RECIPE MENU"
450 LOCATE 7,TB
460 PRINT "1.   ADD RECIPE TO LIST"
470 LOCATE 9,TB
480 PRINT "2.   SELECT RECIPE FROM LIST"
490 LOCATE 11,TB
500 PRINT "3.   END PROGRAM"
510 LOCATE 13,TB
520 INPUT "Which number";NB
530 IF NB = 1 THEN 1000
540 IF NB = 2 THEN 2000
550 IF NB = 3 THEN KEY ON:END
560 PRINT "INCORRECT NUMBER!"
570 GOTO 510: REM Ask again
580 :
590 :
```

```
1000 REM **--ADD TO RECIPE LIST--**
1010 R = 1
1020 CLS: LOCATE 5,1
1030 INPUT "Name of the recipe please";REC$(R)
1040 I = 1
1050 PRINT: PRINT "Type in `END' when finished."
1060 LOCATE 15,1
1070 PRINT "Type in ingredient #";I;" below this line."
1080 INPUT ING$(I)
1090 IF ING$(I) = "END" OR ING$(I) = "end" THEN 1130: RE
     M Display
1100 I = I + 1
1110 CLS: LOCATE 6,1: GOTO 1050: REM Get another ingred.
1120 :
1130 REM Display For Correction
1140 CLS: LOCATE 5,1: PRINT REC$(R)
1150 FOR J = 1 TO I - 1
1160 LOCATE 5 + J,1
1170 PRINT J;" ";ING$(J)
1180 NEXT J
1190 LOCATE 5 + (J + 1),1
1200 INPUT "Is this correct";YES$
1210 IF YES$ = "Y" OR YES$ = "y" THEN 1260: REM Combine
     if ok
1220 PRINT: INPUT "Which number is wrong";WR
1230 PRINT "Type in the correct information for ingredie
     nt #";WR
1240 INPUT ING$(WR)
1250 GOTO 1140: REM Ask again
1260 REC$(R) = REC$(R) + "!" + STR$(INGNBR) + "*" + STR$
     (I - 1)
1270 FOR J = 1 TO I - 1
1280 IG$(R,J) = ING$(J)
1290 NEXT J
1300 INGNBR = INGNBR + (I - 1)
1310 R = R + 1
1320 PRINT
1330 INPUT "Do you want to add more recipes";YES$
1340 IF YES$ = "Y" OR YES$ = "y" THEN 1020: REM Another
     recipe
1350 :
1360 RECNBR = RECNBR + (R - 1)
1370 LY = LEN(STR$(RECNBR))
1380 LZ = LEN(STR$(INGNBR))
1390 Y$ = RIGHT$(STR$(RECNBR),LY - 1): REM Strip off sig
     n
1400 Z$ = RIGHT$(STR$(INGNBR),LZ - 1): REM Strip off sig
     n
1410 NUMBER$ = Y$ + "*" + Z$
1420 :
1430 REM File output routine
1440 OPEN "RECNAMES.DAT" FOR APPEND AS #1
1450 OPEN "INGRED.DAT" FOR APPEND AS #2
1460 FOR K = 1 TO (R - 1)
```

```
1470 PRINT #1, REC$(K)
1480 LN = LEN (REC$(K))
1490 T = 1
1500 IF MID$ (REC$(K),T,1) = "*" THEN   1520
1510 T = T + 1: GOTO 1500
1520 Q = VAL (MID$(REC$(K),T + 1,LN - T))
1530 FOR H = 1 TO Q
1540 PRINT #2, IG$(K,H)
1550 NEXT H
1560 NEXT K
1570 OPEN "RECPTR.DAT" FOR OUTPUT AS #3
1580 PRINT #3, NUMBER$
1590 CLOSE #1,#2,#3
1600 GOTO 410: REM Menu
1610 :
1620 :
2000 REM **--SELECT RECIPE--**
2010 CLS: LOCATE 5,1
2020 REM Input Recipe Names
2030 OPEN "RECNAMES.DAT" FOR INPUT AS #1
2040 FOR I = 1 TO RECNBR
2050 LINE INPUT# 1,RC$(I)
2060 T = 1
2070 IF MID$(RC$(I),T,1) = "I" THEN 2090
2080 T = T + 1: GOTO 2070
2090 RZ$(I) = LEFT$(RC$(I),T - 1): REM Just Name
2100 NEXT I
2110 CLOSE #1
2120 FOR I = 1 TO RECNBR
2130 PRINT I;" ";RZ$(I)
2140 NEXT I
2150 :
2160 PRINT: PRINT
2170 INPUT "Which recipe";RC
2180 LN = LEN (RC$(RC))
2190 T = 1
2200 IF MID$(RC$(RC),T,1) = "I" THEN 2220
2210 T = T + 1: GOTO 2200
2220 T1 = T
2230 IF MID$(RC$(RC),T1,1) = "*" THEN 2250
2240 T1 = T1 + 1: GOTO 2230
2250 REM Add `2' to bypass sign of numeric value
2260 IGNB = VAL (MID$(RC$(RC),T + 2,T1 - 1)) + 1
2270 LIGNB = VAL (MID$(RC$(RC),T1 + 2,LN - T1))
2280 :
2290 REM Input & Display Ingred.
2300 CLS: PRINT RZ$(RC)
2310 OPEN "INGRED.DAT" FOR INPUT AS #1
2320 FOR K = 1 TO IGNB
2330 LINE INPUT #1,ID$
2340 NEXT K
2350 FOR K = 1 TO LIGNB
2360 LINE INPUT #1, ID$(K)
2370 PRINT ID$(K)
```

```
2380 NEXT K
2390 CLOSE #1
2400 PRINT: PRINT
2410 INPUT "Press `ENTER' when ready to continue";L$
2420 INPUT "Select another recipe";YES$
2430 IF YES$ = "Y" OR YES$ = "y" THEN 2450
2440 GOTO 410: REM Return to RECIPE MENU
2450 CLS:GOTO 2120: REM Select another
2460 END
2470 :
2480 :
10000 REM **--FIRST TIME USE ONLY!--**
10010 REM Program originally contains--270 GOTO 10000
10020 OPEN "RECPTR.DAT" FOR OUTPUT AS #1
10030 PRINT #1, "0*0"
10040 OPEN "INGRED.DAT" FOR OUTPUT AS #2
10050 PRINT #2, "RECIPE INGREDENTS"
10060 CLOSE #1,#2
10070 PRINT"PRESS `ENTER' ONCE AND THEN THE `F2' KEY"
10080 PRINT
10090 PRINT"SAVE"Q$"RECIPES
10100 LOCATE(CSRLIN-2),1: REM Current screen line - 2
10110 DELETE 270
```

CREATEQA

```
100 REM ***--INPUT Q & A--***
110 :
120 :
130 DIM Q$(50),A$(50)
140 I = 1
150 :
160 :
170 REM **--INPUT ROUTINE--**
180 CLS: LOCATE 5,1
190 INPUT "Subject Name";SUB$
200 SUB$ = SUB$ + ".DAT"
210 CLS: LOCATE 5,1
220 PRINT "Type `END' when finished."
230 PRINT:PRINT
240 PRINT "QUESTION #";I
250 PRINT
260 LINE INPUT Q$(I)
270 IF Q$(I) = "END" OR Q$(I) = "end" THEN 430
280 PRINT
290 PRINT "ANSWER"
300 PRINT
310 LINE INPUT A$(I)
320 CLS: LOCATE 5,1
330 PRINT Q$(I)
340 PRINT
350 PRINT A$(I)
360 PRINT
370 INPUT "Is this correct";Y$
380 PRINT
390 IF Y$ = "N" OR Y$ = "n" THEN 240
400 I = I + 1: GOTO 210
410 :
420 :
430 REM **--FILE OUTPUT ROUTINE--**
440 OPEN SUB$ FOR OUTPUT AS #1
450 PRINT #1,I - 1
460 FOR J = 1 TO I - 1
470 PRINT #1,Q$(J)
480 PRINT #1,A$(J)
490 NEXT J
500 CLOSE #1
510 END
```

DRILLQA

```
100 REM ***--DRILL & PRACTICE--***
110 :
120 :
130 DIM Q$(50),A$(50),QP(11),AP(11)
140 Z = 0
150 :
160 :
170 REM **--FILE INPUT ROUTINE--**
180 CLS: LOCATE 5,1
190 INPUT "Subject Name";SUB$
200 SUB$ = SUB$ + ".DAT": PRINT
210 OPEN SUB$ FOR INPUT AS #1
220 INPUT #1,J
230 FOR I = 1 TO J
240 LINE INPUT #1,Q$(I)
250 LINE INPUT #1,A$(I)
260 NEXT I
270 CLOSE #1
280 :
290 :
300 REM **--GET Q & A--**
310 RD = VAL (RIGHT$(TIME$,2))
320 RANDOMIZE RD
330 I = RND (1) * 10: I = INT (I)
340 IF I > J OR I < 1 THEN 330
350 CLS: LOCATE 7,1
360 PRINT "Type `END' when finished."
370 PRINT: PRINT
380 PRINT Q$(I)
390 PRINT: PRINT
400 INPUT "Your answer is";ANS$
410 CVT$ = ANS$: GOSUB 1000: ANS$ = CVT$
420 CVT$ = A$(I): GOSUB 1000: A$(I) = CVT$
430 PRINT
440 IF ANS$ = "END" THEN 600
450 IF ANS$ = A$(I) THEN PRINT "CORRECT": A = A + 1: GOTO
    540
460 IF Z > 0 THEN 520
470 PRINT "No, try once more."
480 PRINT
490 Z = 1
500 A2 = A2 + 1
510 GOTO 400
520 PRINT "No, the answer is: ";A$(I)
530 M = M + 1
540 Z = 0
550 PRINT
560 FOR K = 1 TO 1000: NEXT K
570 GOTO 330
580 :
590 :
```

```
600 REM **--DISPLAY SCORE--**
610 A2 = A2 - M
620 A = A - A2
630 CLS: LOCATE 5,1
640 PRINT "You got";A;"right on the first try"
650 PRINT: PRINT
660 PRINT "You got";A2;"right on the second try"
670 PRINT: PRINT
680 PRINT "You missed";M;"answers."
690 END
700 :
710 :
1000 REM **--CONVERT TO UPPERCASE ROUTINE--**
1010 FOR CV = 1 TO LEN(CVT$)
1020 X = ASC (MID$(CVT$,CV,1))
1030 IF X > 96 AND X < 123 THEN X = X - 32
1040 CVTUP$ = CVTUP$ + CHR$(X)
1050 NEXT CV
1060 CVT$ = CVTUP$
1070 CVTUP$ = ""
1080 RETURN
```

9
DIF Files

One of the more exciting possibilities in file handling is the prospect of a standard format for transferring file information. At least one such standard is now being supported by a number of major pieces of application software. The DIF™ file format was developed by Software Arts, writers of VisiCalc.® It is important to keep in mind the intent of this standard. The standard does not suggest that all files be stored according to the DIF format. Such a requirement would place an impossible burden on too many applications to make the standard truly acceptable. Instead, the standard suggests a specific format for file transfer.

If you never expect to transfer your file information from one program to another, you have no real need to use DIF, but if you wish to have different programs share the same data, then a standard such as DIF is very valuable. For example, if you never expect to use another program with your MAILING LIST SYSTEM names and addresses, then there is no reason to store those names and addresses according to the DIF format. On the other hand, if you want to use VisiCalc with the scores obtained from the MATH SYSTEM, then the DIF format becomes important. Without the standard, it would be necessary to type all the scores into the VisiCalc program. With DIF, VisiCalc can read the scores directly from the disk. On a small file, retyping is not a big consideration, but as the file grows, it becomes a major problem. Regardless of the file size, rekeying the information for every application program that makes use of the same data is annoying, incon-

---

DIF™ is a trademark of Software Arts, Inc.
VisiCalc® is a registered trademark of VisiCorp.

venient, and unnecessary. If an application program such as VisiCalc makes use of, or supports the DIF file format, any information stored according to that standard can be used by that application program.

Most application programs supporting DIF actually offer you two methods of saving your information or data. The first, or standard, method is the most efficient and effective way to store information for the specific program. The second method is the DIF format. In other words, the file is saved twice, once in the normal manner, according to the program needs, and secondly, in a format that allows other programs to access and use the information. This two-method system is necessary because the DIF format (or any standard format) is not a very efficient way of storing and retrieving information. Let's look at the DIF format and use it to store the scores from the MATH SYSTEM so that VisiCalc can directly access those scores.

Before getting into the exact way DIF files are stored, it is necessary to understand that in order to make a standard method of saving information, the file must contain information about itself: where it starts and ends, whether the information is numeric or alphabetic, label information, or actual data. The creators of DIF decided that all DIF files must be divided into two basic parts. The first part contains information about the file itself, and the second contains the actual data. The first part is called the Header Section, and the second part the Data Section. Next, since there are many ways of displaying information, the DIF creators decided to group all information into two categories: Vectors and Tuples. Basically, Vectors and Tuples are just columns and rows. Finally, each piece of information must carry with it the type of information it is: numeric, alphabetic (alphanumeric), or special (descriptive). To distinguish between these types of information, they assigned the following codes: a "0" indicates numeric information, a "1" indicates alphanumeric information, and a "−1" indicates special or descriptive file information.

The only other major decision to be made was the exact organization of the file. This organizational decision is indeed more complex, but it does follow a logical pattern and can be learned with practice. The Header Section (the part of the file that carries information about itself) comes first. Obviously then, the Data Section comes after the Header Section. The beginning and ending of each of these sections must then be indicated in some way.

If you remember, we used two symbols as separators in the MAIL-ING LIST SYSTEM, the "!" and the "*" (see Chapter 4). In much the same way, the creators of DIF have used symbols to set off the beginning and end points of the two file sections. The word "TABLE" is used to begin the file and is the first entry in the Header Section. The

characters "EOD" (End of Data) are used as the last entry of the file
and the end of the Data Section.

Finally, something must divide the two sections. The DIF creators
decided that the division should occur in the Header Section and had
to be the last entry in that section. That last entry then, has to follow
the pattern for the Header Section. This means that the division
between the Header Section and the Data Section needs to be in the
following format:

```
DATA
0, 0
" "
```

We now have the beginning and end of the file and the division
between the two sections.

```
REM  **--HEADER SECTION--**
           TABLE
             .
             .
             .
             .
             .
           DATA
           0, 0
           " "
REM  **--DATA SECTION--**
             .
             .
             .
             .
             .
           EOD
```

The two sections are organized in slightly different ways. The Header
Section requires three lines of information for each entry, while the
Data Section uses two lines of information for each entry.

HEADER SECTION

The first line in each entry of the Header Section gives the topic of
the entry. TABLE, VECTORS, TUPLES, and DATA are the usual
topic lines. The second line in each entry gives numeric information
about each topic, such as the number of VECTORS and the number of

TUPLES. The third line allows for a name for each topic if a name is necessary. A typical Header Section might look like the following:

```
TABLE
0, 1
"SCORES"
:
VECTORS
0, 5
" "
:
TUPLES
0, 4
" "
:
LABEL
1, 0
"SESSION #"
:
LABEL
2, 0
"OPERATION"
:
LABEL
3, 0
"DIGITS"
:
LABEL
4, 0
"# CORRECT"
:
LABEL
5, 0
"# WRONG"
:
DATA
0, 0
" "
```

(I have added the colons to separate the individual entries.)

Remember that this is the way the information would look in the file and that this section contains information about the file itself. Since VECTORS and TUPLES are basically columns and rows, it is not too difficult to understand the numeric information required in the second line of information in each entry of the Header Section. The first number is the VECTOR, or column, number. The second number is a specific value related to the topic of the entry.

MATH SCORES

SESSION #	OPERATION	DIGITS	CORRECT	WRONG
1	ADD	2	8	2
2	MUL	3	12	8
3	DIV	3	7	13
4	SUB	5	24	1

For example, in a table of five columns, the second line of information under the topic of VECTORS would be "0,5". Since the topic "VECTORS" is not actually in the table, it does not have a column number (Vector name), so the "0" is first. The "5" indicates the value relating to the topic, VECTORS, or five columns. Under the topic of LABEL, you can list the actual names of the columns, their relative positions, and any specific value. With a LABEL, the value is usually "0" in a simple table. TUPLES, or rows, might have a second line of "0,4" indicating that the topic TUPLES was not actually in the table but had a value of 4; i.e., 4 rows. The value for the topic TABLE is the version number and must be a "1". So we see that the Header Section describes a file of information that, in our example, consists of 5 columns and 4 rows (5 VECTORS and 4 TUPLES).

DATA SECTION

Each entry of the Data Section consists of two lines of information. The first line is numeric and gives two pieces of information: the type of information and the value associated with that information. The second line provides alphabetic information associated with the entry. For instance, if the information being stored was the number "62.5", the Data Section entry would be:

0, 62. 5
V

If the information being stored was the word "PERCENT", the entry would be:

1, 0
"PERCENT"

In the first example, the information or data is numeric, so the first number in the first line of this entry is a "0". The value associated with this entry is the information itself, "62.5". The second line of a numeric piece of information can have one of five possibilities: (1) V for a numeric value, (2) NA for not available, the numeric value is 0, (3) ERROR when an invalid calculation has resulted in an error, the numeric value is 0, (4) *True* for the logical value, the numeric value is 1, and (5) *False* for the logical value, the numeric value being 0. These five possibilities lend greater flexibility to those who may have need for complex data manipulation. In simpler files, numeric information will usually have a second line of "V".

In the second example, the information being stored is alphabetic, so the first number in the first line of this entry is a "1". The value associated with alphabetic information is usually "0" so that the first line is "1,0". The second line provides alphabetic information about the entry, and since the information is alphabetic, this second line is the information itself. In other words, if the information is alphanumeric (a "1" is indicated in the first line of the entry), the second line contains that alphanumeric information.

The other possibility for an entry in the Data Section is that of a "special value." There are two special values: one for the beginning of each Tuple and one for the end of the Data Section. Information is grouped within the Data Section by TUPLES (rows) with a special entry marking the beginning of each TUPLE. The entry for this beginning is:

```
-1,0
BOT
```

And the entry for the end of the Data Section is:

```
-1,0
EOD
```

The first number in the first line is the type of information (a "−1" indicating a special entry), and the second is the value associated with that entry (a "0" for special entries). The second line contains either a BOT for Beginning Of Tuple or EOD for End Of Data.

We should now be able to write out a sample TUPLE for the file using the scores from the MATH SYSTEM.

```
-1,0    (beginning of tuple)
BOT
:
0,1        (math session number)
V
```

```
:
1,0       (type of operation)
"ADD"
:
0,2       (number of digits)
V
:
0,8       (number correct)
V
:
0,2       (number wrong)
V
:
-1,0  (beginning of next tuple)
BOT
```

The words in parentheses would not be included in the file. They are there to help explain each entry. Again, I have added the colons to separate each entry.

The organization of the Header Section and the Data Section allows for a large variety in file manipulation, far more variety than I have gone into with this explanation. Further information on the structure and flexibility of DIF files can be obtained from: (1) the DIF Clearinghouse, POB 527, Cambridge, Ma. 02139, or (2) by reading the information contained in the VisiCalc program, or (3) by reading "DIF: A format for Data Exchange between Applications Programs," BYTE Magazine, November 1981, p. 174.

Now we should be able to write a simple program that will reformat our math scores file in such a way that it conforms to the DIF standard. The first part of this program reads the scores into memory. The second part does the reformatting.

```
100   REM   ***--CREATE DIF SCORES FILE--***
110   :
120   :
130   DIM S$(100), DT(100), CR(100), WR(100)
140   Q$ = CHR$(34):REM Quotation mark
150   I = 1
160   CLS: LOCATE 5,1
170   INPUT "Student's Name Please";NAMES$
180   :
190   :
200   REM **--FILE INPUT ROUTINE--**
210   OPEN NAMES$ + ".DAT" FOR INPUT AS #1
220   IF EOF (1) THEN 330
```

```
230   INPUT #1, S$(I): REM SIGN OF OPERATION
240   INPUT #1, DT(I): REM # of DIGITS
250   INPUT #1, CR(I): REM # CORRECT
260   INPUT #1, WR(I): REM # WRONG
270   IF S$(I) = "+" THEN S$(I) = "ADD"
280   IF S$(I) = "-" THEN S$(I) = "SUB"
290   IF S$(I) = "X" THEN S$(I) = "MLT"
300   IF S$(I) = "/" THEN S$(I) = "DIV"
310   I = I + 1
320   GOTO 220
330   CLOSE #1
340   :
350   :
```

With the exception of line 140, this is virtually the same routine used for the SCORES program. Line 140 has been added because we need to put quotation marks within quotation marks. The next part of the program is designed by following the necessary organization of either the Header Section or the Data Section.

```
360 REM **--DIF ROUTINE--**
370 J = I - 1: NV = 5: NT = I - 1
380 REM J = COUNTER
390 REM NV = NUMBER OF VECTORS
400 REM NT = NUMBER OF TUPLES
410 FILE$ = NAMES$ + ".DIF"
420 OPEN FILE$ FOR OUTPUT AS #1
430 :
440 REM **--HEADER SECTION--**
450 :
460 PRINT #1, "TABLE"
470 PRINT #1, "0, 1"
480 PRINT #1, Q$NAME$Q$
490 :
500 PRINT #1, "VECTORS"
510 PRINT #1, "0, "; NV
520 PRINT #1, Q$Q$
530 :
540 PRINT #1, "TUPLES"
550 PRINT #1, "0, "; NT
560 PRINT #1, Q$Q$
570 :
580 PRINT #1, "LABEL"
590 PRINT #1, "1, 0"
600 PRINT #1, Q$"SESSION #"Q$
```

```
610 :
620 PRINT #1, "LABEL"
630 PRINT #1, "2, 0"
640 PRINT #1, Q$"OPERATION"Q$
650 :
660 PRINT #1, "LABEL"
670 PRINT #1, "3, 0"
680 PRINT #1, Q$"DIGITS"Q$
690 :
700 PRINT #1, "LABEL"
710 PRINT #1, "4, 0"
720 PRINT #1, Q$"CORRECT"Q$
730 :
740 PRINT #1, "LABEL"
750 PRINT #1, "5, 0"
760 PRINT #1, Q$"WRONG"Q$
770 :
780 PRINT #1, "DATA"
790 PRINT #1, "0, 0"
800 PRINT #1, Q$Q$
810 :
```

These lines create the Header Section. They follow the rules of the Header Section in that each entry has three lines: the topic line, the numeric line, and the title or string line. The label entries are optional. The instructions at line 370 could be handled with input variable statements instead of constants. Line 410 combines the name of the file with the suffix ".DIF" to distinguish between the two files. This suffix may be required for some application programs. The next section of code creates the Data Section.

```
820 REM **--DATA SECTION--**
830 :
840 PRINT #1, "-1, 0"
850 PRINT #1, "BOT"
860 :
870 PRINT #1, "1, 0"
880 PRINT #1, Q$"SESSION #"Q$
890 :
900 PRINT #1, "1, 0"
910 PRINT #1, Q$"OPERATION"Q$
920 :
930 PRINT #1, "1, 0"
940 PRINT #1, Q$"DIGITS"Q$
950 :
```

```
960 PRINT #1,"1,0"
970 PRINT #1,Q$"CORRECT"Q$
980 :
990 PRINT #1,"1,0"
1000 PRINT #1,Q$"WRONG"Q$
1010 :
1020 FOR I = 1 TO J
1030 :
1040 PRINT #1,"-1,0"
1050 PRINT #1,"BOT"
1060 :
1070 PRINT #1,"0,";I  :REM MATH SESSION #
1080 PRINT #1,"V"
1090 :
1100 PRINT #1,"1,0":REM OPERATION
1110 PRINT #1,S$(I)
1120 :
1130 PRINT #1,"0,";DT(I):REM # OF DIGITS
1140 PRINT #1,"V"
1150 :
1160 PRINT #1,"0,";CR(I):REM # CORRECT
1170 PRINT #1,"V"
1180 :
1190 PRINT #1,"0,";WR(I):REM # WRONG
1200 PRINT #1,"V"
1210 :
1220 NEXT I
1230 PRINT #1,"-1,0"
1240 PRINT #1,"EOD"
1250 :
1260 CLOSE #1
```

We include the labels with the Data Section so that VisiCalc will view them as data and include them in the display. (VisiCalc does not support the "LABEL" topic in the Header Section.) Once the label information has been included, we write out the actual data by printing the contents of the various arrays. We use a loop to accomplish this. When the loop is finished, the "special entry," EOD, is written and the file closed. Now we should have a program that will create a duplicate file of an individual's math scores in the DIF file format.

We are able to create a DIF file that can be accessed by DIF supporting application programs. One other step remains. We may need to use data obtained with an application program. This requires creating a program that reads DIF files. Reading a DIF file is simply reading a sequential file that has its information stored in a specific order. The following program will read a VisiCalc DIF file. The display portion of the program is left in its original form since each file may require a different display format.

```
100  REM ***--DIF READER--***
110  :
120  :
130  DIM A$(200),S(200),N(200)
140  I = 1
150  CLS: LOCATE 5,1
160  INPUT "File name please";FILE$
170  FILE$ = FILE$ + ".DIF"
180  :
190  :
200  REM **--FILE INPUT ROUTINE--**
210  OPEN FILE$ FOR INPUT AS #1
220  LINE INPUT #1,T$: REM Read the Topic Name
230  INPUT #1, S,N: REM Read the Vector #, Value
240  INPUT #1, S$: REM The string value
250  IF T$ = "VECTORS" THEN NV = N
260  IF T$ = "TUPLES"  THEN NT = N
270  IF T$ < > "DATA" THEN 220
280  K = 1
290  INPUT #1,S(K),N(K)
300  LINE INPUT #1,A$(K)
310  IF A$(K) = "EOD" THEN 330
320  K = K + 1: GOTO 290
330  CLOSE #1
340  :
350  :
360  REM **--DISPLAY ROUTINE--**
370  FOR J = 1 TO K
380  PRINT S(J);",";N(J)
390  PRINT A$(J)
400  NEXT J
410  END
```

The display routine is left in its elementary form since the point of the program is to show how to access files from DIF supporting application programs. All these lines should be familiar. Line 270 tells the computer to go back to line 220 until T$ equals "DATA". At that time, the computer is to drop down to the loop used to read and store the Data Section information (lines 280 through 330). When A$(K) reads the value "EOD", we know that the file is finished, and we need to CLOSE the file and proceed to the display routine.

As with all programs, there are other ways of writing a DIF reader program and obtaining essentially the same results. We could have read and saved all the information contained in the Header Section, or we could have used a number of GOSUBS (especially in the DIF creator program). Most of the differences, however, are stylistic differences and not substantive differences.

You now have the ability to read and write DIF files. That ability may not prove immediately useful, but I think you will find that this may eventually be the most valuable thing you have learned in this book. If you are not completely sure you understand the format, a second look through this chapter and additional work with DIF creator or reader programs should make you comfortable with DIF.

I have not tried to explain all the possibilities or variations of DIF. This chapter is intended only as an introduction to this file transfer standard. I firmly believe that some such standard is essential if micros are to be taken seriously.

I will conclude this chapter with a tutorial on the specific procedure necessary to transfer the information stored in the scores files to the VisiCalc program. This section will be useful to you only if you have VisiCalc and have actually typed in and run the MATH SYSTEM programs. You will need to have typed in the DIFCREAT program discussed in this chapter also. (A disk containing all the programs in this book is available for those who do not want to type in every program.)

Step 1: Type: LOAD "DIFCREAT

Step 2: Press the F2 key or type RUN and press the ENTER key.

Step 3: Answer the question with your name if you have used the MATH SYSTEM, or with the name of someone who has used the MATH SYSTEM.

Step 4: The disk comes on. Soon the OK prompt returns. Nothing else appears on the screen.

Step 5: Place the VisiCalc diskette in DRIVE A and the diskette containing the newly created DIF file in DRIVE B. (Single drive users should check the VisiCalc manual for the procedure on when to switch diskettes.)

Step 6: Boot the system either by turning on the computer or by resetting it with the CTRL, ALT, and DEL keys (see Chapter 1). Read the screen and press any key, if necessary.

Step 7: After the VisiCalc display appears, press the / key. *Do not press the ENTER key!* Do not press the ENTER key from this point on unless given specific instructions to do so.

Step 8: Next press the S key.

Step 9: Now type the # key by using the shift key and pressing the 3 key on the top row of the keyboard.

Step 10: Press the L key.

Step 11: Type the following exactly B: and press the ENTER key.

Step 12: The B DRIVE comes on briefly and the name of the first file stored in the DIF format is displayed near the top of the screen following the B:

Step 13: If this is the file name you want, press the ENTER key. If it is not the file name you want, strike the right arrow key repeatedly until the desired file name is displayed and then press the ENTER key.

Step 14: The B DRIVE comes on briefly and then the computer displays the following near the top of the screen:
Data load: R C or ENTER.

Step 15: Press the C key.

Step 16: The B DRIVE comes back on and soon the screen displays information that originally came from the MATH SYSTEM programs.

Step 17: Press the / key again.

Step 18: Press the G key.

Step 19: Press the F key.

Step 20: Finally, press the L key. The numbers should now be lined up under the proper column titles. Further adjustment can be made to the column widths etc.

At this point, the scores obtained under the MATH SYSTEM can be manipulated in any fashion desired within the bounds of the VisiCalc program.

No attempt is made to explain the reason for each step. If you want to understand why various keys are pressed while in VisiCalc, obtain a copy of the VisiCalc manual or purchase one or more of the books that are being published on the use of VisiCalc.

QUESTIONS

1. *True or False:* DIF suggests a standard way of saving all files.
2. Name the two parts of a DIF file.
3. Which part contains information about the file itself?
4. Which part contains the actual file information?
5. How many lines are associated with each entry in the Header Section?
6. How many lines are associated with each entry in the Data Section?
7. What value is used to indicate numeric information in the Data Section?
8. What value is used to indicate alphanumeric information in the Data Section?
9. What characters are used as the last entry in a DIF file?

ANSWERS

1. False
2. Header Section and Data Section
3. Header Section
4. Data Section
5. 3
6. 2
7. 0
8. 1
9. EOD

DIFCREAT

```
100 REM ***--CREATE SCORES DIF FILE--***
110 :
120 :
130 DIM S$(100),DT(100),CR(100),WR(100)
140 Q$ = CHR$(34): REM Quotation mark
150 I = 1
160 CLS: LOCATE 5,1
170 INPUT "Student's Name Please";NAMES$
180 :
190 :
200 REM **--FILE INPUT ROUTINE--**
210 OPEN NAMES$ + ".DAT" FOR INPUT AS #1
220 IF EOF(1) THEN 330
230 INPUT #1,S$(I): REM SIGN OF OPERATION
240 INPUT #1,DT(I): REM # OF DIGITS
250 INPUT #1,CR(I): REM # CORRECT
260 INPUT #1,WR(I): REM # WRONG
270 IF S$(I) = "+" THEN S$(I) = "ADD"
280 IF S$(I) = "-" THEN S$(I) = "SUB"
290 IF S$(I) = "X" THEN S$(I) = "MLT"
300 IF S$(I) = "/" THEN S$(I) = "DIV"
310 I = I + 1
320 GOTO 220
330 CLOSE #1
340 :
350 :
360 REM **--DIF ROUTINE--**
370 J = I - 1: NV = 5 : NT = I - 1
380 REM J  = COUNTER
390 REM NV = NUMBER OF VECTORS
400 REM NT = NUMBER OF TUPLES
410 FILE$  = NAMES$ +".DIF"
420 OPEN FILE$ FOR OUTPUT AS #1
430 :
440 REM **--HEADER SECTION--**
450 :
460 PRINT #1,"TABLE"
470 PRINT #1,"O,1"
480 PRINT #1,Q$NAMES$Q$
490 :
500 PRINT #1,"VECTORS"
510 PRINT #1,"0,";NV
520 PRINT #1,Q$Q$
530 :
540 PRINT #1,"TUPLES"
550 PRINT #1,"0,";NT
560 PRINT #1,Q$Q$
570 :
580 PRINT #1,"LABEL"
590 PRINT #1,"1,0"
```

```
600 PRINT #1,Q$"SESSION #"Q$
610 :
620 PRINT #1,"LABEL"
630 PRINT #1,"2,0"
640 PRINT #1,Q$"OPERATION"Q$
650 :
660 PRINT #1,"LABEL"
670 PRINT #1,"3,0"
680 PRINT #1,Q$"DIGITS"Q$
690 :
700 PRINT #1,"LABEL"
710 PRINT #1,"4,0"
720 PRINT #1,Q$"CORRECT"Q$
730 :
740 PRINT #1,"LABEL"
750 PRINT #1,"5,0"
760 PRINT #1,Q$"WRONG"Q$
770 :
780 PRINT #1,"DATA"
790 PRINT #1,"0,0"
800 PRINT #1,Q$Q$
810 :
820 REM **--DATA SECTION--**
830 :
840 PRINT #1,"-1,0"
850 PRINT #1,"BOT"
860 :
870 PRINT #1,"1,0"
880 PRINT #1,Q$"SESSION"Q$
890 :
900 PRINT #1,"1,0"
910 PRINT #1,Q$"OPERATION"Q$
920 :
930 PRINT #1,"1,0"
940 PRINT #1,Q$"DIGITS"Q$
950 :
960 PRINT #1,"1,0"
970 PRINT #1,Q$"CORRECT"Q$
980 :
990 PRINT #1,"1,0"
1000 PRINT #1,Q$"WRONG"Q$
1010 :
1020 FOR I = 1 TO J
1030 :
1040 PRINT #1,"-1,0"
1050 PRINT #1,"BOT"
1060 :
1070 PRINT #1,"0,";I: REM MATH SESSION #
1080 PRINT #1,"V"
1090 :
1100 PRINT #1,"1,0": REM OPERATION
1110 PRINT #1,S$(I)
1120 :
1130 PRINT #1,"0,";DT(I): REM # OF DIGITS
```

```
1140 PRINT #1,"V"
1150 :
1160 PRINT #1,"0,";CR(I): REM # CORRECT
1170 PRINT #1,"V"
1180 :
1190 PRINT #1,"0,";WR(I): REM # WRONG
1200 PRINT #1,"V"
1210 :
1220 NEXT I
1230 PRINT #1,"-1,0"
1240 PRINT #1,"EOD"
1250 :
1260 CLOSE #1
```

DIFREAD

```
100 REM ***--DIF READER--***
110 :
120 :
130 DIM A$(200),S(200),N(200)
140 I = 1
150 CLS: LOCATE 5,1
160 INPUT "File name please";FILE$
170 FILE$ = FILE$ + ".DIF"
180 :
190 :
200 REM **--FILE INPUT ROUTINE--**
210 OPEN FILE$ FOR INPUT AS #1
220 LINE INPUT #1,T$: REM Read the Topic Name
230 INPUT #1,S,N: REM Read the Vector #, Value
240 INPUT #1,S$: REM The string value
250 IF T$ = "VECTORS" THEN NV = N
260 IF T$ = "TUPLES" THEN NT = N
270 IF T$ < > "DATA" THEN 220
280 K = 1
290 INPUT #1,S(K),N(K)
300 LINE INPUT #1,A$(K)
310 IF A$(K) = "EOD" THEN 330
320 K = K + 1: GOTO 290
330 CLOSE #1
340 :
350 :
360 REM **--DISPLAY ROUTINE--**
370 FOR J = 1 TO K
380 PRINT S(J);",";N(J)
390 PRINT A$(J)
400 NEXT J
410 END
```

10
Random File Introduction

The biggest barrier I have found in explaining random access files is fear. People are afraid that random access is too hard to learn. Actually, once you understand the principles behind sequential access, learning to work with random access is not that difficult. I believe that if you have followed all the examples in the previous chapters, you will be able to learn to work with random files. Do not become intimidated by the different approach random access requires.

There are two kinds of random access files: random files that consist of undivided equal length records, and random files that consist of divided equal length records. Notice the only difference is that in one kind, the records are divided into parts, while in the other kind, the records remain as a whole. This latter kind is the easier to explain and use, so I will discuss it first.

UNDIVIDED RANDOM FILES

IBM calls these undivided random files "pseudo-sequential" files because this type of random file is very similar to sequential files. The main difference between the two is that with these random files, we can now access any record in any order. With the sequential files, it is necessary to begin with the first record and proceed past all intervening records until we come to the record we want. Now, with random files, we are able to go directly to the desired record.

```
10 OPEN "TEST.DAT" AS #1 LEN = 50
20 FOR I = 1 TO 100
30 PRINT #1, "ABCDE"
```

```
40  PUT  #1
50  NEXT  I
60  CLOSE  #1
```

In this example, you can see how easy it is to use random files of the undivided kind. There are basically three differences between this program and a similar program to create a sequential file. The first two differences occur in line 10. In random file programs, you do not need to specify the kind of access; i.e., INPUT or OUTPUT. But you must specify the length of each record within the file. Once you open the file properly, you are able to directly read or write to any record you choose in any order you choose. Please notice the qualification about opening the file properly.

Both kinds of random files must consist of equal length records. This means that you must decide on the length of the longest record you will ever have. For instance, in our MAILING LIST SYSTEM, each line had a maximum length of 255 characters because that is the maximum number of characters allowed in a single string variable. Probably none of your lines (or records) actually had the maximum length, but that was the length possible for each record. You did not need to specify this number because, in sequential files, the next record begins immediately after the end of the last character and the record delimiter, no matter what the actual length of the record. You must specify the maximum length in random files because the next record does not begin immediately after the last character in the previous record. It actually begins the specified record length after the beginning of the previous record, regardless of the number of characters in that record.

In our above example, the length is given as "50". That means that each record has a maximum of 50 characters possible and that each record begins 50 characters (spaces), or bytes, from the start of the previous record. If the first record begins at byte 0, the second begins at 50, the third record at 100, etc. You do not need to be concerned with the actual location on the disk. It is important to understand that since each record must be of equal length, it is very easy for the computer to calculate the starting position of each record and possible for you to specify any record in any order. You must provide the computer with that maximum length by assigning a value after the LEN parameter in random files. (If no value is specified, the computer defaults to a value of 128.) The number given after the LEN in an OPEN statement indicates the maximum number of characters, or bytes, you expect in any record in that file. It also indicates that each record will be that number of characters, or bytes, long.

If you have a record that is not as long as the number given after the LEN, then you will have a certain amount of disk space that is unused, so it is important to figure carefully and keep the number after LEN as low as possible. If the number is very large but most of your records are rather small, then you will be wasting a lot of disk space (as in the above example). A certain amount of wasted disk space is inevitable in using random files, since few files will contain information of exactly .equal length. In using random files, you are willing to waste a little disk space in order to gain the advantage of much faster disk access.

The third difference comes in line 40. The PRINT #1 in line 30 fills the buffer but does not actually write anything to the diskette. The PUT #1 in line 40 is necessary to actually write the information to the diskette. If, as in the above example, no number is specified after the file number, the computer defaults to the next record, proceeding in sequence through the file. As you will see, any record can be accessed by simply giving the record number after the file number in either a PUT or a GET statement.

```
70 OPEN "TEST.DAT" AS #1 LEN=50
80 CLS: LOCATE 5,1
90 FOR I = 1 TO 100
100 GET #1
110 INPUT #1,A$
120 PRINT A$
130 NEXT I
140 CLOSE #1
```

In order to read back what was just written, we must either close the file (line 60) and then reopen it (line 70), or specify a record number after the file number in line 100. In addition, before printing the value of A$, the value must be brought from the buffer (line 110). Otherwise, this display routine looks very similar to what a sequential file routine would look like. Once again, the main difference occurs in the first line of the routine.

Combining both input and output into one routine we see the following:

```
150 OPEN "TEST.DAT" AS #1 LEN=50
160 INPUT "RECORD NUMBER PLEASE ";REC
170 PRINT #1, "XXXXX"
180 PUT #1,REC
190 FOR I = REC - 10 TO REC + 10
200 GET #1,I
210 INPUT #1,A$
```

```
220  PRINT A$
230  NEXT I
240  CLOSE #1
```

In this combined input and output routine, the file is opened and closed once. It is not necessary to close the file and open it again between the two access routines. Lines 170 and 180 access the record specified by the user in line 160 and write the value "XXXXX" in place of the value "ABCDE" written by our first output routine. Lines 190 through 230 then loop through the file beginning with the record that is 10 records before the record specified by the user in line 160 (REC − 10) and proceeding to 10 records past the identified record. The purpose here is to show that we can access specific records in both read and write modes.

As you can see, there is not too much difference in learning to use sequential access files and learning to use random access files of the undivided kind. Our MAILING LIST SYSTEM would be somewhat easer to work with now, but it would still be a good idea to include some kind of separator between addresses and phone numbers and also between sets of information. We would still have some difficulty picking out just the zip code or first name or city or any other part of a record if we needed just that part. It can be done with enough good programming, but an easier way is to use the second kind of random access files—the divided equal length record.

DIVIDED RANDOM FILES

The divided random file consists of records that are broken into varying-length parts or fields. Each record is the same length, but within each record, the fields or parts of the record can be of varying lengths. In other words, a random access file that consists of records with a length of 100 characters or bytes can have each record divided into parts of equal or unequal lengths. The first field might be 25 bytes long, the second field 10 bytes, the third field 15 bytes, and the last field 50 bytes. The total number of bytes or characters equals 100, but no two fields need be the same length.

In our MAILING LIST SYSTEM example, with random files that contained divided records, we could specify a certain length for the first name and other lengths for the last name, city, zip code, etc. Each record, therefore, could contain a complete set of the information needed for the MAILING LIST SYSTEM. For instance, if we decide that each line of information or each record would have no more than

150 characters in it, we could further decide that the first field of each record would exist from byte 0 to byte 10, the second from byte 11 to byte 15, the third field from byte 16 to byte 30, etc. Each record could contain the first name in the first field, the middle initial in the second field, the last name in the third field, the numerical address in the fourth field, the street address in the fifth field, any apartment number, etc. in the sixth field, the city in the seventh field, the state in the eighth field, and the zip code in the ninth field. Under this set up, it would be easy to access any part of any record in any order we desired. For example, if we just wanted the zip code and first name in that order, we would have no trouble accessing just that information.

I have been using the term "byte" in connection with the word "character" so that you might get used to the idea that the length of a record is measured in bytes. Each character or number is one byte. If a file has equal length records of 50, that is 50 bytes. If the second field begins 27 characters from the first character, that is the 27th byte of the file. To access that byte we use another statement—the FIELD statement. For example:

```
200  OPEN "TEST.DAT" AS #1 LEN=75
220  FIELD #1,25 AS A$,  50 AS B$
240  GET #1,44
260  PRINT B$
280  CLOSE #1
```

This example would open the existing file called "TEST.DAT" whose length for each record is 75 bytes. Line 220 defines each record in file #1 as containing two fields, identified as A$ and B$. The first field contains 25 bytes and the second field has 50 bytes. Line 240 brings information in from the 44th record, and line 260 displays the information contained in the second field of that record. Notice that when we use the FIELD statement, it is not necessary to input information from the random file buffer before displaying it.

MEDICAL RECORDS SYSTEM

With this background, we are going to go over what I hope is a useful program. The example is a file used to store personal family medical records. In these random file examples, I will not go over all the routines as I did in the sequential file examples. Instead, I will concentrate on the file routines. The complete listing for the program will be found at the end of the chapter.

If you take a look at the complete listing, you will see that we begin with a menu routine. The first thing that needs to be done the first time the program is used is to set the value of the record pointer to zero and write that value out to a sequential file. After setting the pointer value that first time, the program instructions automatically update the pointer value.

FILE OUTPUT ROUTINE

Next comes a keyboard input routine in order to obtain our original information. We are asking the user to supply: (1) the name of the individual (NAMES$); (2) the date (DT$); (3) the type of record, i.e. whether it is a record of a Dr. Visit, Medication, Illness, Accident or Injury, Shot or Immunization, or X-ray (TYPE$); and (4) any miscellaneous information such as the name of the medication and frequency of use, the kind of illness, location of injury, etc. (MISC$). Once we have all our information and have verified that it is correct, we are ready to write that information out to the disk file.

```
1570 REM **--FILE OUTPUT ROUTINE--**
1580 OPEN "MEDPTR.DAT" FOR INPUT AS #1
1590 INPUT #1,PTR
1600 CLOSE #1
1610 PTR = PTR + 1
1620 OPEN "MEDRECS.DAT" AS #2 LEN=50
1630 FIELD #2,15 as N$,10 AS D$,1 AS T$,24 AS M$
1640 LSET N$ = NAMES$
1650 LSET D$ = DT$
1660 LSET T$ = TYPE$
1670 LSET M$ = MISC$
1680 PUT #2,PTR
1690 CLOSE #2
1700 OPEN "MEDPTR.DAT" FOR OUTPUT AS #1
1710 PRINT #1,PTR
1720 CLOSE #1
1730 GOTO 170: REM Menu
```

There are three parts to this output routine. The first part (lines 1580−1610) accesses the pointer file and updates the pointer value. The second part (lines 1620−1690) defines the data file and writes the information to it. Finally, the last part (lines 1700−1730) again accesses the pointer file, this time to write out the new value of the pointer. We are concerned with the second part since that is the part that deals with a random access file.

Line 1620 defines the random access file, MEDRECS.DAT, as the second file we are working with and a file with a length of 50 characters, or bytes, in each record. Line 1630 defines the fields within each record: the first field is 15 bytes long and will be identified as N$; the second field is 10 bytes or characters in length and is called D$; the third field has only one character in it, identified as T$; and the last field contains 24 bytes and is identified as M$. Lines 1640 to 1670 may seem strange. These lines allow the programmer to position the data within the actual file. LSET simply means to left justify the information contained on the side opposite the equal sign. In other words, if a piece of information contains less characters than the space allotted for it, LSETing that information insures that the information will always begin at the left edge of the space allotted for the information. RSET will right justify or line everything up on the right side of the space allotted. Due to the fact that the computer first moves information into a buffer and then onto the diskette, we should not use the same variable names for both operations. That is the reason for LSETing N$ to equal NAMES$, etc. Line 1680 PUTs the information in the random file buffer out to the diskette at the specified PTR position or record number. Finally, in line 1690, we close the file.

There is one point that should be emphasized before moving on. Notice that it is not necessary to use string arrays: NAMES$(). We do not have to use string arrays because of the versatility of random files. In this program, the information for a complete record is written to the disk before additional information is obtained from the user. The idea that we can use the disk without extensive use of string arrays will become more apparent with the section on reading and displaying our medical information.

FILE INPUT ROUTINE

We move now to the section of our program that allows us to see the information we have stored in the MEDRECS.DAT file. In this first section, we read the file and immediately display the information.

```
2000 REM **--READ FILE ROUTINE--**
2010 CLS
2020 OPEN "MEDPTR.DAT" FOR INPUT AS #1
2030 INPUT #1,PTR
2040 CLOSE #1
2050 OPEN "MEDRECS.DAT" AS #2 LEN=50
```

```
2060 FIELD #2,15 AS NAMES$,10 AS DT$,1 AS TYPE$,24
     AS MISC$
2070 FOR I = 1 TO PTR
2080 GET #2,I
2090 TP$ = TYPE: GOSUB 20000: REM Type subroutine
2100 PRINT NAMES$ TAB(20) DT$ TAB(35) TP$ TAB(55)
     MISC$
2110 PRINT
2120 NEXT I
2130 CLOSE #2
2140 INPUT "Press the 'ENTER' key to continue";L$
2150 GOTO 170: REM Menu
```

The first thing that is done is to name the routine (line 2000) and clear the screen (line 2010). Next, the pointer file is accessed, and the value of the pointer (the number of records currently in the data file) is stored in the numeric variable PTR. It is not necessary to immediately close the pointer file (MEDPTR.DAT), but it is a good programming habit. In line 2050, the data file MEDRECS.DAT is opened as our second accessed file and defined as having records of 50 bytes, or characters, in length. Line 2060 is identical to line 1630 except we can now use our standard names for the string variables. Line 2070 establishes the boundaries of our loop while 2080 GETs the record determined by the value of I. The instruction in line 2090 may look unusual. We first set the string variable TP$ equal to the string variable TYPE$. Control is then transferred to a subroutine located in lines 20000 to 20070. The purpose of this subroutine is to match the single character symbol with its complete corresponding TYPE name: for example, exchange "D" for "Dr. Visit". Once the exchange has been made, control is returned to the statement immediately following the GOSUB statement. This is one of the few times that multiple statements on the same instruction line may clarify the purpose of the instructions. The idea is to use a common variable, go to a routine that uses that common variable, and return from that routine with a new value. We will use this procedure in other programs.

Line 2100 displays the information obtained from the accessed record. The information can be displayed in any order the programmer chooses and with a variety of programming statements. In this case, I have used the TAB statement to format the display. The parenthesis after the TAB statement must come immediately after the B; i.e., no intervening spaces. Line 2110 displays a blank line in order to double space those lines with information. In lines 2130 to 2150, we close the file and wait until the user has typed something before returning to the menu portion of the program.

The only section of the program left to examine is the search routine. Lines 3000 to 3230 establish exactly what we will be searching for, and lines 3300 through 3550 conduct the actual search and display the results.

```
3300 REM **--FILE INPUT ROUTINE--**
3310 CLS: LOCATE 5,1
3320 OPEN "MEDPTR.DAT" FOR INPUT AS #1
3330 INPUT #1,PTR
3340 CLOSE #1
3350 OPEN "MEDRECS.DAT" AS #2 LEN=50
3360 FIELD #2,15 AS FIND$(1),10 AS FIND$(2),1 AS
     FIND$(3),24 AS FIND$(4)
3370 LN = LEN(SRCH$)
3380 FOR I = 1 TO PTR
3390 GET #2,I
3400 :
3410 CVT$ = LEFT$(FIND$(NB),LN)
3420 GOSUB 10000: REM Convert to uppercase
3430 :
3440 IF SRCH$ < > CVT$ THEN 3510: REM Next I
3450 TP$ = FIND$(3): GOSUB 20000: REM Type subrout
     ine
3460 PRINT FIND$(1);"   ";
3470 PRINT FIND$(2);"   ";
3480 PRINT    TP$;     "   ";
3490 PRINT FIND$(4);"   ";
3500 PRINT
3510 NEXT I
3520 CLOSE #2
3530 PRINT: PRINT
3540 INPUT "Press 'ENTER' to continue.";L$
3550 GOTO 3000: REM Search again
```

This is an elementary search and display routine. Lines 3320 to 3340 open the pointer file and obtain the value of the pointer. The data file is then opened (line 3350) and defined (line 3360). This time we define the fields within each record by a string variable array: FIND$(). This is done so that we need only search a particular field.

Next comes a little technique that allows the user to search for just the beginning portion of a field in case the user does not know the complete spelling of the entire field. The search is limited to just the number of characters the user has supplied in answer to the question in line 3230 (see the program listing at the end of this chapter). We determine this number and then use the number in 3410 to limit the number of characters that will go through the process of conversion to upper case. Once those characters have been converted to upper case, we can compare them to the characters supplied by the user (SRCH$). If they are not equal, the computer is instructed to increment the value of I and proceed.

Line 3380 establishes the boundaries for a loop. Within that loop, we look for just the desired part of each record. When that part is located, the rest of the information associated with that part is displayed (lines 3460 to 3490). Those instruction-lines are skipped for information that does not match or equal the string variable for which we are searching. When the entire file has been searched, the file is closed, and control is transferred back to the beginning of the search routine to see if the user wishes to search for more information.

This program provides a reasonable example of the techniques involved with creating, adding to, and reading from a random access file. It does not get too fancy yet is a useful program. You may want to supply additional routines such as a printer routine. I have included a DIF TRANSLATION routine for further practice with the DIF method of file handling. The method given in the last chapter for loading a DIF file into VisiCalc will work for this DIF file also. There may not be much point in loading this type of information into VisiCalc, but if other application programs (such as data base systems) make use of the DIF standard, you should be able to use their expanded capabilities without the necessity of rekeying all your data.

At this point, you should find yourself capable of "reading" a program listing. As we progress through the book, the amount of text decreases while the amount of program instructions that you should "read" increases. In the following chapter, we will use random files in a more elaborate manner.

One additional comment needs to be made in concluding this chapter. There are a variety of ways for using random access files of either the divided or undivided kind. The method presented in this chapter is not meant to suggest itself as the only method or even the best method. It is a method that does work and is understandable. In working with files, I have found that comprehension is of more value than program efficiency or speed. And one cautionary note: things don't always function as it seems they logically should, especially when working with random files of the undivided kind. Part of the reason for this involves the use of the random file buffer and the lack of a FIELD statement. For this reason, I would not encourage extensive use of the undivided type of random files until you are very comfortable with the way they operate.

QUESTIONS

1. Name the two kinds of random files.

2. What term does IBM use to refer to undivided random files?

3. *True or False:* Random files can contain records of different lengths.

4. What are the two BASIC words used to obtain information from a diskette and place information on a diskette?

5. *True or False:* In random files, the next record begins immediately after the last character in the previous record.

6. What parameter must an OPEN command have in a random file?

7. *True or False:* Random files waste disk space but have much faster disk access than do sequential files.

8. *True or False:* The relationship that exists between the various parts of a divided random access file can be defined in the following way: A random access file consists of equal length records. Each record may consist of equal and/or unequal length fields. The number following the BASIC word LEN in an OPEN statement indicates the length of each record. The information in a FIELD statement, defines and names the various fields within each record.

9. What is the length of each record measured in?

10. *True or False:* Random files require greater use of string arrays than do sequential files.

11. What BASIC word is used to left justify strings for random access files?

ANSWERS

1. Divided and undivided random files
2. Pseudo-sequential
3. False
4. GET and PUT
5. False
6. LEN
7. True
8. True
9. Bytes
10. False
11. LSET

MEDREC

```
100 REM ***--MEDICAL RECORDS SYSTEM--***
110 :
120 :
130 TB = 25: REM Tab value
140 KEY OFF
150 :
160 :
170 REM **--MEDICAL RECORDS MENU--**
180 CLS
190 LOCATE 3,TB
200 PRINT "MEDICAL RECORDS"
210 LOCATE 6,TB
220 PRINT "1.  WRITE RECORD"
230 LOCATE 8,TB
240 PRINT "2.  READ RECORD"
250 LOCATE 10,TB
260 PRINT "3.  SEARCH RECORD"
270 LOCATE 12,TB
280 PRINT "4.  SET POINTER"
290 LOCATE 14,TB
300 PRINT "5.  DIF TRANSLATION"
310 LOCATE 16,TB
320 PRINT "6.  END"
330 LOCATE 18,TB
340 INPUT "WHICH NUMBER";NUMBER
350 IF NUMBER < 1 OR NUMBER > 6 THEN GOSUB 7000: REM Inc
    orrect number msg.
360 IF NUMBER = 1 THEN 1000
370 IF NUMBER = 2 THEN 2000
380 IF NUMBER = 3 THEN 3000
390 IF NUMBER = 4 THEN 4000
400 IF NUMBER = 5 THEN 5000
410 IF NUMBER = 6 THEN KEY ON: END
420 GOTO 190: REM Ask again
430 :
440 :
1000 REM **--WRITE RECORD ROUTINE--**
1010 CLS: LOCATE 10,1
1020 LINE INPUT "Type in individual's name please: ";NAM
     ES$
1030 IF LEN (NAMES$) > 15 THEN NAMES$ = LEFT$(NAMES$,15)
1040 PRINT
1050 LINE INPUT "Type in the date in the form: 2-9-83. ";
     DT$
1060 IF LEN (DT$) >10 THEN DT$ = LEFT$(DT$,10)
1070 CLS: LOCATE 5,1
1080 LOCATE 5,TB
1090 PRINT "Type Of Record"
1100 LOCATE 7,TB
1110 PRINT "D--Dr. visit"
```

```
1120 LOCATE 9,TB
1130 PRINT "M--Medication"
1140 LOCATE 11,TB
1150 PRINT "I--Illness"
1160 LOCATE 13,TB
1170 PRINT "A--Accident/injury"
1180 LOCATE 15,TB
1190 PRINT "S--Shot/immunization"
1200 LOCATE 17,TB
1210 PRINT "X--X-Ray"
1220 LOCATE 19,TB
1230 INPUT "Which type of record";TYPE$
1240 :
1250 CVT$ = TYPE$
1260 GOSUB 10000: REM Convert to uppercase
1270 TYPE$ = CVT$
1280 :
1290 CLS
1300 LOCATE 5,TB
1310 PRINT "Type in any misc. information"
1320 LOCATE 10,TB
1330 FOR I = 1 TO 22
1340 PRINT "_";: REM Underline or CHR$(95)
1350 NEXT I
1360 LOCATE 10,TB
1370 INPUT "",MISC$: REM Input over underline
1380 IF LEN(MISC$) > 22 THEN 8000: REM Too long msg.
1390 CLS
1400 LOCATE 5,1
1410 PRINT TAB(TB) NAMES$
1420 PRINT
1430 PRINT TAB(TB) DT$
1440 PRINT
1450 TP$ = TYPE$: GOSUB 20000: REM Type subroutine
1460 PRINT TAB(TB) TP$
1470 PRINT
1480 PRINT TAB(TB) MISC$
1490 PRINT
1500 PRINT TAB(TB);:INPUT "Is this correct ";YES$
1510 CVT$ = YES$
1520 GOSUB 10000: REM Convert to uppercase
1530 YES$ = CVT$
1540 IF YES$ < > "Y" THEN 1000: REM Start over
1550 :
1560 :
1570 REM **--FILE OUTPUT ROUTINE--**
1580 OPEN "MEDPTR.DAT" FOR INPUT AS #1
1590 INPUT #1,PTR
1600 CLOSE #1
1610 PTR = PTR + 1
1620 OPEN "MEDRECS.DAT" AS #2 LEN=50
1630 FIELD #2,15 AS N$,10 AS D$,1 AS T$,24 AS M$
1640 LSET N$ = NAMES$
1650 LSET D$ = DT$
```

```
1660 LSET T$ = TYPE$
1670 LSET M$ = MISC$
1680 PUT #2,PTR
1690 CLOSE #2
1700 OPEN "MEDPTR.DAT" FOR OUTPUT AS #1
1710 PRINT #1,PTR
1720 CLOSE #1
1730 GOTO 170: REM Menu
1740 :
1750 :
2000 REM **--READ FILE ROUTINE--**
2010 CLS
2020 OPEN "MEDPTR.DAT" FOR INPUT AS #1
2030 INPUT #1,PTR
2040 CLOSE #1
2050 OPEN "MEDRECS.DAT" AS #2 LEN=50
2060 FIELD #2,15 AS NAMES$,10 AS DT$,1 AS TYPE$,24 AS MI
     SC$
2070 FOR I = 1 TO PTR
2080 GET #2,I
2090 TP$ = TYPE$: GOSUB 20000: REM Type subroutine
2100 PRINT NAMES$ TAB(20) DT$ TAB(35) TP$ TAB(55) MISC$
2110 PRINT
2120 NEXT I
2130 CLOSE #2
2140 INPUT "Press the `ENTER' key to continue";L$
2150 GOTO 170: REM MENU
2160 :
2170 :
3000 REM **--SEARCH ROUTINE--**
3010 CLS
3020 LOCATE 5,TB
3030 PRINT "SEARCH FOR..."
3040 LOCATE 7,TB
3050 PRINT "1.  NAME"
3060 LOCATE 9,TB
3070 PRINT "2.  DATE"
3080 LOCATE 11,TB
3090 PRINT "3.  TYPE"
3100 LOCATE 13,TB
3110 PRINT "4.  MISC"
3120 LOCATE 15,TB
3130 PRINT "5. END SEARCH"
3140 LOCATE 17,TB
3150 INPUT "Which Number ";NB
3160 IF NB = 1 THEN B$ = "Name"
3170 IF NB = 2 THEN B$ = "Date"
3180 IF NB = 3 THEN B$ = "Type"
3190 IF NB = 4 THEN B$ = "Misc"
3200 IF NB = 5 THEN 170: REM Menu
3210 IF NB < 1 OR NB > 5 THEN GOSUB 7000: GOTO 3020: REM
     Incorrect number msg.
3220 LOCATE 19,TB
3230 PRINT "Which ";B$;:INPUT "";SRCH$
```

```
3240 :
3250 CVT$ = SRCH$
3260 GOSUB 10000: REM Convert to uppercase
3270 SRCH$ = CVT$
3280 :
3290 :
3300 REM **--FILE INPUT ROUTINE--**
3310 CLS:LOCATE 5,1
3320 OPEN "MEDPTR.DAT" FOR INPUT AS #1
3330 INPUT #1,PTR
3340 CLOSE #1
3350 OPEN "MEDRECS.DAT" AS #2 LEN=50
3360 FIELD #2,15 AS FIND$(1),10 AS FIND$(2),1 AS FIND$(3
     ),24 AS FIND$(4)
3370 LN = LEN(SRCH$)
3380 FOR I = 1 TO PTR
3390 GET #2,I
3400 :
3410 CVT$ = LEFT$(FIND$(NB),LN)
3420 GOSUB 10000: REM Convert to uppercase
3430 :
3440 IF SRCH$ < > CVT$ THEN 3510: REM Next I
3450 TP$ = FIND$(3): GOSUB 20000: REM Type subroutine
3460 PRINT FIND$(1);"   ";
3470 PRINT FIND$(2);"   ";
3480 PRINT TP$;"   ";
3490 PRINT FIND$(4)
3500 PRINT
3510 NEXT I
3520 CLOSE #2
3530 PRINT: PRINT
3540 INPUT "Press `ENTER' to continue.";L$
3550 GOTO 3000: REM Search again
3560 :
3570 :
4000 REM **--SET POINTER ROUTINE--**
4010 CLS
4020 LOCATE 5,1
4030 PRINT "You should only need to set the pointer the
     first time the program"
4040 PRINT
4050 PRINT "is used. That first time, the value should b
     e set to a `0'. After"
4060 PRINT
4070 PRINT "that, if the pointer file `MEDPTR.DAT' is no
     t erased, this routine"
4080 PRINT
4090 PRINT "should not be needed. If the pointer file is
     erased, use this routine"
4100 PRINT
4110 PRINT "to reset the value of the pointer to the cor
     rect number of records."
4120 PRINT: PRINT
4130 INPUT "Do you want to set a value for the pointer "
     ;YES$
```

```
4140 :
4150 CVT$ = YES$
4160 GOSUB 10000: REM Convert to uppercase
4170 YES$ = CVT$
4180 :
4190 IF YES$ = "Y" THEN 4210
4200 GOTO 170: REM Menu
4210 PRINT
4220 INPUT "Type in a value for the pointer ";PTR
4230 PRINT
4240 PRINT "Is this the correct value: ";PTR
4250 INPUT "Type `YES' if it is. ",YES$
4260 :
4270 CVT$ = YES$
4280 GOSUB 10000: REM Convert to uppercase
4290 YES$ = CVT$
4300 :
4310 IF YES$ = "YES" THEN 4330
4320 GOTO 4000: REM Begin again
4330 OPEN "MEDPTR.DAT" FOR OUTPUT AS #1
4340 PRINT #1,PTR
4350 CLOSE #1
4360 PRINT
4370 PRINT "The pointer has now been set to";PTR
4380 FOR I = 1 TO 2000: NEXT I
4390 GOTO 170: REM Menu
4400 :
4410 :
5000 REM **--DIF TRANSLATION--**
5010 CLS:LOCATE 5,15
5020 PRINT "DIF TRANSLATION IN PROGRESS. PLEASE DO NOT TO
     UCH!!"
5030 Q$ = CHR$(34): REM Quotation mark
5040 OPEN "MEDPTR.DAT" FOR INPUT AS #1
5050 INPUT #1,PTR
5060 CLOSE #1
5070 NV = 4: NT = PTR + 1
5080 REM NV = NUMBER OF VECTORS
5090 REM NT = NUMBER OF TUPLES
5100 :
5110 OPEN "MEDRECS.DAT" AS #2 LEN=50
5120 OPEN "MEDRECS.DIF" FOR OUTPUT AS #3
5130 FIELD #2,15 AS NAMES$,10 AS DT$,1 AS TYPE$,24 AS MIS
     C$
5140 :
5150 REM **--HEADER SECTION--**
5160 :
5170 PRINT #3,"TABLE"
5180 PRINT #3,"0,1"
5190 PRINT #3,Q$"MEDICAL RECORDS"Q$
5200 :
5210 PRINT #3,"VECTORS"
5220 PRINT #3,"0,";NV
5230 PRINT #3,Q$Q$
```

```
5240 :
5250 PRINT #3,"TUPLES"
5260 PRINT #3,"0,";NT
5270 PRINT #3,Q$Q$
5280 :
5290 PRINT #3,"LABEL"
5300 PRINT #3,"1,0"
5310 PRINT #3,Q$"NAME"Q$
5320 :
5330 PRINT #3,"LABEL"
5340 PRINT #3,"2,0"
5350 PRINT #3,Q$"DATE"Q$
5360 :
5370 PRINT #3,"LABEL"
5380 PRINT #3,"3,0"
5390 PRINT #3,Q$"TYPE"Q$
5400 :
5410 PRINT #3,"LABEL"
5420 PRINT #3,"4,0"
5430 PRINT #3,Q$"MISC."Q$
5440 :
5450 PRINT #3,"DATA"
5460 PRINT #3,"0,0"
5470 PRINT #3,Q$Q$
5480 :
5490 REM **--DATA SECTION--**
5500 :
5510 PRINT #3,"-1,0"
5520 PRINT #3,"BOT"
5530 :
5540 PRINT #3,"1,0"
5550 PRINT #3,Q$"NAME"Q$
5560 :
5570 PRINT #3,"1,0"
5580 PRINT #3,Q$"DATE"Q$
5590 :
5600 PRINT #3,"1,0"
5610 PRINT #3,Q$"TYPE"Q$
5620 :
5630 PRINT #3,"1,0"
5640 PRINT #3,Q$"MISC."Q$
5650 :
5660 FOR I = 1 TO PTR
5670 :
5680 GET #2,I
5690 TP$ = TYPE$: GOSUB 20000: REM Type subroutine
5700 :
5710 PRINT #3,"-1,0"
5720 PRINT #3,"BOT"
5730 :
5740 PRINT #3,"1,0"
5750 PRINT #3,NAME$
5760 :
5770 PRINT #3,"1,0"
```

```
5780 PRINT #3,DT$
5790 :
5800 PRINT #3,"1,0"
5810 PRINT #3,TP$
5820 :
5830 PRINT #3,"1,0"
5840 PRINT #3,MISC$
5850 :
5860 NEXT I
5870 PRINT #3,"-1,0"
5880 PRINT #3,"EOD"
5890 :
5900 CLOSE #2,#3
5910 FILES
5920 PRINT: PRINT
5930 PRINT "DIF TRANSLATION COMPLETE!"
5940 INPUT "Press `ENTER' when ready to continue ",L$
5950 GOTO 170: REM Menu
5960 :
5970 :
7000 REM **--INCORRECT NUMBER ROUTINE--**
7010 LOCATE 22,TB
7020 PRINT "INCORRECT NUMBER. PLEASE CHOOSE AGAIN."
7030 RETURN
7040 :
7050 :
8000 REM **--ERROR MESSAGE--**
8010 PRINT "Too long!"
8020 PRINT
8030 PRINT "Do not go beyond the end of the dashes."
8040 FOR I = 1 TO 3000: NEXT I
8050 GOTO 1290
8060 :
8070 :
10000 REM **--CONVERT TO UPPERCASE ROUTINE--**
10010 FOR CV = 1 TO LEN(CVT$)
10020 X = ASC (MID$(CVT$,CV,1))
10030 IF X > 96 AND X < 123 THEN X = X - 32
10040 CVTUP$ = CVTUP$ + CHR$(X)
10050 NEXT CV
10060 CVT$ = CVTUP$
10070 CVTUP$ = ""
10080 RETURN
10090 :
10100 :
20000 REM **--TYPE SUBROUTINE--**
20010 IF TP$ = "D" THEN TP$ = "Dr. visit"
20020 IF TP$ = "M" THEN TP$ = "Medication"
20030 IF TP$ = "I" THEN TP$ = "Illness"
20040 IF TP$ = "A" THEN TP$ = "Accident/injury"
20050 IF TP$ = "S" THEN TP$ = "Shot/immunization"
20060 IF TP$ = "X" THEN TP$ = "X-Rays"
20070 RETURN
```

11

Home Inventory System

Advanced Random Access
File Manipulation

We are going to look at a simple, yet fairly complete, random access system for home inventory. We will examine the file handling portions of the various programs in detail with the expectation of modifying them for use with other applications. The purpose of such modification is to suggest the possibility of the development of a general purpose data base system.

There are six programs in this HOME INVENTORY SYSTEM: INVMENU, WRITEINV, READINV, SRCHINV, CRECTINV, and TRANSINV. Each program name attempts to describe the main function of the particular program. INVMENU is the general menu that allows the user to switch easily among the other programs. WRITEINV is used to create and add to the inventory file. READINV displays the entire inventory file in the order the information was entered. SRCHINV is really the heart of the system. This program has a menu of its own with seven options. Six of these options relate to pulling specific information from the file and displaying it. The next program, CRECTINV, allows the user to change or delete information in the inventory file. The last program, TRANSINV, provides a translation of the inventory file into the DIF format.

CREATE HOME INVENTORY

The INVMENU and TRANSINV programs do not contain any new programming code, so they will not be discussed. The first program we will look at is the WRITEINV program. The complete listing for this program is given at the end of this chapter. You will probably find it helpful to first look over the program before reading this description.

There are two pieces of code that may be worth explaining. Each of the input sections includes an SP value. This SP value is the number of spaces that the various inputs are allowed in the file. This value is checked to see that the user does not exceed the allotted amount. Each input statement first contains empty quotation marks. Without those quotation marks, a question mark is printed for each input. I thought the format looked better without the question mark and so have included these empty quotation marks. The GOSUB routine is used to print the varying number of underline spaces.

Lines 1000 to 2000 are the instructions used to check the information and allow the user to change anything before the information is written to the disk.

Lines 2000 to 3000 are the file handling lines and will be discussed in detail.

```
2000 REM **--FILE OUTPUT ROUTINE--**
2010 ON ERROR GOTO 3000
2030 OPEN "INVPTR.DAT" FOR INPUT AS #1
2030 INPUT #1,PTR
2040 PTR = PTR + 1
2050 CLOSE #1
2060 :
2070 OPEN "HOMEINV.DAT" AS #2 LEN=100
2080 FIELD #2, 25 AS I$, 15 AS S$, 10 AS C$, 20
     AS R$, 30 AS D$
2090 LSET I$ = ITEM$
2100 LSET S$ = SERIAL$
2110 LSET C$ = CST$
2120 LSET R$ = ROOM$
2130 LSET D$ = DESC$
2140 PUT #2,PTR
2150 CLOSE #2
2160 :
2170 OPEN "INVPTR.DAT" FOR OUTPUT AS #1
2180 PRINT #1,PTR
2190 CLOSE #1
2200 :
2210 CLS
2220 PRINT "Do you want to add more items?"
2230 PRINT
```

```
2240 INPUT "Type 'NO' to stop ";NO$
2250 IF NO$ = "NO" OR NO$ = "no" THEN RUN "INVMENU"
2260 GOTO 100: REM Begin again
```

Line 2010 is our method of checking whether or not the file has already been created. If the file exists, then no error should occur in bringing in the value of the pointer. But if this is the first time the program has been used, an error will occur. The error will occur when line 2030 tries to bring in a value for PTR, since no such value has yet been written to the disk. We do not wish the program to halt when this error happens; rather, we want the problem fixed. We use the routine located between lines 3000 and 4000 to write out a value for PTR and then return to the beginning of the FILE OUTPUT ROUTINE to start the process over. After use of this error routine, a value does exist on the disk, and line 2030 can input a value for PTR without an error occurring. Once we have a value for the pointer, we add one to that value.

Lines 2070 to 2150 instruct the computer to write out the information collected from the user to the inventory file. Each piece of information is given a certain maximum number of spaces. Most information will not take up the maximum, so some space in each field will be left blank. ITEM$ information (identified as I$ in the FIELD statement, line 2080), can contain up to 25 characters, or bytes, of information. SERIAL$ information (S$ in the FIELD statement) can have up to 15 bytes of information. CST$ (cost or C$) information has a maximum of 10 bytes, ROOM$ information (R$) 20 bytes, and DESC$ (description or D$) can have up to 30 bytes of information.

When all the information has been transferred to the disk, the pointer value is written out to its sequential file. The user is queried about adding more information to the file and the appropriate action taken upon obtaining a response.

DISPLAY HOME INVENTORY

The READINV program is really the reverse of the routine just covered. The word GET is substituted for the word PUT, and the values of the variables are formatted for display on the screen rather than written to the disk. Otherwise, the routines are very similar. Each field of each record is read into the computer from the disk and displayed. When all records have been read in and displayed, the total value of all items is given, and the user is transferred to the INVMENU program.

SEARCH/SORT HOME INVENTORY

The main program of this HOME INVENTORY SYSTEM is the SRCHINV program. There are six sort or search routines and an option to return to the main HOME INVENTORY MENU.

1. SEARCH FOR ITEM

2. SEARCH FOR SERIAL NUMBER

3. SEARCH FOR COST

4. SEARCH FOR ROOM ITEMS

5. SORT ITEMS ALPHABETICALLY

6. SORT ITEMS BY SERIAL NUMBER

7. RETURN TO MAIN MENU

Numbers 1, 2, and 4 use a common search subroutine. The two sort options (numbers 5 and 6) use a common sort subroutine, the Shell-Metzner sort. Number 3 uses its own search routines for both parts of this selection. We will cover the common search subroutine first.

```
10000 REM **--COMMON SEARCH SUBROUTINE--**
10010 OPEN "HOMEINV.DAT" AS #2 LEN=100
10020 FIELD #2, 25 AS FIND$(1), 15 AS FIND$(2),
      10 AS FIND$(3), 20 AS FIND$(4), 30 AS FIND$(5)
10030 LN = LEN(SRCH$)
10040 GET #2, I
10050 :
10060 CVT$ = LEFT$(FIND$(NUMBER), LN)
10070 GOSUB 20000: REM Convert to upper case
10080 :
10090 IF SRCH$ = CVT$ THEN 10200
10100 I = I + 1
10110 IF I < PTR OR I = PTR THEN 10040
10120 REM Clear line 22
10130 LOCATE 22,HT: FOR SP = 1 TO 80: PRINT " ";
      : NEXT SP
10140 LOCATE 22,HT: PRINT "SEARCH COMPLETED!"
10150 CSR = 1: REM Set search completed flag
10160 FOR K = 1 TO 1000: NEXT K
10170 CLOSE #2
10180 RETURN
10190 :
```

```
10200 ITEM$    = FIND$(1)
10210 SERIAL$  = FIND$(2)
10220 CST$     = FIND$(3)
10230 ROOM$    = FIND$(4)
10240 DESC$    = FIND$(5)
10250 I = I + 1
10260 CLOSE #2
10270 RETURN
10280 :
10290 :
```

This subroutine is common to the first two options and to the room search option. Each of the option routines that uses this subroutine establishes the necessary conditions prior to entering the subroutine. The values of SRCH$ and NUMBER are determined prior to the GOSUB statement in each of the option routines. Both of these values also go through the conversion to upper case process. Once these values are known, the specified part of the file can be searched for any match (line 10090). If a match occurs, control passes to the instructions at lines 10200 to 10270. These instructions read in from the buffer the information associated with the item searched for. The RETURN statement in line 10270 returns control to the instruction following the GOSUB statement in the original option routine—1, 2, or 4. When a match does not occur, the record counter (I) is first incremented by one, then the record counter is checked to see that its value does not exceed the value of the total number of records (PTR). Finally, the process is repeated.

The next section of code discussed is part one of the Search For Cost option. In lines 3000 to 3100, a decision is made by the user: whether to search for items above a certain cost or items below a certain cost. The appropriate part of this option routine is then given control. The following code is for items above a specific value.

```
3130 REM **--ITEMS ABOVE $ AMOUNT--**
3140 LOCATE VT + 10,HT: INPUT "Above which amount
     ";AMT
3150 CLS
3160 LOCATE VT,HT: PRINT "ITEMS ABOVE ";
3170 PRINT USING "$$####,.##,";AMT
3180 PRINT: PRINT
3190 GOSUB 15000: REM Open file
3200 FOR I = 1 TO PTR
3210 GET #2,I
3220 C$ = CST$
```

```
3230 IF LEFT$ (C$, 7) = "DELETED" THEN 3290: REM
     Next I
3240 IF LEFT$ (C$, 1) = "$" THEN GOSUB 12000: REM
     Strip $ sign
3250 IF VAL (C$) > AMT THEN 3270
3260 GOTO 3290: REM Next I
3270 TTLAMT = TTLAMT + VAL (C$)
3280 PRINT ITEM$ TAB (30) CST$
3290 NEXT I
3300 PRINT
3310 PRINT "TOTAL VALUE = ";
3320 PRINT USING "$$####,.##"; TTLAMT
3330 GOSUB 16000: REM Close file
3340 GOSUB 9000: REM Housekeeping
3350 GOTO 240: REM Menu
```

The items that are valued above a certain amount are searched for in
line 3250. The amount is previously determined in line 3140 and
displayed in 3160 and 3170. Line 3200 begins a loop that extends
through 3290. Each record is searched for costs that exceed the specified amount. Line 3250 says that if the cost of the record being examined exceeds the amount specified, then control is passed to line 3270.
When such an item has been found: (1) a running total is kept of the
cumulative value of these items (line 3270), and (2) the item and its
value are displayed on the screen (line 3280). After all the records
have been examined, the total value of all items above the specific
amount is given (line 3310), and control is transferred to the file closing (line 3330) and housekeeping subroutines (line 3340). Finally,
control is shifted back to the menu for further instructions (line 3350).

The routine to find items below a certain value is virtually the
same as that just given. The only significant difference occurs in line
3500 where the sign is reversed. We are looking for items whose value
is less than the specified amount. Those items whose value is greater
than the specified amount are passed over.

We have looked briefly at the first four options, the search options.
The next two options are sort options and use a common sort subroutine, the Shell-Metzner sort. I will explain only the procedures
involved in setting up using a sort subroutine with IBM BASIC disk
files. We will look first at the alphabetizing routine.

```
5000 REM **--SORT ITEMS ALPHABETICALLY--**
5010 CLS
5020 LOCATE VT, HT: PRINT "WORKING--PLEASE DON'T
     TOUCH!!"
5030 Q = 1 REM Valid record counter
```

```
5040 GOSUB 15000: REM Open file
5050 FOR I = 1 TO PTR
5060 GET #2, I
5070 I$ = ITEM$: REM Get string from buffer
5080 IF LEFT$(I$,7) = "DELETED" THEN 5140: REM Nex
     t I
5090 CVT$ = I$
5100 GOSUB 20000: REM Convert to upper case
5110 I$ = CVT$
5120 A$(Q) = I$: REM Store in array for internal
     sort
5130 Q = Q + 1
5140 NEXT I
5150 GOSUB 16000: REM Close file
5160 N = Q - 1
5170 LOCATE VT + 5, HT: PRINT "STILL WORKING--PLEAS
     E WAIT!"
5180 GOSUB 25000: REM Sort routine
5190 :
5200 REM DISPLAY RESULTS
5210 CLS
5220 LOCATE VT, 1
5230 FOR I = 1 TO Q - 1
5240 PRINT I; A$(I)
5250 NEXT I
5260 GOSUB 9000: REM Houskeeping
5270 GOTO 240: REM Menu
```

The keys to this routine are: (1) reading in only the item names,
(2) storing them in a string array, (3) sorting them with the sort subroutine located between lines 25000 and 25150, and (4) displaying
them in their now-alphabetized order.

A separate record counter is used (line 5030) to keep track of the
valid records since there may be some records that have been deleted
and now contain the value "DELETED". If there are such records,
they are skipped and the loop (I) is increased by one. But the valid
record counter (Q) is not increased. If the record is not valid (it contains "DELETED"), it is also not included in the string array of valid
records to be sorted. Once the loop is completed, the string array A$()
should contain all the valid item names. A new warning message is
displayed (line 5170), and control is transferred to the sort subroutine.
When the sorting has been completed, the results are displayed
through another loop (lines 5230 to 5250).

The last two lines in this routine (lines 5260 and 5270) are common to all the routines and simply "clean up" various conditions that may have been "set" during execution of the routine. If you look closely at the instructions in this housekeeping subroutine, one of the instructions restores something that no instruction in this program has changed. I have done so purposely for the following reasons: (1) for the reader to figure out which instruction does not really need to be included in this housekeeping routine, (2) to suggest to the reader a possible use for this apparently useless instruction, and (3) to inspire some of you to modify this program so that this now useless housekeeping instruction becomes worthwhile.

The last of the options, sort by serial number, again makes use of the LEFT$ and MID$ string array commands. It is also the longest of the routines. The routine sorts by serial number and then displays the resulting list in serial number order, along with the associated item name. It is conceivable that an individual or insurance company would need all of the associated information instead of just the item name. Therefore, if you are interested in developing a completely useful HOME INVENTORY SYSTEM, you might wish to add the code necessary to display all related information in both serial number order and alphabetical order.

```
6000 REM **--SORT ITEMS BY SERIAL NUMBER--**
6010 CLS
6020 LOCATE VT,HT: PRINT "WORKING--PLEASE DON'T
     TOUCH!!"
6030 Q = 1: REM Valid record counter
6040 GOSUB 15000: REM Open file
6050 FOR I = 1 TO PTR
6060 GET #2,I
6070 S$ = SERIAL$
6080 I$ = ITEM$
6090 IF LEFT$(I$,7) = "DELETED" THEN 6150
6100 CVT$ = S$
6110 GOSUB 20000: REM Convert to upper case
6120 S$ = CVT$
6130 A$(Q) = S$ + "*" + I$: REM Combine for sort
6140 Q = Q + 1
6150 NEXT I
6160 GOSUB 16000: REM Close file
6170 N = Q - 1
6180 LOCATE VT + 5,HT: PRINT "STILL WORKING--PLEASE
     WAIT!!"
6190 GOSUB 25000: REM Sort routine
6200 :
```

```
6210 REM DISPLAY RESULTS
6220 CLS
6230 LOCATE VT, 1
6240 FOR I = 1 TO Q - 1
6250 REM Separate and display
6260 LA = LEN(A$(I))
6270 PRINT I;" ";
6280 IF MID$ (A$(I),J,1) = "*" THEN 6300
6290 J = J + 1: GOTO 6280
6300 PRINT LEFT$(A$(I),J - 1).;
6310 PRINT TAB(25) MID$(A$(I),J + 1,LA)
6320 J = 1
6330 NEXT I
6340 GOSUB 9000: REM Houskeeping
6350 GOTO 240: REM Menu
```

Lines 6060 to 6080 bring in the serial number of each item. If the serial number has been deleted (contains the word "DELETED"), the record is skipped as in the prevoius routine. In fact, the two sort routines have nearly identical beginnings. The main difference occurs in lines 6100 to 6120 when the serial number instead of the item name goes through the conversion to upper case. The only other major difference occurs when the item name is concatenated (joined) to the serial number. Line 6130 combines: (1) the existing value of S$ (the serial number), (2) the current value of I$ (the item name), and (3) a separator (the asterisk) into one new string array value, A$(Q).

Once the entire file is read and the correct number of valid records determined, control is passed to the sort subroutine (line 6190). Lines 6210 to 6330 are used to display the results of the sort. Here again, we need to make use of the power of the LEFT$, MID$ and LEN functions. The numeric variable LN is set to equal the length of each of the string arrays (line 6260). The MID$ function is used to determine where in the string the asterisk is located (line 6280). (The BASIC reserved word INSTR could have been used instead.) The LEFT$ and MID$ functions are used to print out the desired parts of the string in an acceptable format (lines 6300 to 6310). This sequence is repeated until all valid records have been displayed in serial number order. The end of this routine is the same as the end of the other five routines.

This concludes the discussion of the SEARCH/SORT HOME INVENTORY (SRCHINV) program. There are a number of other points that could be discussed, but those points relate mainly to different techniques of programming in BASIC rather than techniques for working with IBM BASIC files. By now, if you have worked through all of the programs, you should be able to "read" a program and recognize some of the different techniques used.

CORRECT HOME INVENTORY

The next program in this HOME INVENTORY SYSTEM provides the ability to change or delete information in the HOMEINV.DAT file. Both parts of this program make use of two routines: a FILE OUTPUT ROUTINE and a FILE INPUT ROUTINE. These two routines have been used in our other programs in this system. The CORRECT RECORD routine (lines 1000 to 2000) is essentially the same as the correction routine in the WRITEINV program (lines 1000 to 2000). The difference is that in the WRITEINV program, the information being checked for accuracy comes from the keyboard. In the CRECTINV program, the information comes from the disk. That is the reason for line 1070. This line transfers control to the FILE INPUT ROUTINE which inputs from the specified record on the disk the values for ITEM$, SERIAL$, CST$, ROOM$, and DESC$. These values are then displayed, and a check is made to see if they are correct.

At this point, one other new line of code is encountered (line 1020). Lines 1020, 1200, 1210, and 1430 are all related. All deal with a string variable called FLAG$. Line 1020 sets the original value of FLAG$ equal to the word "NO". This indicates that no information has yet been changed. Lines 1200 and 1210 check the value of FLAG$ and direct the computer accordingly. If the information is correct and no change has been made, the value of FLAG$ is still "NO", and the computer is directed to start this routine over again. If the information has been changed, the value of FLAG$ will have been changed by line 1430 to "YES" indicating altered information. If the information is correct and has been changed, we are now ready to write that information back out to the file on the disk (the FILE OUTPUT ROUTINE). This technique allows the user to scan through the records if he/she is not sure of the record number of the incorrect information.

The deletion routine is a relatively uncomplicated routine. The suspected record is brought in from disk (line 2060) and displayed (lines 2080 to 2110). A request is made of the user to see if this is the information to be deleted. If it is not, the deletion routine starts again. If the information is to be deleted, the user is required to type the word "YES" rather than just the "Y". If "YES" is typed, all string variables are given the value "DELETED", and control is passed to the FILE OUTPUT ROUTINE where "DELETED" replaces the now deleted information. Notice that the entire file does not need to be resequenced and rewritten to the disk. Instead, only the information requiring change is affected.

The change and delete routines for random access files are considerably easier than similar routines for sequential access files. This ease is one of the major strengths of random files. Access is direct to any part of the file desired. In fact, in a very large inventory system, it is possible to read from disk and check only the desired part of the record, rather than the entire record. Programming can often be simpler and easier to read. There is less need for string arrays and, therefore, less need for large amounts of internal computer memory. The disk can be used as an extension of the internal memory with random files since the same principles are involved. The major difference is in the time involved, disk access being much slower than internal memory access.

At the end of the chapter, I have included another system, a BACK ORDER SYSTEM, created by modifying this current HOME INVENTORY SYSTEM. The modification is not extensive. The main reason for including the BACK ORDER SYSTEM is to suggest the possibility of a general purpose data base program. All our systems have included some method for: (1) creating and adding to a file, (2) displaying information from that file in various ways, and (3) editing the file. These are the essential characteristics in any data base system. It should be possible to create a general purpose data base system that would request certain necessary information from the user. Based on the supplied information, this general data base system would create a file and set up the procedures to display and edit information in that file.

The better commercial data base programs have expanded on these essential characteristics. They have added "features" that some users may need but others will never use. One feature that I feel is essential is transportability of file information. If a data base system does not allow some method of universal access to the files created under its system, I believe that system is severely limited in its usefulness to anyone other than the casual user. *Files created under a general data base system must be able to be accessed by other commercial application programs!* Without such access, the user must re-enter data in each application program used with the file information. This is the reason DIF is so important (see Chapter 9). Some of the general purpose data base systems do support DIF while others at least make their files available through normal IBM DOS file structure.

In the Preface, I said that "Reading this book will not make you capable of creating complete data base programs . . .," but at this point, you should have an appreciation of the effort that goes into creating a good general purpose data base system. For your individual use, you may find that you can create a semi-general purpose data base system, a system that can serve your needs but would not be universal in meeting the needs of everyone. This is the reason for including the BACK ORDER SYSTEM as a modification of the HOME INVEN-TORY SYSTEM. Structured carefully, with enough user supplied variables, this series of programs can form the basis for such a personal data base system.

The next chapter will deal with the planning necessary in creating the programs for any file system. The example will be a STOCK MARKET SYSTEM for keeping track of the price and volume changes of certain issues.

QUESTIONS

1. What BASIC reserved phrase is only used the first time the WRITEINV program is run?

2. Give the name of the string array variable that allows us to use one search routine for three different program modules.

3. What sort routine is used in both systems in this chapter?

4. Which housekeeping instruction restores something that no instruction in the SRCHINV program changed?

5. What word means joining string variables together?

6. *True or False*: It is more difficult to change information in a random access file than in a sequential file.

ANSWERS

1. ON ERROR GOTO
2. FIND$()
3. Shell-Metzner
4. DISPLAY$ = "SCRN:"
5. CONCATENATE
6. False

INVMENU

```
100 REM **--HOME INVENTORY SYSTEM--**
110 HT = 25: REM Horizontal tab
120 VT =  2: REM Vertical tab
130 KEY OFF
140 :
150 :
160 REM **--MENU ROUTINE--**
170 CLS
180 LOCATE VT,     HT: PRINT "HOME INVENTORY SYSTEM"
190 LOCATE VT +  2,HT: PRINT "1.   WRITE RECORD"
200 LOCATE VT +  4,HT: PRINT "2.   READ RECORD"
210 LOCATE VT +  6,HT: PRINT "3.   SEARCH RECORD"
220 LOCATE VT +  8,HT: PRINT "4.   CORRECT RECORD"
230 LOCATE VT + 10,HT: PRINT "5.   TRANSLATE RECORD"
240 LOCATE VT + 12,HT: PRINT "6.   LIST FILES"
250 LOCATE VT + 14,HT: PRINT "7.   END"
260 LOCATE VT + 16,HT: INPUT "Which number ";NUMBER
270 IF NUMBER = 1 THEN 1000
280 IF NUMBER = 2 THEN 2000
290 IF NUMBER = 3 THEN 3000
300 IF NUMBER = 4 THEN 4000
310 IF NUMBER = 5 THEN 5000
320 IF NUMBER = 6 THEN 6000
330 IF NUMBER = 7 THEN KEY ON: END
340 LOCATE 22,HT: PRINT "INCORRECT NUMBER! PLEASE CHOOSE
    AGAIN."
350 GOTO 180
360 :
370 :
1000 REM **--WRITE RECORD PROGRAM--**
1010 RUN "WRITEINV"
1990 :
1995 :
2000 REM **--READ RECORD PROGRAM--**
2010 RUN "READINV"
2990 :
2995 :
3000 REM **--SEARCH RECORD PROGRAM--**
3010 RUN "SRCHINV"
3990 :
3995 :
4000 REM **--CORRECT RECORD PROGRAM--**
4010 RUN "CRECTINV"
4990 :
4995 :
5000 REM **--TRANSLATE RECORD PROGRAM--**
5010 RUN "TRANSINV"
5990 :
5995 :
```

```
6000 REM **--LIST OF FILES ROUTINE--**
6010 CLS
6020 LOCATE 5,1
6030 FILES
6040 PRINT: PRINT
6050 INPUT "Press the `ENTER' key when ready to continue";L$
6070 GOTO 160: REM Menu
```

WRITEINV

```
100 REM ***--WRITE INVENTORY RECORD--**
110 :
120 :
130 HT = 25: REM Horizontal tab
140 VT =  5: REM Vertical tab
150 :
160 :
170 CLS
180 LOCATE  VT,HT: PRINT "ADD TO HOME INVENTORY"
190 :
200 :
210 REM **--NAME ROUTINE--**
220 LOCATE 10,HT
230 PRINT "ITEM'S NAME PLEASE."
240 SP = 25
250 GOSUB 5000: REM Input subroutine
260 LOCATE 15,HT
270 INPUT "",ITEM$
280 IF LEN (ITEM$) > SP THEN BEEP: GOTO 210
290 S$ = ITEM$: GOSUB 6000: ITEM$ = S$
300 :
310 :
320 REM **--SERIAL NUMBER ROUTINE--**
330 GOSUB 7000: REM Clear lower part of screen
340 LOCATE 10,HT
350 PRINT "ITEM'S SERIAL NUMBER PLEASE"
360 SP = 15
370 GOSUB 5000: REM Input subroutine
380 LOCATE 15,HT
390 INPUT "",SERIAL$
400 IF LEN(SERIAL$) > SP THEN BEEP: GOTO 320
410 S$ = SERIAL$: GOSUB 6000: SERIAL$ = S$
420 :
430 :
440 REM **--ITEM'S COST ROUTINE--**
450 GOSUB 7000: REM Clear lower part of screen
460 LOCATE 10,HT
470 PRINT "ITEM'S COST PLEASE"
480 SP = 10
490 GOSUB 5000: REM Input subroutine
```

```
500 LOCATE 15,HT
510 INPUT "",CST$
520 IF LEN(CST$) > SP THEN BEEP: GOTO 440
530 S$ = CST$: GOSUB 6000: CST$ = S$
540 :
550 :
560 REM **--ITEM'S ROOM ROUTINE--**
570 GOSUB 7000: REM Clear lower part of screen
580 LOCATE 10,HT
590 PRINT "ITEM'S ROOM PLEASE"
600 SP = 20
610 GOSUB 5000: REM Input subroutine
620 LOCATE 15,HT
630 INPUT "",ROOM$
640 IF LEN(ROOM$) > SP THEN BEEP: GOTO 560
650 S$ = ROOM$: GOSUB 6000: ROOM$ = S$
660 :
670 :
680 REM **--ITEM'S DESCRIPTION--**
690 GOSUB 7000: REM Clear lower part of screen
700 LOCATE 10,HT
710 PRINT "ITEM'S DESCRIPTION PLEASE"
720 SP = 30
730 GOSUB 5000: REM Input subroutine
740 LOCATE 15,HT
750 INPUT "",DESC$
760 IF LEN(DESC$) > SP THEN BEEP: GOTO 680
770 S$ = DESC$: GOSUB 6000: DESC$ = S$
780 :
790 :
1000 REM **--DISPLAY FOR CORRECTION--**
1010 CLS
1020 LOCATE VT,     HT: PRINT "1.  ";ITEM$
1030 LOCATE VT +  2,HT: PRINT "2.  ";SERIAL$
1040 LOCATE VT +  4,HT: PRINT "3.  ";CST$
1050 LOCATE VT +  6,HT: PRINT "4.  ";ROOM$
1060 LOCATE VT +  8,HT: PRINT "5.  ";DESC$
1070 LOCATE VT + 10,HT: INPUT "Is this correct (`Y' or `N
     ') ";YES$
1080 IF YES$ = "Y" OR YES$ = "y" THEN 2000: REM File outp
     ut routine
1090 LOCATE VT + 12,HT: INPUT "Which number is wrong ";NB
1100 IF NB = 1 THEN SP = 25
1110 IF NB = 2 THEN SP = 15
1120 IF NB = 3 THEN SP = 10
1130 IF NB = 4 THEN SP = 20
1140 IF NB = 5 THEN SP = 30
1150 IF NB < 1 OR NB > 5 THEN PRINT "INCORRECT CHOICE!":
     GOTO 1090
1160 CLS: LOCATE 10,HT
1170 PRINT "Type in the correct information:"
1180 GOSUB 5000: REM Underline subroutine
1190 LOCATE 15,HT
```

```
1200 INPUT "",CT$(NB)
1210 IF LEN(CT$(NB)) > SP THEN BEEP: GOTO 1160
1220 IF NB = 1 THEN ITEM$   = CT$(NB)
1230 IF NB = 2 THEN SERIAL$ = CT$(NB)
1240 IF NB = 3 THEN CST$    = CT$(NB)
1250 IF NB = 4 THEN ROOM$   = CT$(NB)
1260 IF NB = 5 THEN DESC$   = CT$(NB)
1270 GOTO 1000: REM Check again
1280 :
1290 :
2000 REM **--FILE OUTPUT ROUTINE--**
2010 ON ERROR GOTO 3000
2020 OPEN "INVPTR.DAT" FOR INPUT AS #1
2030 INPUT #1,PTR
2040 PTR = PTR + 1
2050 CLOSE #1
2060 :
2070 OPEN "HOMEINV.DAT" AS #2 LEN=100
2080 FIELD #2,25 AS I$,15 AS S$,10 AS C$,20 AS R$,30 AS D$
2090 LSET I$ = ITEM$
2100 LSET S$ = SERIAL$
2110 LSET C$ = CST$
2120 LSET R$ = ROOM$
2130 LSET D$ = DESC$
2140 PUT #2,PTR
2150 CLOSE #2
2160 :
2170 OPEN "INVPTR.DAT" FOR OUTPUT AS #1
2180 PRINT #1,PTR
2190 CLOSE #1
2200 :
2210 CLS
2220 PRINT "Do you want to add more items?"
2230 PRINT
2240 INPUT "Type `NO' to stop ";NO$
2250 IF NO$ = "NO" OR NO$ = "no" THEN RUN "INVMENU
2260 GOTO 100: REM Begin again
2270 :
2280 :
3000 REM **--FIRST TIME USE ONLY--**
3010 OPEN "INVPTR.DAT" FOR OUTPUT AS #1
3020 PRINT #1,"0"
3030 CLOSE #1
3040 PRINT
3050 GOTO 2000: REM Begin file routine again
3060 :
3070 :
5000 REM **--UNDERLINE ROUTINE--**
5010 LOCATE 15,HT
5020 FOR I = 1 TO SP
5030 PRINT "_";
5040 NEXT I
5050 RETURN
```

```
5060 :
5070 :
6000 REM **--STRIP EXCESS UNDERLINE CHAR--**
6010 S2$ = S$
6020 I = 1
6030 IF MID$(S2$,I,1)  = "_" THEN 6070
6040 I = I + 1
6050 IF I > SP THEN 6070
6060 GOTO 6030
6070 S$ = LEFT$(S2$,I - 1)
6080 RETURN
6090 :
6100 :
7000 REM **--CLEAR LOWER PART OF SCREEN--**
7010 LOCATE 10,1
7020 FOR V = 10 TO 15 STEP 5
7030 FOR H = 0 TO 7
7040 LOCATE V,(H * 10) + 1
7050 PRINT "             ";: REM 10 spaces
7060 NEXT H
7070 NEXT V
7080 RETURN
```

READINV

```
100 REM ***--DISPLAY HOME INVENTORY--***
110 :
120 :
130 REM **--FILE INPUT ROUTINE--**
140 OPEN "INVPTR.DAT" FOR INPUT AS #1
150 INPUT #1,PTR
160 CLOSE #1
170 :
180 OPEN "HOMEINV.DAT" AS #2 LEN=100
190 FIELD #2,25 AS ITEM$,15 AS SERIAL$,10 AS CST$,20 AS
    ROOM$,30 AS DESC$
200 CLS
210 FOR I = 1 TO PTR
220 GET #2,I
230 IF LEFT$(ITEM$,7) = "DELETED" THEN 300: REM Next I
240 PRINT I;ITEM$ TAB(30) SERIAL$ TAB(45) CST$ TAB(55) R
    OOM$
250 PRINT TAB(45) DESC$
260 PRINT
270 C$ = CST$
280 IF LEFT$(C$,1) = "$" THEN GOSUB 1000
290 TTLCST = TTLCST + VAL (C$)
300 NEXT I
310 CLOSE #2
320 PRINT: PRINT "Total value of items =";
330 PRINT USING "$$#####,.##";TTLCST
340 PRINT
350 INPUT "Press `ENTER' to return to the program menu";
    L$
360 RUN "INVMENU"
370 :
380 :
1000 REM **--STRIP $ SIGN--**
1010 LN = LEN (C$)
1020 A$ = RIGHT$(C$,LN-1)
1030 C$ = A$
1040 RETURN
```

SRCHINV

```
100 REM ***--SEARCH/SORT HOME INVENTORY--**
110 :
120 :
130 REM **--INPUT POINTER VALUE--**
140 OPEN "INVPTR.DAT" FOR INPUT AS #1
150 INPUT #1,PTR
160 CLOSE #1
170 :
180 :
190 DIM A$(PTR)
200 VT =  2: REM Vertical tab
210 HT = 25: REM Horizontal tab
220 :
230 :
240 REM **--MENU ROUTINE--**
250 CLS
260 LOCATE VT,    HT: PRINT "SEARCH/SORT MENU"
270 LOCATE VT +  2,HT: PRINT "1.   SEARCH FOR ITEM"
280 LOCATE VT +  4,HT: PRINT "2.   SEARCH FOR SERIAL NUMB
    ER"
290 LOCATE VT +  6,HT: PRINT "3.   SEARCH FOR COST"
300 LOCATE VT +  8,HT: PRINT "4.   SEARCH FOR ROOM ITEMS"
310 LOCATE VT + 10,HT: PRINT "5.   SORT ITEMS ALPHABETICA
    LLY"
320 LOCATE VT + 12,HT: PRINT "6.   SORT ITEMS BY SERIAL N
    UMBER"
330 LOCATE VT + 14,HT: PRINT "7.   RETURN TO MAIN MENU"
340 LOCATE VT + 16,HT: INPUT "Which number";NUMBER
350 IF NUMBER = 1 THEN 1000
360 IF NUMBER = 2 THEN 2000
370 IF NUMBER = 3 THEN 3000
380 IF NUMBER = 4 THEN 4000
390 IF NUMBER = 5 THEN 5000
400 IF NUMBER = 6 THEN 6000
410 IF NUMBER = 7 THEN 7000
420 LOCATE 22,HT: PRINT "INCORRECT NUMBER! PLEASE CHOOSE
    AGAIN."
430 GOTO 340: REM Ask again
440 :
450 :
1000 REM **--SEARCH FOR ITEM--**
1010 CLS
1020 LOCATE VT,HT: INPUT "Which item ";SRCH$
1030 CVT$ = SRCH$: GOSUB 20000: REM Convert to uppercase
1040 SRCH$ = CVT$
1050 I = 1
1060 CLS
1070 GOSUB 10000: REM Common Search Routine
1080 IF CSR = 1 THEN 1110: REM Search completed
1090 PRINT ITEM$ TAB(30) SERIAL$ TAB(45) CST$ TAB(55) RO
     OM$
```

```
1100 PRINT TAB(45) DESC$
1110 ITEM$ = "": SERIAL$ = "": CST$ = "": ROOM$ = "": DE
     SC$ = ""
1120 IF I = PTR OR I > PTR THEN 1140
1130 GOTO 1070: REM Continue search
1140 GOSUB 9000: REM Housekeeping
1150 GOTO 240: REM Menu
1160 :
1170 :
2000 REM **--SEARCH FOR SERIAL NUMBER--**
2010 CLS
2020 LOCATE VT,HT: INPUT "Which serial number ";SRCH$
2030 CVT$ = SRCH$: GOSUB 20000: REM Convert to uppercase
2040 SRCH$ = CVT$
2050 I = 1
2060 CLS
2070 GOSUB 10000: REM Common Search Routine
2080 PRINT SERIAL$ TAB(20) ITEM$
2090 GOSUB 9000: REM Housekeeping
2100 GOTO 240: REM Menu
2110 :
2120 :
3000 REM **--SEARCH FOR COST--**
3010 CLS
3020 TTLAMT = 0: FIND$ = ""
3030 LOCATE VT,    HT: PRINT "SEARCH FOR ITEMS..."
3040 LOCATE VT + 2,HT: PRINT "A...Above a certain amount"
3050 LOCATE VT + 4,HT: PRINT "B...Below a certain amount"
3060 LOCATE VT + 6,HT: INPUT "Which letter `A' or `B' ";L
     T$
3070 IF LT$ = "A" OR LT$ = "a" THEN 3130
3080 IF LT$ = "B" OR LT$ = "b" THEN 3380
3090 LOCATE 22,HT: PRINT "INCORRECT CHOICE"
3100 GOTO 3060: REM Ask again
3110 :
3120 :
3130 REM **--ITEMS ABOVE $ AMOUNT--**
3140 LOCATE VT + 10,HT: INPUT "Above which amount ";AMT
3150 CLS
3160 LOCATE VT,HT: PRINT "ITEMS ABOVE ";
3170 PRINT USING "$$####,.##";AMT
3180 PRINT: PRINT
3190 GOSUB 15000: REM Open file
3200 FOR I = 1 TO PTR
3210 GET #2,I
3220 C$ = CST$
3230 IF LEFT$(C$,7) = "DELETED" THEN 3290: REM Next I
3240 IF LEFT$(C$,1) = "$" THEN GOSUB 12000: REM Strip $ s
     ign
3250 IF VAL(C$) > AMT THEN 3270
3260 GOTO 3290: REM Next I
3270 TTLAMT = TTLAMT + VAL(C$)
3280 PRINT ITEM$ TAB(30) CST$
3290 NEXT I
3300 PRINT
```

```
3310 PRINT "TOTAL VALUE =";
3320 PRINT USING "$$####,.##";TTLAMT
3330 GOSUB 16000: REM Close file
3340 GOSUB 9000: REM Housekeeping
3350 GOTO 240: REM Menu
3360 :
3370 :
3380 REM **--ITEMS BELOW $ AMOUNT--**
3390 LOCATE VT + 10,HT: INPUT "Below which amount ";AMT
3400 CLS
3410 LOCATE VT,HT: PRINT "ITEMS BELOW ";
3420 PRINT USING "$$####,.##";AMT
3430 PRINT: PRINT
3440 GOSUB 15000: REM Open file
3450 FOR I = 1 TO PTR
3460 GET #2,I
3470 C$ = CST$
3480 IF LEFT$(C$,7) = "DELETED" THEN 3540: REM Next I
3490 IF LEFT$(C$,1) = "$" THEN GOSUB 12000: REM Strip $
     sign
3500 IF VAL(C$) < AMT THEN 3520
3510 GOTO 3540: REM Next I
3520 TTLAMT = TTLAMT + VAL(C$)
3530 PRINT  ITEM$ TAB(30) CST$
3540 NEXT I
3550 PRINT
3560 PRINT "TOTAL VALUE =";
3570 PRINT USING "$$####,.##";TTLAMT
3580 GOSUB 16000: REM Close file
3590 GOSUB 9000: REM Housekeeping
3600 GOTO 240: REM Menu
3610 :
3620 :
4000 REM **--SEARCH FOR ROOM ITEMS--**
4010 CLS
4020 TLROOM = 0
4030 LOCATE VT,HT: INPUT "Which room ";SRCH$
4040 CVT$ = SRCH$: GOSUB 20000: REM Convert to uppercase
4050 SRCH$ = CVT$
4060 I = 1
4070 CLS
4080 GOSUB 10000: REM Common Search Routine
4090 IF CSR = 1 THEN 4160: REM Search completed
4100 PRINT ITEM$ TAB(30) SERIAL$ TAB(45) CST$
4110 PRINT TAB(45) DESC$
4120 C$ = CST$: R$ = ROOM$
4130 IF LEFT$(C$,1) = "$" THEN GOSUB 12000: REM Strip $
     sign
4140 TLROOM = TLROOM + VAL(C$)
4150 Y = CSRLIN
4160 ITEM$ = "": SERIAL$ = "": CST$ = "": DESC$ = ""
4170 IF I = PTR OR I > PTR THEN 4200
4180 LOCATE Y + 1,1
4190 GOTO 4080: REM Continue Search
```

```
4200 GOSUB 9000: REM Housekeeping
4210 REM Strip extra spaces
4220 R1 =1
4230 IF MID$(R$,R1,2) = "  " THEN 4250
4240 R1 = R1 + 1: GOTO 4230
4250 R1$ = LEFT$(R$,R1 - 1)
4260 :
4270 REM Display total value for room
4280 CLS: LOCATE 10,25
4290 PRINT "Total value for ";R1$;" = ";
4300 PRINT USING "$$####,.##";TLROOM
4310 GOSUB 9000: REM Housekeeping
4320 GOTO 240: REM Menu
4330 :
4340 :
5000 REM **--SORT ITEMS ALPHABETICALLY--**
5010 CLS
5020 LOCATE VT,HT: PRINT "WORKING--PLEASE DON'T TOUCH!!"
5030 Q = 1: REM Valid record counter
5040 GOSUB 15000: REM Open file
5050 FOR I = 1 TO PTR
5060 GET #2,I
5070 I$ = ITEM$: REM Get string from buffer
5080 IF LEFT$(I$,7) = "DELETED" THEN 5140: REM Next I
5090 CVT$ = I$
5100 GOSUB 20000: REM Convert to uppercase
5110 I$ = CVT$
5120 A$(Q) = I$: REM Store in array for internal sort
5130 Q = Q + 1
5140 NEXT I
5150 GOSUB 16000: REM Close file
5160 N = Q - 1
5170 LOCATE VT + 5,HT: PRINT "STILL WORKING--PLEASE WAIT!"
5180 GOSUB 25000: REM Sort routine
5190 :
5200 REM DISPLAY RESULTS
5210 CLS
5220 LOCATE VT,1
5230 FOR I = 1 TO Q - 1
5240 PRINT I;A$(I)
5250 NEXT I
5260 GOSUB 9000: REM Housekeeping
5270 GOTO 240: REM Menu
5280 :
5290 :
6000 REM **--SORT ITEMS BY SERIAL NUMBER--**
6010 CLS
6020 LOCATE VT,HT: PRINT "WORKING--PLEASE DON'T TOUCH!!"
6030 Q = 1: REM Valid record counter
6040 GOSUB 15000: REM Open file
6050 FOR I = 1 TO PTR
6060 GET #2,I
6070 S$ = SERIAL$
6080 I$ = ITEM$
```

```
6090 IF LEFT$(I$,7) = "DELETED" THEN 6150
6100 CVT$ = S$
6110 GOSUB 20000: REM Convert to uppercase
6120 S$ = CVT$
6130 A$(Q) = S$ + "*" + I$: REM Combine for sort
6140 Q = Q + 1
6150 NEXT I
6160 GOSUB 16000: REM Close file
6170 N = Q - 1
6180 LOCATE VT + 5,HT: PRINT "STILL WORKING--PLEASE WAIT!"
6190 GOSUB 25000: REM Sort routine
6200 :
6210 REM DISPLAY RESULTS
6220 CLS
6230 LOCATE VT,1
6240 FOR I = 1 TO Q - 1
6250 REM Separate and display
6260 LA = LEN(A$(I))
6270 PRINT I;"   ";
6280 IF MID$(A$(I),J,1) = "*" THEN 6300
6290 J = J + 1: GOTO 6280
6300 PRINT LEFT$(A$(I),J - 1);
6310 PRINT TAB(25) MID$(A$(I),J + 1,LA)
6320 J = 1
6330 NEXT I
6340 GOSUB 9000: REM Housekeeping
6350 GOTO 240: REM Menu
6360 :
6370 :
7000 REM **--RETURN TO MAIN MENU--**
7010 RUN "INVMENU"
7020 :
7030 :
9000 REM **--HOUSEKEEPING ROUTINE--**
9010 ITEM$    = ""
9020 SERIAL$  = ""
9030 CST$     = ""
9040 ROOM$    = ""
9050 DESC$    = ""
9060 DISPLAY$ = "SCRN:"
9070 CSR = 0
9080 :
9090 REM Clear line 22
9100 LOCATE 22,HT: FOR SP = 1 TO 80: PRINT " ";: NEXT SP
9110 LOCATE 22,HT: INPUT "Press `ENTER' to continue";L$
9120 RETURN
9130 :
9140 :
10000 REM **--COMMON SEARCH ROUTINE--**
10010 OPEN "HOMEINV.DAT" AS #2 LEN=100
10020 FIELD #2,25 AS FIND$(1),15 AS FIND$(2),10 AS FIND$
      (3), 20 AS FIND$(4),30 AS FIND$(5)
10030 LN = LEN(SRCH$)
10040 GET #2,I
```

```
10050 :
10060 CVT$ = LEFT$(FIND$(NUMBER),LN)
10070 GOSUB 20000: REM Convert to uppercase
10080 :
10090 IF SRCH$ = CVT$ THEN 10200
10100 I = I + 1
10110 IF I < PTR OR I = PTR THEN 10040
10120 REM Clear line 22
10130 LOCATE 22,HT: FOR SP = 1 TO 80: PRINT " ";: NEXT SP
10140 LOCATE 22,HT: PRINT "SEARCH COMPLETED!"
10150 CSR = 1: REM Set search completed flag
10160 FOR K = 1 TO 1000: NEXT K
10170 CLOSE #2
10180 RETURN
10190 :
10200 ITEM$    = FIND$(1)
10210 SERIAL$  = FIND$(2)
10220 CST$     = FIND$(3)
10230 ROOM$    = FIND$(4)
10240 DESC$    = FIND$(5)
10250 I = I + 1
10260 CLOSE #2
10270 RETURN
10280 :
10290 :
12000 REM **--STRIP $ SIGN--**
12010 LC = LEN (C$)
12020 A$ = RIGHT$(C$,LC-1)
12030 C$ = A$
12040 RETURN
12050 :
12060 :
15000 REM **--OPEN RANDOM ACCESS FILE--**
15010 OPEN "HOMEINV.DAT" AS #2 LEN=100
15020 FIELD #2,25 AS ITEM$,15 AS SERIAL$,10 AS CST$,20 AS
      ROOM$,30 AS DESC$
15030 RETURN
15040 :
15050 :
16000 REM **--CLOSE RANDOM ACCESS FILE--**
16010 CLOSE #2
16020 RETURN
16030 :
16040 :
20000 REM **--CONVERT TO UPPERCASE ROUTINE--**
20010 FOR CV = 1 TO LEN(CVT$)
20020 X = ASC (MID$(CVT$,CV,1))
20030 IF X > 96 AND X < 123 THEN X = X - 32
20040 CVTUP$ = CVTUP$ + CHR$(X)
20050 NEXT CV
20060 CVT$ = CVTUP$
20070 CVTUP$ = ""
20080 RETURN
20090 :
```

```
20100 :
25000 REM **--SORT ROUTINE--**
25010 M = N
25020 M = INT (M / 2)
25030 IF M = 0 THEN 25150
25040 J = 1: K = N - M
25050 I = J
25060 L = I + M
25070 IF A$(I) < A$(L) THEN 25120
25080 T$ = A$(I): A$(I) = A$(L): A$(L) = T$
25090 I = I - M
25100 IF I < 1 THEN 25120
25110 GOTO 25060
25120 J = J + 1
25130 IF J > K THEN 25020
25140 GOTO 25050
25150 RETURN
```

CRECTINV

```
100 REM ***--CORRECT INVENTORY RECORD--**
110 :
120 :
130 HT = 25: REM Horizontal tab
140 VT =  5: REM Vertical tab
150 :
160 :
170 OPEN "INVPTR.DAT" FOR INPUT AS #1
180 INPUT #1,PTR
190 CLOSE #1
200 :
210 :
220 REM **--MENU ROUTINE--**
230 CLS
240 LOCATE VT,     HT: PRINT "CORRECT/DELETE MENU"
250 LOCATE VT +  2,HT: PRINT "C....Correct Inventory Rec
    ord"
260 LOCATE VT +  4,HT: PRINT "D....Delete  Inventory Rec
    ord"
270 LOCATE VT +  6,HT: PRINT "R....Return To Main Menu"
280 LOCATE VT +  8,HT: INPUT "Which letter please ";LT$
290 IF LT$ = "C" OR LT$ = "c" THEN 1000
300 IF LT$ = "D" OR LT$ = "d" THEN 2000
310 IF LT$ = "R" OR LT$ = "r" THEN 3000
320 LOCATE VT + 10,HT: PRINT "INCORRECT CHOICE"
330 GOTO 280: REM Ask again
340 :
350 :
1000 REM **--CORRECT RECORD--**
1010 CLS
1020 FLAG$ = "NO": REM Information has yet to be changed
```

```
1030 LOCATE 10,HT: PRINT "Type a `0' to return to the Me
     nu"
1040 LOCATE 12,HT: INPUT "Correct which record ";REC
1050 IF REC = 0 THEN 220: REM Menu
1060 IF REC > PTR THEN LOCATE 22,HT: PRINT "NOT THAT MAN
     Y RECORDS!": GOTO 1040
1070 GOSUB 5000: REM Read file
1080 :
1090 REM **--DISPLAY FOR CORRECTION--**
1100 CLS
1110 LOCATE VT,      HT: PRINT "1.   ";ITEM$
1120 LOCATE VT +  2,HT: PRINT "2.   ";SERIAL$
1130 LOCATE VT +  4,HT: PRINT "3.   ";CST$
1140 LOCATE VT +  6,HT: PRINT "4.   ";ROOM$
1150 LOCATE VT +  8,HT: PRINT "5.   ";DESC$
1160 LOCATE VT + 10,HT: INPUT "Is this correct (`Y' or `
     N') ";YES$
1170 IF YES$ = "Y" OR YES$ = "y" THEN 1200
1180 GOTO 1230: REM negative response
1190 :
1200 IF FLAG$ = "YES" THEN 6000: REM Info changed--write
     it out
1210 IF FLAG$ = "NO" THEN 1000: REM Info not changed--ge
     t another
1220 :
1230 LOCATE VT + 12,HT: INPUT "Which number is wrong ";N
     B
1240 IF NB = 1 THEN SP = 25
1250 IF NB = 2 THEN SP = 15
1260 IF NB = 3 THEN SP = 10
1270 IF NB = 4 THEN SP = 20
1280 IF NB = 5 THEN SP = 30
1290 IF NB < 1 OR NB > 5 THEN PRINT "INCORRECT CHOICE!":
     GOTO 1230
1300 :
1310 CLS: LOCATE 10,HT
1320 PRINT "Type in the correct information:"
1330 GOSUB 7000: REM Underline subroutine
1340 LOCATE 15,HT
1350 INPUT "",CT$(NB)
1360 IF LEN(CT$(NB)) > SP THEN BEEP: GOTO 1310
1370 IF NB = 1 THEN ITEM$   = CT$(NB)
1380 IF NB = 2 THEN SERIAL$ = CT$(NB)
1390 IF NB = 3 THEN CST$    = CT$(NB)
1400 IF NB = 4 THEN ROOM$   = CT$(NB)
1410 IF NB = 5 THEN DESC$   = CT$(NB)
1420 FLAG$ = "YES": REM Information has been changed
1430 GOTO 1090: REM Check again
1440 :
1450 :
2000 REM **--DELETE RECORD--**
2010 CLS
2020 LOCATE 10,HT: PRINT "Type a `0' to return to the Me
     nu"
```

```
2030 LOCATE 12,HT: INPUT "Delete which record ";REC
2040 IF REC = 0 THEN 220: REM Menu
2050 IF REC > PTR THEN LOCATE 22,HT: PRINT "NOT THAT MAN
     Y RECORDS!": GOTO 2030
2060 GOSUB 5000: REM Read file
2070 :
2080 CLS
2090 LOCATE VT,1: PRINT ITEM$ TAB(30) SERIAL$ TAB(45) CS
     T$ TAB(55) ROOM$
2100 PRINT TAB(45) DESC$
2110 PRINT: PRINT
2120 INPUT "Delete this Record ";YES$
2130 IF YES$ = "Y" OR YES$ = "y" THEN 2150
2140 GOTO 2000: REM Ask again
2150 INPUT "Are you sure? Type 'YES' to delete this reco
     rd.";YES$
2160 IF YES$ = "YES" OR YES$ = "yes" THEN 2180
2170 GOTO 2000: REM Ask again
2180 ITEM$    = "DELETED"
2190 SERIAL$  = "DELETED"
2200 CST$     = "DELETED"
2210 ROOM$    = "DELETED"
2220 DESC$    = "DELETED"
2230 GOTO 6000: REM File output routine
2240 :
2250 :
3000 REM **--RETURN TO MAIN MENU--**
3010 RUN "INVMENU
3020 :
3030 :
5000 REM **--FILE INPUT ROUTINE--**
5010 OPEN "HOMEINV.DAT" AS #2 LEN=100
5020 FIELD #2,25 AS I$,15 AS S$,10 AS C$,20 AS R$,30 AS D$
5030 GET #2,REC
5040 ITEM$    = I$
5050 SERIAL$ = S$
5060 CST$     = C$
5070 ROOM$    = R$
5080 DESC$    = D$
5090 CLOSE #2
5100 RETURN
5110 :
5120 :
6000 REM **--FILE OUTPUT ROUTINE--**
6010 OPEN "HOMEINV.DAT" AS #2 LEN=100
6020 FIELD #2,25 AS I$,15 AS S$,10 AS C$,20 AS R$,30 AS D$
6030 LSET I$ = ITEM$
6040 LSET S$ = SERIAL$
6050 LSET C$ = CST$
6060 LSET R$ = ROOM$
6070 LSET D$ = DESC$
6080 PUT #2,REC
6090 CLOSE #2
```

```
6100 GOTO 220: REM Menu
6110 :
6120 :
7000 REM **--UNDERLINE ROUTINE--**
7010 LOCATE 15,HT
7020 FOR I = 1 TO SP
7030 PRINT "_";
7040 NEXT I
7050 RETURN
```

TRANSINV

```
100 REM ***--INVENTORY DIF TRANSLATION--***
110 :
120 :
130 CLS:
140 LOCATE 5,15
150 PRINT "DIF TRANSLATION IN PROGRESS. PLEASE DO NOT TO
    UCH!!"
160 Q$ = CHR$(34): REM Quotation mark
170 OPEN "INVPTR.DAT" FOR INPUT AS #1
180 INPUT #1,PTR
190 CLOSE #1
200 NV = 5: NT = PTR + 1
210 REM NV = NUMBER OF VECTORS
220 REM NT = NUMBER OF TUPLES
230 :
240 OPEN "HOMEINV.DAT" AS #2 LEN=100
250 OPEN "HOMEINV.DIF" FOR OUTPUT AS #3
260 FIELD #2,25 AS ITEM$,15 AS SERIAL$,10 AS CST$,20 AS
    ROOM$,30 AS DESC$
270 :
280 REM **--HEADER SECTION--**
290 :
300 PRINT #3,"TABLE"
310 PRINT #3,"0,1"
320 PRINT #3,Q$"INVENTORY"Q$
330 :
340 PRINT #3,"VECTORS"
350 PRINT #3,"0,";NV
360 PRINT #3,Q$Q$
370 :
380 PRINT #3,"TUPLES"
390 PRINT #3,"0,";NT
400 PRINT #3,Q$Q$
410 :
420 PRINT #3,"LABEL"
430 PRINT #3,"1,0"
440 PRINT #3,Q$"ITEM"Q$
450 :
```

```
460 PRINT #3,"LABEL"
470 PRINT #3,"2,0"
480 PRINT #3,Q$"SERIAL #"Q$
490 :
500 PRINT #3,"LABEL"
510 PRINT #3,"3,0"
520 PRINT #3,Q$"COST"Q$
530 :
540 PRINT #3,"LABEL"
550 PRINT #3,"4,0"
560 PRINT #3,Q$"ROOM"Q$
570 :
580 PRINT #3,"LABEL"
590 PRINT #3,"5,0"
600 PRINT #3,Q$"DESC."Q$
610 :
620 PRINT #3,"DATA"
630 PRINT #3,"0,0"
640 PRINT #3,Q$Q$
650 :
660 REM **--DATA SECTION--**
670 :
680 PRINT #3,"-1,0"
690 PRINT #3,"BOT"
700 :
710 PRINT #3,"1,0"
720 PRINT #3,Q$"ITEM"Q$
730 :
740 PRINT #3,"1,0"
750 PRINT #3,Q$"SERIAL #"Q$
760 :
770 PRINT #3,"1,0"
780 PRINT #3,Q$"COST"Q$
790 :
800 PRINT #3,"1,0"
810 PRINT #3,Q$"ROOM"Q$
820 :
830 PRINT #3,"1,0"
840 PRINT #3,Q$"DESC."Q$
850 :
860 FOR I = 1 TO PTR
870 :
880 GET #2,I
890 :
900 I$ = ITEM$
910 IF LEFT$(I$,7) = "DELETED" THEN 1170: REM Next I
920 C$ = CST$
930 IF LEFT$(C$,1) = "$" THEN 950
940 GOTO 990
950 LC = LEN (C$)
960 A$ = RIGHT$(C$,LC - 1)
970 C$ = A$
980 :
990 PRINT #3,"-1,0"
```

```
1000 PRINT #3,"BOT"
1010 :
1020 PRINT #3,"1,0"
1030 PRINT #3,ITEM$
1040 :
1050 PRINT #3,"1,0"
1060 PRINT #3,SERIAL$
1070 :
1080 PRINT #3,"0,";VAL(C$)
1090 PRINT #3,"V"
1100 :
1110 PRINT #3,"1,0"
1120 PRINT #3,ROOM$
1130 :
1140 PRINT #3,"1,0"
1150 PRINT #3,DESC$
1160 :
1170 NEXT I
1180 PRINT #3,"-1,0"
1190 PRINT #3,"EOD"
1200 :
1210 CLOSE #2,#3
1220 FILES
1230 PRINT: PRINT
1240 PRINT"DIF TRANSLATION COMPLETE!"
1250 INPUT "Press `ENTER' when ready to continue ";L$
1260 RUN "INVMENU"
```

BKOMENU

```
100 REM **--BACK ORDER SYSTEM--**
110 HT = 25: REM Horizontal tab
120 VT =  2: REM Vertical tab
130 KEY OFF
140 :
150 :
160 REM **--MENU ROUTINE--**
170 CLS
180 LOCATE VT,      HT: PRINT "BACK ORDER SYSTEM"
190 LOCATE VT +  2,HT: PRINT "1.   WRITE RECORD"
200 LOCATE VT +  4,HT: PRINT "2.   READ RECORD"
210 LOCATE VT +  6,HT: PRINT "3.   SEARCH RECORD"
220 LOCATE VT +  8,HT: PRINT "4.   CORRECT RECORD"
230 LOCATE VT + 10,HT: PRINT "5.   TRANSLATE RECORD"
240 LOCATE VT + 12,HT: PRINT "6.   LIST FILES"
250 LOCATE VT + 14,HT: PRINT "7.   END"
260 LOCATE VT + 16,HT: INPUT "Which number ";NUMBER
270 IF NUMBER = 1 THEN 1000
280 IF NUMBER = 2 THEN 2000
290 IF NUMBER = 3 THEN 3000
300 IF NUMBER = 4 THEN 4000
310 IF NUMBER = 5 THEN 5000
320 IF NUMBER = 6 THEN 6000
330 IF NUMBER = 7 THEN KEY ON: END
340 LOCATE 22,HT: PRINT "INCORRECT NUMBER! PLEASE CHOOSE
    AGAIN."
350 GOTO 180
360 :
370 :
1000 REM **--WRITE RECORD PROGRAM--**
1010 RUN "WRITEBKO"
1990 :
1995 :
2000 REM **--READ RECORD PROGRAM--**
2010 RUN "READBKO"
2990 :
2995 :
3000 REM **--SEARCH RECORD PROGRAM--**
3010 RUN "SRCHBKO"
3990 :
3995 :
4000 REM **--CORRECT RECORD PROGRAM--**
4010 RUN "CRECTBKO"
4990 :
4995 :
5000 REM **--TRANSLATE RECORD PROGRAM--**
5010 RUN "TRANSBKO"
5990 :
5995 :
```

```
6000 REM **--LIST OF FILES ROUTINE--**
6010 CLS
6020 LOCATE 5,1
6030 FILES
6040 PRINT: PRINT
6050 INPUT "Press the `ENTER' key when ready to continue";L$
6070 GOTO 160: REM Menu
```

WRITEBKO

```
100 REM ***--WRITE BACKORDER RECORD--**
110 :
120 :
130 HT = 20: REM Horizontal tab
140 VT =  2: REM Vertical tab
150 :
160 :
170 CLS
180 LOCATE  VT,HT: PRINT "ADD TO BACK ORDER RECORDS"
185 LOCATE VT + 2,HT: PRINT "Press `ENTER' to duplicate
    last entry"
187 LOCATE VT + 4,HT: PRINT "Type `-' for no value."
190 :
200 :
210 REM **--ITEM'S NAME ROUTINE--**
220 LOCATE 10,HT
230 PRINT "ITEM'S NAME PLEASE."
240 SP = 25
250 GOSUB 5000: REM Input subroutine
260 LOCATE 15,HT
270 INPUT "",ITEM$
280 IF LEN (ITEM$) > SP THEN BEEP: GOTO 210
290 S$ = ITEM$: GOSUB 6000: ITEM$ = S$
295 IF ITEM$ = "" THEN ITEM$ = A1$
297 A1$ = ITEM$
300 :
310 :
320 REM **--DESCRIPTION ROUTINE--**
330 GOSUB 7000: REM Clear lower part of screen
340 LOCATE 10,HT
350 PRINT "ITEM'S DESCRIPTION PLEASE"
360 SP = 30
370 GOSUB 5000: REM Input subroutine
380 LOCATE 15,HT
390 INPUT "",DESC$
400 IF LEN(DESC$) > SP THEN BEEP: GOTO 320
410 S$ = DESC$: GOSUB 6000: DESC$ = S$
415 IF DESC$ = "" THEN DESC$ = B1$
417 B1$ = DESC$
420 :
```

```
430 :
440 REM **--INDIVIDUAL'S NAME ROUTINE--**
450 GOSUB 7000: REM Clear lower part of screen
460 LOCATE 10,HT
470 PRINT "INDIVIDUAL'S NAME PLEASE"
480 SP = 20
490 GOSUB 5000: REM Input subroutine
500 LOCATE 15,HT
510 INPUT "",NAMES$
520 IF LEN(NAMES$) > SP THEN BEEP: GOTO 440
530 S$ = NAMES$: GOSUB 6000: NAMES$ = S$
535 IF NAMES$ = "" THEN NAMES$ = C1$
537 C1$ = NAMES$
540 :
550 :
560 REM **--PHONE NUMBER ROUTINE--**
570 GOSUB 7000: REM Clear lower part of screen
580 LOCATE 10,HT
590 PRINT "PHONE NUMBER PLEASE"
600 SP = 20
610 GOSUB 5000: REM Input subroutine
620 LOCATE 15,HT
630 INPUT "",PHNE$
640 IF LEN(PHNE$) > SP THEN BEEP: GOTO 560
650 S$ = PHNE$: GOSUB 6000: PHNE$ = S$
655 IF PHNE$ = "" THEN PHNE$ = D1$
657 D1$ = PHNE$
660 :
670 :
680 REM **--DATE ORDERED--**
690 GOSUB 7000: REM Clear lower part of screen
700 LOCATE 10,HT
710 PRINT "DATE REQUEST WAS MADE"
720 SP = 10
730 GOSUB 5000: REM Input subroutine
740 LOCATE 15,HT
750 INPUT "",DTE$
760 IF LEN(DTE$) > SP THEN BEEP: GOTO 680
770 S$ = DTE$: GOSUB 6000: DTE$ = S$
775 IF DTE$ = "" THEN DTE$ = E1$
777 E1$ = DTE$
780 :
790 :
800 REM **--ORDERED YET?--**
810 GOSUB 7000: REM Clear lower part of screen
820 LOCATE 10,HT
830 PRINT "ORDERED YET (`Y' OR `N')"
840 SP = 1
850 GOSUB 5000: REM Input subroutine
860 LOCATE 15,HT
870 INPUT "",OD$
880 IF LEN(OD$) > SP THEN BEEP: GOTO 800
890 S$ = OD$: GOSUB 6000: OD$ = S$
895 IF OD$ = "" THEN OD$ = F1$
```

```
897 F1$ = OD$
898 :
899 :
900 REM **--AMOUNT DEPOSITED--**
910 GOSUB 7000: REM Clear lower part of screen
920 LOCATE 10,HT
930 PRINT "AMOUNT DEPOSITED"
940 SP = 10
950 GOSUB 5000: REM Input subroutine
960 LOCATE 15,HT
970 INPUT "",AMT$
980 IF LEN(AMT$) > SP THEN BEEP: GOTO 800
990 S$ = AMT$: GOSUB 6000: AMT$ = S$
995 IF AMT$ = "" THEN AMT$ = G1$
997 G1$ = AMT$
998 :
999 :
1000 REM **--DISPLAY FOR CORRECTION--**
1010 CLS
1020 LOCATE VT,      HT: PRINT "1.   ";ITEM$
1030 LOCATE VT +  2,HT: PRINT "2.   ";DESC$
1040 LOCATE VT +  4,HT: PRINT "3.   ";NAMES$
1050 LOCATE VT +  6,HT: PRINT "4.   ";PHNE$
1060 LOCATE VT +  8,HT: PRINT "5.   ";DTE$
1062 LOCATE VT + 10,HT: PRINT "6.   ";OD$
1064 LOCATE VT + 12,HT: PRINT "7.   ";AMT$
1070 LOCATE VT + 14,HT: INPUT "Is this correct (`Y' or `N
     ') ";YES$
1080 IF YES$ = "Y" OR YES$ = "y" THEN 2000: REM File outp
     ut routine
1090 LOCATE VT + 16,HT: INPUT "Which number is wrong ";NB
1100 IF NB = 1 THEN SP = 25
1110 IF NB = 2 THEN SP = 30
1120 IF NB = 3 THEN SP = 20
1130 IF NB = 4 THEN SP = 20
1140 IF NB = 5 THEN SP = 10
1142 IF NB = 6 THEN SP = 1
1144 IF NB = 7 THEN SP = 10
1150 IF NB < 1 OR NB > 7 THEN PRINT "INCORRECT CHOICE!":
     GOTO 1090
1160 CLS: LOCATE 10,HT
1170 PRINT "Type in the correct information:"
1180 GOSUB 5000: REM Underline subroutine
1190 LOCATE 15,HT
1200 INPUT "",CT$(NB)
1210 IF LEN(CT$(NB)) > SP THEN BEEP: GOTO 1160
1220 IF NB = 1 THEN ITEM$   =   CT$(NB)
1230 IF NB = 2 THEN DESC$   =   CT$(NB)
1240 IF NB = 3 THEN NAMES$  =   CT$(NB)
1250 IF NB = 4 THEN PHNE$   =   CT$(NB)
1260 IF NB = 5 THEN DTE$    =   CT$(NB)
1262 IF NB = 6 THEN OD$     =   CT$(NB)
1264 IF NB = 7 THEN AMT$    =   CT$(NB)
```

```
1270 GOTO 1000: REM Check again
1280 :
1290 :
2000 REM **--FILE OUTPUT ROUTINE--**
2010 ON ERROR GOTO 3000
2020 OPEN "BKOPTR.DAT" FOR INPUT AS #1
2030 INPUT #1,PTR
2040 PTR = PTR + 1
2050 CLOSE #1
2060 :
2070 OPEN "BACKORD.DAT" AS #2 LEN=116
2080 FIELD #2,25 AS I$,30 AS D$,20 AS N$,20 AS P$,10 AS
     T$,1 AS O$,10 AS A$
2090 LSET I$ = ITEM$
2100 LSET D$ = DESC$
2110 LSET N$ = NAMES$
2120 LSET P$ = PHNE$
2130 LSET T$ = DTE$
2132 LSET O$ = OD$
2134 LSET A$ = AMT$
2140 PUT #2,PTR
2150 CLOSE #2
2160 :
2170 OPEN "BKOPTR.DAT" FOR OUTPUT AS #1
2180 PRINT #1,PTR
2190 CLOSE #1
2200 :
2210 CLS
2212 LOCATE VT,HT: PRINT "Do you want to add more items?"
2214 LOCATE VT + 2,HT: INPUT "Type `NO' to stop ";NO$
2216 IF NO$ = "NO" OR NO$ = "no" THEN RUN "BKOMENU"
2218 GOTO 170: REM Begin again
2220 :
2230 :
3000 REM **--FIRST TIME USE ONLY--**
3010 OPEN "BKOPTR.DAT" FOR OUTPUT AS #1
3020 PRINT #1,"0"
3030 CLOSE #1
3040 PRINT
3050 GOTO 2000: REM Begin file routine again
3060 :
3070 :
5000 REM **--UNDERLINE ROUTINE--**
5010 LOCATE 15,HT
5020 FOR I = 1 TO SP
5030 PRINT "_";
5040 NEXT I
5050 RETURN
5060 :
5070 :
6000 REM **--STRIP EXCESS UNDERLINE CHAR--**
6010 S2$ = S$
6020 I = 1
6030 IF MID$(S2$,I,1)  = "_" THEN 6070
```

```
6040 I = I + 1
6050 IF I > SP THEN 6070
6060 GOTO 6030
6070 S$ = LEFT$(S2$,I - 1)
6080 RETURN
6090 :
6100 :
7000 REM **--CLEAR LOWER PART OF SCREEN--**
7010 LOCATE 10,1
7020 FOR V = 10 TO 15 STEP 5
7030 FOR H = 0 TO 7
7040 LOCATE V,(H * 10) + 1
7050 PRINT "          ";: REM 10 spaces
7060 NEXT H
7070 NEXT V
7080 RETURN
```

READBKO

```
100 REM ***--DISPLAY BACK ORDER--***
110 :
120 :
130 REM **--FILE INPUT ROUTINE--**
140 OPEN "BKOPTR.DAT" FOR INPUT AS #1
150 INPUT #1,PTR
160 CLOSE #1
170 :
180 OPEN "BACKORD.DAT" AS #2 LEN=116
190 FIELD #2,25 AS ITEM$,30 AS DESC$,20 AS NAMES$,
            20 AS PHNE$,10 AS DTE$,1 AS OD$,10 AS AMT$
200 CLS
210 FOR I = 1 TO PTR
220 GET #2,I
230 IF LEFT$(ITEM$,7) = "DELETED" THEN 300: REM Next I
240 PRINT I;ITEM$ TAB(30) DESC$
245 PRINT TAB(30) NAMES$ TAB(55) PHNE$
247 PRINT TAB(30) DTE$ TAB(50) OD$ TAB(55) AMT$
260 PRINT
270 C$ = AMT$
280 IF LEFT$(C$,1) = "$" THEN GOSUB 1000
290 TTLCST = TTLCST + VAL (C$)
300 NEXT I
310 CLOSE #2
320 PRINT: PRINT "Total value of items =";
330 PRINT USING "$$#####,.##";TTLCST
340 PRINT
350 INPUT "Press `ENTER' to return to the program menu";L$
360 RUN "BKOMENU"
370 :
380 :
```

```
1000 REM **--STRIP $ SIGN--**
1010 LN = LEN (C$)
1020 A$ = RIGHT$(C$,LN-1)
1030 C$ = A$
1040 RETURN
```

SRCHBKO

```
100 REM ***--SEARCH/SORT BACKORDERS--**
110 :
120 :
130 REM **--INPUT POINTER VALUE--**
140 OPEN "BKOPTR.DAT" FOR INPUT AS #1
150 INPUT #1,PTR
160 CLOSE #1
170 :
180 :
190 DIM AP$(PTR)
200 VT =  2: REM Vertical tab
210 HT = 25: REM Horizontal tab
220 :
230 :
240 REM **--MENU ROUTINE--**
250 CLS
260 LOCATE VT,     HT: PRINT "SEARCH/SORT MENU"
270 LOCATE VT +  2,HT: PRINT "1.   SEARCH FOR ITEM"
280 LOCATE VT +  4,HT: PRINT "2.   SEARCH FOR INDIVDUAL'S
    NAME"
290 LOCATE VT +  6,HT: PRINT "3.   SEARCH FOR DATE"
300 LOCATE VT +  8,HT: PRINT "4.   SEARCH FOR ITEMS NOT Y
    ET ORDERED"
310 LOCATE VT + 10,HT: PRINT "5.   SORT ITEMS ALPHABETICA
    LLY"
320 LOCATE VT + 12,HT: PRINT "6.   SORT BY NAME"
330 LOCATE VT + 14,HT: PRINT "7.   RETURN TO MAIN MENU"
340 LOCATE VT + 16,HT: INPUT "Which number";NUMBER
350 IF NUMBER = 1 THEN 1000
360 IF NUMBER = 2 THEN 2000
370 IF NUMBER = 3 THEN 3000
380 IF NUMBER = 4 THEN 4000
390 IF NUMBER = 5 THEN 6000
400 IF NUMBER = 6 THEN 6000
410 IF NUMBER = 7 THEN 7000
420 LOCATE 22,HT: PRINT "INCORRECT NUMBER! PLEASE CHOOSE
    AGAIN."
430 GOTO 340: REM Ask again
440 :
450 :
1000 REM **--SEARCH FOR ITEM--**
1010 CLS
```

```
1020 LOCATE VT,HT: INPUT "Which item ";SRCH$
1030 CVT$ = SRCH$: GOSUB 20000: REM Convert to uppercase
1040 SRCH$ = CVT$
1050 I = 1
1060 CLS
1065 GOSUB 8000: REM Printer routine
1070 GOSUB 10000: REM Common Search Routine
1080 IF CSR = 1 THEN 1110: REM Search completed
1090 PRINT ITEM$ TAB(30) NAMES$ TAB(55) DTE$
1092 PRINT TAB(30) PHNE$ TAB(55) AMT$
1094 PRINT TAB(30) DESC$ TAB(65) OD$
1100 REM
1110 ITEM$ = "": NAMES$ = "": DTE$ = "": PHNE$ = "": DES
     C$ = ""
1111 OD$ = "": AMT$ = ""
1120 IF I > PTR THEN 1140
1130 GOTO 1070: REM Continue search
1140 GOSUB 9000: REM Housekeeping
1150 GOTO 240: REM Menu
1160 :
1170 :
2000 REM **--SEARCH FOR CUSTOMER'S NAME--**
2010 CLS
2020 LOCATE VT,HT: INPUT "Customer's name please";SRCH$
2030 CVT$ = SRCH$: GOSUB 20000: REM Convert to uppercase
2040 SRCH$ = CVT$
2050 I = 1: NUMBER = 3
2060 CLS
2065 GOSUB 8000: REM Printer routine
2070 GOSUB 10000:.REM Common Search Routine
2075 IF CSR = 1 THEN 2090
2080 PRINT NAMES$ TAB(30) ITEM$ TAB(55) DTE$
2085 GOTO 2070: REM Continue search
2090 GOSUB 9000: REM Housekeeping
2100 GOTO 240: REM Menu
2110 :
2120 :
3000 REM **--SEARCH FOR DATE--**
3010 CLS
3020 FIND$ = ""
3030 LOCATE VT,    HT: PRINT "SEARCH FOR ITEMS..."
3040 LOCATE VT + 2,HT: PRINT "A...After a certain date"
3050 LOCATE VT + 4,HT: PRINT "B...Before a certain date"
3060 LOCATE VT + 6,HT: INPUT "Which letter `A' or `B' ";
     LT$
3070 IF LT$ = "A" OR LT$ = "a" THEN 3130
3080 IF LT$ = "B" OR LT$ = "b" THEN 3380
3090 LOCATE 22,HT: PRINT "INCORRECT CHOICE"
3100 GOTO 3060: REM Ask again
3110 :
3120 :
3130 REM **--ITEMS AFTER CERTAIN DATE--**
3140 LOCATE VT + 10,HT: INPUT "After which date ";DT$
3150 CLS
```

```
3160 LOCATE VT,HT: PRINT "ORDERS AFTER ";DT$
3180 PRINT: PRINT
3190 GOSUB 15000: REM Open file
3200 FOR I = 1 TO PTR
3210 GET #2,I
3220 F$ = DTE$
3230 IF LEFT$(F$,7) = "DELETED" THEN 3290: REM Next I
3250 IF VAL(F$) => VAL(DT$) THEN 3280
3260 GOTO 3290: REM Next I
3280 PRINT ITEM$ TAB(40) DTE$
3290 NEXT I
3300 PRINT
3330 GOSUB 16000: REM Close file
3340 GOSUB 9000: REM Housekeeping
3350 GOTO 240: REM Menu
3360 :
3370 :
3380 REM **--ITEMS BEFORE A CERTAIN DATE--**
3390 LOCATE VT + 10,HT: INPUT "Before which date ";DT$
3400 CLS
3410 LOCATE VT,HT: PRINT "ORDERS BEFORE ";DT$
3430 PRINT: PRINT
3440 GOSUB 15000: REM Open file
3450 FOR I = 1 TO PTR
3460 GET #2,I
3470 F$ = DTE$
3480 IF LEFT$(F$,7) = "DELETED" THEN 3540: REM Next I
3500 IF VAL(F$) < VAL(DT$) THEN 3520
3510 GOTO 3540: REM Next I
3520 REM
3530 PRINT  ITEM$ TAB(40) DTE$
3540 NEXT I
3550 PRINT
3580 GOSUB 16000: REM Close file
3590 GOSUB 9000: REM Housekeeping
3600 GOTO 240: REM Menu
3610 :
3620 :
4000 REM **--SEARCH FOR ITEM NOT ORDERED--**
4010 CLS
4020 LOCATE VT,HT: PRINT "ITEM'S NOT ORDERED"
4030 SRCH$ = "N"
4060 I = 1: NUMBER = 6
4070 CLS
4075 GOSUB 8000: REM Printer routine
4080 GOSUB 10000: REM Common Search Routine
4090 IF CSR = 1 THEN 4160: REM Search completed
4100 PRINT ITEM$ TAB(27) NAMES$ TAB(49) DESC$
4160 ITEM$ = "": NAMES$ = "":
4170 IF I > PTR THEN 4200
4190 GOTO 4080: REM Continue Search
4200 GOSUB 9000: REM Housekeeping
4320 GOTO 240: REM Menu
```

```
4330 :
4340 :
6000 REM **--COMMON SORT ROUTINE--**
6010 CLS
6020 LOCATE VT,HT: PRINT "WORKING--PLEASE DON'T TOUCH!!"
6030 Q = 1: REM Valid record counter
6040 GOSUB 15000: REM Open file
6050 FOR I = 1 TO PTR
6060 GET #2,I
6070 IF NUMBER = 5 THEN F$ = ITEM$
6080 IF NUMBER = 6 THEN F$ = NAMES$
6090 IF LEFT$(F$,7) = "DELETED" THEN 6150
6100 CVT$ = F$
6110 GOSUB 20000: REM Convert to uppercase
6120 F$ = CVT$
6130 AP$(Q) = F$ + "*" + STR$(I): REM Combine for sort
6140 Q = Q + 1
6150 NEXT I
6160 GOSUB 16000: REM Close file
6170 N = Q - 1
6180 LOCATE VT + 5,HT: PRINT "STILL WORKING--PLEASE WAIT!"
6190 GOSUB 25000: REM Sort routine
6200 :
6210 REM DISPLAY RESULTS
6220 CLS
6225 GOSUB 15000
6230 LOCATE VT,1
6240 FOR I = 1 TO Q - 1
6250 REM Separate and display
6260 LA = LEN(AP$(I))
6270 PRINT I;"   ";
6280 IF MID$(AP$(I),J,1) = "*" THEN 6300
6290 J = J + 1: GOTO 6280
6300 REM
6315 K$ = MID$(AP$(I),J + 1)
6316 KP = VAL(K$)
6317 GET #2,KP
6318 IF NUMBER = 5 THEN PRINT ITEM$ TAB(40) NAMES$ TAB(65)
     DTE$
6319 IF NUMBER = 6 THEN PRINT NAMES$ TAB(40) ITEM$ TAB(65)
     DTE$
6320 J = 1
6330 NEXT I
6335 GOSUB 16000
6340 GOSUB 9000: REM Housekeeping
6350 GOTO 240: REM Menu
6360 :
6370 :
7000 REM **--RETURN TO MAIN MENU--**
7010 RUN "BKOMENU"
7020 :
7030 :
8000 RETURN
```

```
9000 REM **--HOUSEKEEPING ROUTINE--**
9010 ITEM$     = ""
9020 DESC$     = ""
9030 NAMES$    = ""
9040 PHNE$     = ""
9050 DTE$      = ""
9052 OD$       = ""
9054 AMT$      = ""
9060 DISPLAY$  = "SCRN:"
9070 CSR = Ø
9080 :
9090 REM Clear line 22
9100 LOCATE 22,HT: FOR SP = 1 TO 80: PRINT " ";: NEXT SP
9110 LOCATE 22,HT: INPUT "Press `ENTER' to continue";L$
9120 RETURN
9130 :
9140 :
10000 REM **--COMMON SEARCH ROUTINE--**
10010 OPEN "BACKORD.DAT" AS #2 LEN=116
10020 FIELD #2,25 AS FIND$(1),30 AS FIND$(2),20 AS FIND$
      (3),20 AS FIND$(4),10 AS FIND$(5),1 AS FIND$(6),10
      AS FIND$(7)
10030 LN = LEN(SRCH$)
10040 GET #2,I
10050 :
10060 CVT$ = LEFT$(FIND$(NUMBER),LN)
10070 GOSUB 20000: REM Convert to uppercase
10080 :
10090 IF SRCH$ = CVT$ THEN 10200
10100 I = I + 1
10110 IF I < PTR OR I = PTR THEN 10040
10120 REM Clear line 22
10130 LOCATE 22,HT: FOR SP = 1 TO 80: PRINT " ";: NEXT SP
10140 LOCATE 22,HT: PRINT "SEARCH COMPLETED!"
10150 CSR = 1: REM Set search completed flag
10160 FOR K = 1 TO 1000: NEXT K
10170 CLOSE #2
10180 RETURN
10190 :
10200 ITEM$    = FIND$(1)
10210 DESC$    = FIND$(2)
10220 NAMES$   = FIND$(3)
10230 PHNE$    = FIND$(4)
10240 DTE$     = FIND$(5)
10242 OD$      = FIND$(6)
10244 AMT$     = FIND$(7)
10250 I = I + 1
10260 CLOSE #2
10270 RETURN
10280 :
10290 :
12000 REM **--STRIP $ SIGN--**
12010 LC = LEN (C$)
12020 A$ = RIGHT$(C$,LC-1)
```

```
12030 C$ = A$
12040 RETURN
12050 :
12060 :
15000 REM **--OPEN RANDOM ACCESS FILE--**
15010 OPEN "BACKORD.DAT" AS #2 LEN=116
15020 FIELD #2,25 AS ITEM$,30 AS DESC$,20 AS NAMES$,20 A
      S PHNE$,10 AS DTE$,1 AS OD$,10 AS AMT$
15030 RETURN
15040 :
15050 :
16000 REM **--CLOSE RANDOM ACCESS FILE--**
16010 CLOSE #2
16020 RETURN
16030 :
16040 :
20000 REM **--CONVERT TO UPPERCASE ROUTINE--**
20010 FOR CV = 1 TO LEN(CVT$)
20020 X = ASC (MID$(CVT$,CV,1))
20030 IF X > 96 AND X < 123 THEN X = X - 32
20040 CVTUP$ = CVTUP$ + CHR$(X)
20050 NEXT CV
20060 CVT$ = CVTUP$
20070 CVTUP$ = ""
20080 RETURN
20090 :
20100 :
25000 REM **--SORT ROUTINE--**
25010 M = N
25020 M = INT (M / 2)
25030 IF M = 0 THEN 25150
25040 J = 1: K = N - M
25050 I = J
25060 L = I + M
25070 IF AP$(I) < AP$(L) THEN 25120
25080 TP$ = AP$(I): AP$(I) = AP$(L): AP$(L) = TP$
25090 I = I - M
25100 IF I < 1 THEN 25120
25110 GOTO 25060
25120 J = J + 1
25130 IF J > K THEN 25020
25140 GOTO 25050
25150 RETURN
```

CRECTBKO

```
100 REM ***--CORRECT BACKORDER RECORD--**
110 :
120 :
130 HT = 25: REM Horizontal tab
140 VT =  2: REM Vertical tab
150 :
160 :
170 OPEN "BKOPTR.DAT" FOR INPUT AS #1
180 INPUT #1,PTR
190 CLOSE #1
200 :
210 :
220 REM **--MENU ROUTINE--**
230 CLS
240 LOCATE VT,     HT: PRINT "CORRECT/DELETE MENU"
250 LOCATE VT +  2,HT: PRINT "C....Correct Backorder Rec
    ord"
260 LOCATE VT +  4,HT: PRINT "D....Delete  Backorder Rec
    ord"
270 LOCATE VT +  6,HT: PRINT "R....Return To Main Menu"
280 LOCATE VT +  8,HT: INPUT "Which letter please ";LT$
290 IF LT$ = "C" OR LT$ = "c" THEN 1000
300 IF LT$ = "D" OR LT$ = "d" THEN 2000
310 IF LT$ = "R" OR LT$ = "r" THEN 3000
320 LOCATE VT + 10,HT: PRINT "INCORRECT CHOICE"
330 GOTO 280: REM Ask again
340 :
350 :
1000 REM **--CORRECT RECORD--**
1010 CLS
1020 FLAG$ = "NO": REM Information has yet to be changed
1030 LOCATE 10,HT: PRINT "Type a `0' to return to the Me
     nu"
1040 LOCATE 12,HT: INPUT "Correct which record ";REC
1050 IF REC = 0 THEN 220: REM Menu
1060 IF REC > PTR THEN LOCATE 22,HT: PRINT "NOT THAT MAN
     Y RECORDS!": GOTO 1040
1070 GOSUB 5000: REM Read file
1080 :
1090 REM **--DISPLAY FOR CORRECTION--**
1100 CLS
1110 LOCATE VT,     HT: PRINT "1.   ";ITEM$
1120 LOCATE VT +  2,HT: PRINT "2.   ";DESC$
1130 LOCATE VT +  4,HT: PRINT "3.   ";NAMES$
1140 LOCATE VT +  6,HT: PRINT "4.   ";PHNE$
1150 LOCATE VT +  8,HT: PRINT "5.   ";DTE$
1152 LOCATE VT + 10,HT: PRINT "6.   ";OD$
1154 LOCATE VT + 12,HT: PRINT "7.   ";AMT$
1160 LOCATE VT + 14,HT: INPUT "Is this correct (`Y' or `
     N') ";YES$
```

```
1170 IF YES$ = "Y" OR YES$ = "y" THEN 1200
1180 GOTO 1230: REM negative response
1190 :
1200 IF FLAG$ = "YES" THEN 6000: REM Info changed--write
     it out
1210 IF FLAG$ = "NO" THEN 1000: REM Info not changed--ge
     t another
1220 :
1230 LOCATE VT + 16,HT: INPUT "Which number is wrong ";N
     B
1240 IF NB = 1 THEN SP = 25
1250 IF NB = 2 THEN SP = 30
1260 IF NB = 3 THEN SP = 20
1270 IF NB = 4 THEN SP = 20
1280 IF NB = 5 THEN SP = 10
1282 IF NB = 6 THEN SP = 1
1284 IF NB = 7 THEN SP = 10
1290 IF NB < 1 OR NB > 7 THEN PRINT "INCORRECT CHOICE!":
     GOTO 1230
1300 :
1310 CLS: LOCATE 10,HT
1320 PRINT "Type in the correct information:"
1330 GOSUB 7000: REM Underline subroutine
1340 LOCATE 15,HT
1350 INPUT "",CT$(NB)
1360 IF LEN(CT$(NB)) > SP THEN BEEP: GOTO 1310
1370 IF NB = 1 THEN ITEM$    =   CT$(NB)
1380 IF NB = 2 THEN DESC$    =   CT$(NB)
1390 IF NB = 3 THEN NAMES$   =   CT$(NB)
1400 IF NB = 4 THEN PHNE$    =   CT$(NB)
1410 IF NB = 5 THEN DTE$     =   CT$(NB)
1412 IF NB = 6 THEN OD$      =   CT$(NB)
14.4 IF NB = 7 THEN AMT$     =   CT$(NB)
1420 FLAG$ = "YES": REM Information has been changed
1430 GOTO 1090: REM Check again
1440 :
1450 :
2000 REM **--DELETE RECORD--**
2010 CLS
2020 LOCATE 10,HT: PRINT "Type a `0' to return to the Me
     nu"
2030 LOCATE 12,HT: INPUT "Delete which record ";REC
2040 IF REC = 0 THEN 220: REM Menu
2050 IF REC > PTR THEN LOCATE 22,HT: PRINT "NOT THAT MAN
     Y RECORDS!": GOTO 2030
2060 GOSUB 5000: REM Read file
2070 :
2080 CLS
2090 LOCATE VT,HT: PRINT ITEM$
2091 LOCATE VT + 1,HT: PRINT DESC$
2092 LOCATE VT + 2,HT: PRINT NAMES$
2093 LOCATE VT + 3,HT: PRINT PHNE$
2094 LOCATE VT + 4,HT: PRINT DTE$
2095 LOCATE VT + 5,HT: PRINT OD$
```

```
2096 LOCATE VT + 6,HT: PRINT AMT$
2110 PRINT: PRINT
2120 INPUT "Delete this Record ";YES$
2130 IF YES$ = "Y" OR YES$ = "y" THEN 2150
2140 GOTO 2000: REM Ask again
2150 INPUT "Are you sure? Type `YES' to delete this reco
     rd.";YES$
2160 IF YES$ = "YES" OR YES$ = "yes" THEN 2180
2170 GOTO 2000: REM Ask again
2180 ITEM$      = "DELETED"
2190 DESC$      = "DELETED"
2200 NAMES$     = "DELETED"
2210 PHNE$      = "DELETED"
2220 DTE$       = "DELETED"
2222 OD$        = "D"
2224 AMT$       = "DELETED"
2230 GOTO 6000: REM File output routine
2240 :
2250 :
3000 REM **--RETURN TO MAIN MENU--**
3010 RUN "BKOMENU
3020 :
3030 :
5000 REM **--FILE INPUT ROUTINE--**
5010 OPEN "BACKORD.DAT" AS #2 LEN=116
5020 FIELD #2,25 AS I$,30 AS D$,20 AS N$,20 AS P$,10 AS
     T$,1 AS O$,10 AS A$
5030 GET #2,REC
5040 ITEM$      = I$
5050 DESC$      = D$
5060 NAMES$     = N$
5070 PHNE$      = P$
5080 DTE$       = T$
5082 OD$        = O$
5084 AMT$       = A$
5090 CLOSE #2
5100 RETURN
5110 :
5120 :
6000 REM **--FILE OUTPUT ROUTINE--**
6010 OPEN "BACKORD.DAT" AS #2 LEN=116
6020 FIELD #2,25 AS I$,30 AS D$,20 AS N$,20 AS P$,10 AS
     T$,1 AS O$,10 AS A$
6030 LSET I$ = ITEM$
6040 LSET D$ = DESC$
6050 LSET N$ = NAMES$
6060 LSET P$ = PHNE$
6070 LSET T$ = DTE$
6072 LSET O$ = OD$
6074 LSET A$ = AMT$
6080 PUT #2,REC
6090 CLOSE #2
6100 GOTO 220: REM Menu
6110 :
6120 :
```

```
7000 REM **--UNDERLINE ROUTINE--**
7010 LOCATE 15,HT
7020 FOR I = 1 TO SP
7030 PRINT "_";
7040 NEXT I
7050 RETURN
```

TRANSBKO

```
100 REM ***--BACKORDER DIF TRANSLATION--***
110 :
120 :
130 CLS:
140 LOCATE 5,15
150 PRINT "DIF TRANSLATION IN PROGRESS. PLEASE DO NOT TO
    UCH!!"
160 Q$ = CHR$(34): REM Quotation mark
170 OPEN "BKOPTR.DAT" FOR INPUT AS #1
180 INPUT #1,PTR
190 CLOSE #1
200 NV = 7: NT = PTR + 1
210 REM NV = NUMBER OF VECTORS
220 REM NT = NUMBER OF TUPLES
230 :
240 OPEN "BACKORD.DAT" AS #2 LEN=116
250 OPEN "BACKORD.DIF" FOR OUTPUT AS #3
260 FIELD #2,25 AS ITEM$,30 AS DESC$,20 AS NAMES$,20 AS
    PHNE$,10 AS DTE$,1 AS OD$,10 AS AMT$
270 :
280 REM **--HEADER SECTION--**
290 :
300 PRINT #3,"TABLE"
310 PRINT #3,"0,1"
320 PRINT #3,Q$"BACKORDER"Q$
330 :
340 PRINT #3,"VECTORS"
350 PRINT #3,"0,";NV
360 PRINT #3,Q$Q$
370 :
380 PRINT #3,"TUPLES"
390 PRINT #3,"0,";NT
400 PRINT #3,Q$Q$
410 :
420 PRINT #3,"LABEL"
430 PRINT #3,"1,0"
440 PRINT #3,Q$"ITEM"Q$
450 :
460 PRINT #3,"LABEL"
470 PRINT #3,"2,0"
480 PRINT #3,Q$"DESCRIPTION"Q$
490 :
```

```
500 PRINT #3,"LABEL"
510 PRINT #3,"3,0"
520 PRINT #3,Q$"NAME"Q$
530 :
540 PRINT #3,"LABEL"
550 PRINT #3,"4,0"
560 PRINT #3,Q$"PHONE"Q$
570 :
580 PRINT #3,"LABEL"
590 PRINT #3,"5,0"
600 PRINT #3,Q$"DATE"Q$
610 :
620 PRINT #3,"LABEL"
630 PRINT #3,"6,0"
640 PRINT #3,Q$"ORDERED"
650 :
660 PRINT #3,"LABEL"
670 PRINT #3,"7,0"
680 PRINT #3,Q$"AMOUNT"Q$
690 :
700 PRINT #3,"DATA"
710 PRINT #3,"0,0"
720 PRINT #3,Q$Q$
730 :
740 REM **--DATA SECTION--**
750 :
760 PRINT #3,"-1,0"
770 PRINT #3,"BOT"
780 :
790 PRINT #3,"1,0"
800 PRINT #3,Q$"ITEM"Q$
810 :
820 PRINT #3,"1,0"
830 PRINT #3,Q$"DESC."Q$
840 :
850 PRINT #3,"1,0"
860 PRINT #3,Q$"NAME"Q$
870 :
880 PRINT #3,"1,0"
890 PRINT #3,Q$"PHONE"Q$
900 :
910 PRINT #3,"1,0"
920 PRINT #3,Q$"DATE"Q$
930 :
940 PRINT #3,"1,0"
950 PRINT #3,Q$"ORDERED"Q$
960 :
970 PRINT #3,"1,0"
980 PRINT #3,Q$"AMOUNT"Q$
990 :
1000 :
1010 FOR I = 1 TO PTR
1020 :
```

```
1030 GET #2,I
1040 :
1050 I$ = ITEM$
1060 IF LEFT$(I$,7) = "DELETED" THEN 1380: REM Next I
1070 A$ = AMT$
1080 IF LEFT$(A$,1) = "$" THEN 1100
1090 GOTO 1140
1100 LA = LEN (A$)
1110 Z$ = RIGHT$(A$,LA - 1)
1120 A$ = Z$
1130 :
1140 PRINT #3,"-1,0"
1150 PRINT #3,"BOT"
1160 :
1170 PRINT #3,"1,0"
1180 PRINT #3,ITEM$
1190 :
1200 PRINT #3,"1,0"
1210 PRINT #3,DESC$
1220 :
1230 PRINT #3,"1,0"
1240 PRINT #3,NAMES$
1250 :
1260 PRINT #3,"1,0"
1270 PRINT #3,PHNE$
1280 :
1290 PRINT #3,"1,0"
1300 PRINT #3,DTE$
1310 :
1320 PRINT #3,"1,0"
1330 PRINT #3,OD$
1340 :
1350 PRINT #3,"0,";VAL(A$)
1360 PRINT #3,"V"
1370 :
1380 NEXT I
1390 PRINT #3,"-1,0"
1400 PRINT #3,"EOD"
1410 :
1420 CLOSE #2,#3
1430 FILES
1440 PRINT: PRINT
1450 PRINT"DIF TRANSLATION COMPLETE!"
1460 INPUT "Press `ENTER' when ready to continue ";L$
1470 RUN "BKOMENU"
```

12
Planning a File System

Rather than present another chapter explaining the programming of another system, this chapter will present the procedures involved in conceiving and creating a file system. I will use a STOCK MARKET SYSTEM as the example. Although shorter than previous chapters, this chapter is no less important.

There are five main steps involved in conceiving and creating a specific data base system.

1. Know you subject.

2. Plan carefully and organize your thoughts.

3. Make preliminary decisions on the number of main variables, the length of each record, and if necessary, the lengths of fields within each record.

4. Roughly plan the sequence of the data base operation and the code for each part of that operation.

5. Begin on the code for the first part of the system.

Some programmers will argue with either the sequence of the steps or the steps themselves. Some may say that such an outline is too limited. All may be right. I am merely trying to give a limited amount of guidance in the development of a specific file system. Some systems analysts are carried away with the pre-code procedures, but one thing is clear: a certain amount of planning before coding is absolutely necessary!

STOCK MARKET SYSTEM

Results of the previous day's trading activity are printed in most daily newspapers. Normally, these results include such things as 52 week high and low stock price; stock symbol; latest dividend; a yield figure; P/E ratio; sales; daily high, low, and closing price; and, possibly, the amount of price change from the previous day. That information is available for active issues on the New York and American Stock Exchanges. Less information is given for over-the-counter or NASDAQ issues, option, commodity, and bond trading. There are figures for the various averages: NYSE INDEX, DOW, STANDARD & POORS, AMERICAN INDEX, NASDAQ COMPOSITE, and/or INDUSTRIALS, to name just a few. There are other key items to watch: gold, interest rates, value of the dollar overseas, money supply, President's daily intake of vitamins, etc. As you might guess, the list is limitless.

Although an investment record may contain more variables than information maintained on your own library, the principle is the same. You must thoroughly know your subject in order to be able to make decisions concerning the information to be saved. The first step in planning your data base should be deciding which information is of value; i.e., what information to save.

In our STOCK MARKET SYSTEM, I am going to severely limit the amount of information saved. Individuals may wish to keep additional information they believe to be important. For each issue, we will save the daily high, low, and closing price, plus the day's volume, P/E ratio, and date. In addition, we will save any price that makes either a new high or new low for that issue.

Steps 2 and 3 blend together somewhat at this point. In the planning, decisions are made. Most stock prices are under $1000 per share, so I will allow a maximum of three places before the decimal point. Prices are usually given in terms of eighths of a dollar; i.e., 3/8 or 1/2. With a little extra planning and coding, significant disk space can be saved on each issue. If the extreme right figure is always viewed as the decimal portion of the stock price, then four digits will represent all stock prices up to $999 and 7/8 per share, which would be saved on the disk as 9997. Saving the high, low and close each day already means 15 bytes per issue per day—4 bytes for the number plus 1 byte for the leading space that is added to numbers converted to strings, for a total of 5 bytes for each high, low, and closing price. If disk space or double precision accuracy is a matter of concern, then the additional BASIC functions of CVI, CVS, CVD, MKI$, MKS$, and MKD$ should be used. These six functions convert numbers to strings or strings to numbers in either a 2, 4, or 8 byte amount of memory. The use of these functions requires consistency in both input and output access. This consistency requirement can considerably complicate the programming process. In this application, we are not concerned with too little disk space nor do we need accuracy beyond that achieved with the VAL and STR$ functions.

Volume can be handled in somewhat the same way. Most papers indicate the sales volume only in hundreds of shares sold per day. A volume of 2000 shares would be displayed as 20. Since virtually every stock trades under 9,999,900 shares in one day, we can limit the number of places to six—9999 plus one for the leading space implied positive sign. (If the number is negative, the leading space becomes a minus sign.) All P/E ratios are under 999 for any issue. This necessitates another 4 bytes for each issue. Finally, we will save the trading date with each record—10 more bytes. That brings the total number of bytes for each issue to 35: 4 for the P/E ratio, 6 for the volume, 5 for the high, 5 for the low, 5 for the close, and 10 for the date. We will save any new high or new low price in a separate sequential file.

Next, we must decide on the number of issues to follow on a daily basis. This is an individual choice and often depends upon the time available for closely following the market. A reasonable figure to start out with is ten issues. If a number greater than ten is used, then the string array variable chosen for the stock names will need to be dimensioned to the proper number. With the number of stocks determined, we can calculate the maximum number of bytes used for each day's transactions. Ten stocks, each requiring 35 bytes, mean a length of 350 bytes per trading day. Based on approximately 140,000 available bytes on a single-sided diskette, we can store 400 days' trading information. That is about a year and a half of stock market activity for ten issues on a single data diskette.

Step 4 is a rough plan of the sequence of programs and the code within each program. Following the procedures we have used in our previous examples, we need programs that will create the necessary files and daily add to those files. Secondly, we need programs to display, in a variety of ways, the information either stored in the file or derived from the information stored. Finally, we must have correction programs.

I am going to introduce another method of creating random files. I have included a program that will only be used once for each set of stocks followed. The STKMENU program indicates that when the user chooses the first option, the ADDSTOCK program is run. The very first time (and only the first time) the STKMENU program is run and the number one selection is made, the computer will load a program that is called ADDSTOCK. In reality, this is a program used one time to create the STKPTR (stock pointer) file and the HILOW (hi, low) file. It also provides the user with some information on the general operation of the STOCK MARKET SYSTEM. Once these files have been created and the user has indicated that the information has been absorbed, this program renames itself on the diskette so that it now has the program file name OLDADD. Then, it renames a second program from its original ADDREAL file name to the necessary ADDSTOCK file name. Finally, the user is given the choice to either return to the main Stock Menu or to add the first day's trading activity. The STKMENU program always runs a program called ADDSTOCK. The first time it runs one program (originally called ADDSTOCK, renamed OLDADD), but every time after that, it runs another program (originally called ADDREAL, renamed ADD-STOCK). The different programs share the same file name, ADD-STOCK, but at different times. In summary, the first program is designed to create the necessary files and then rename both itself, and the real ADDSTOCK (originally ADDREAL) program is designed to daily update each individual stock's file. The explanation may sound complicated, but the operation itself is suprisingly simple.

Within the file addition program, the sequence of operation is fairly standard. We need to read in: (1) the value of the file pointer (add one to that value), (2) the symbols for the various stocks, and (3) their current high and low price. Next, the previous day's figures must be entered for each issue and checked for accuracy. The previous day's figures must also be compared to the current high and low, and if they exceed those figures, they need to replace the appropriate figure. Finally, all the new information must be written to the disk.

The editing programs should follow a similar pattern but with a few exceptions. The pointer should be determined by an input from the keyboard. The high, low, close, volume, and P/E should come from the disk instead of the keyboard, with corrections coming from the keyboard.

The display programs are more difficult to structure in any absolute manner. The only certain structure is that information comes from the disk and is displayed either on the screen or through the printer. In between, a variety of steps can take place. The information can be used to calculate certain values that may be used to evaluate a particular situation and project the price movement of the stock, or the disk information may simply be formatted for display on either the screen or the printer. The information may be used to graph the price movement of the stock or to compare its movement against that of another stock or average. The display portion of the STOCK MARKET SYSTEM is the core of the system and is usually not a fixed set of programs. User needs change and require that the display programs change. In the system presented, the display programs will be limited in their scope. We will display individual stock histories, along with some calculated figures, averages, price and volume changes, etc. We will not get into graphic representation of stock performance in this book. A future book will deal with graphic representation of data base information. It is such a broad topic that it requires a book of its own.

The final step is coding the programs according to the plans established. At the end of this chapter, you will find minimum programs designed according to the structure outlined in this chapter. You are encouraged to take these minimum programs and expand upon them to fit your own interest, or alter them to cover a topic of your own design. It is only by practical experience that you will learn to create IBM BASIC files.

QUESTIONS

1. *True or False:* Good programmers can just sit down and start writing code.
2. What is the first step in planning a data base system?
3. Give the three main parts of any data base system.
4. Which part must be flexible as user needs change?

ANSWERS

1. False
2. Deciding which information is of value
3. Creation and addition, display, correction
4. Display

STKMENU

```
100 REM ***--STOCK MENU--***
110 :
120 :
130 VT = 2: REM Vertical tab
140 HT = 25: REM Horizontal tab
150 KEY OFF
160 :
170 :
180 CLS
190 LOCATE VT,HT + 4 : PRINT "STOCK MENU"
200 LOCATE VT +  2,HT: PRINT "1.   ADD STOCK INFORMATION"
210 LOCATE VT +  4,HT: PRINT "2.   DISPLAY STOCK INFORMAT
    ION"
220 LOCATE VT +  6,HT: PRINT "3.   DISPLAY HI/LOW VALUES"
230 LOCATE VT +  8,HT: PRINT "4.   CORRECT HI/LOW VALUES"
240 LOCATE VT + 10,HT: PRINT "5.   CORRECT STOCK DATA"
250 LOCATE VT + 12,HT: PRINT "6.   DIF TRANSLATION"
260 LOCATE VT + 14,HT: PRINT "7.   LIST OF FILES"
270 LOCATE VT + 16,HT: PRINT "8.   END"
280 LOCATE VT + 18,HT: INPUT "Which number ";NB
290 :
300 IF NB = 1 THEN RUN "ADDSTOCK"
310 IF NB = 2 THEN RUN "DSPSTOCK"
320 IF NB = 3 THEN RUN "DSPHILOW"
330 IF NB = 4 THEN RUN "CRTHILOW"
340 IF NB = 5 THEN RUN "CRTSTOCK"
350 IF NB = 6 THEN RUN "DIFSTOCK"
360 IF NB = 7 THEN 420
370 IF NB = 8 THEN KEY ON: END
380 LOCATE 22,HT: PRINT "INCORRECT NUMBER! PLEASE CHOOSE
    AGAIN."
390 GOTO 280: REM Ask again
400 :
410 :
420 REM **--LIST OF FILES--**
430 CLS: LOCATE 5,1
440 FILES
450 PRINT: PRINT
460 INPUT "Press `ENTER' to continue ";L$
470 GOTO 180: REM Menu
```

ADDSTOCK

```
100 REM ***--INITALIZE STOCK FILES--***
110 :
120 :
130 REM **--CREATE FILE POINTER--**
140 OPEN "STOCKPTR.DAT" FOR OUTPUT AS #1
150 PRINT #1,"0"
160 CLOSE #1
170 :
180 :
190 REM **--INFORMATION--**
200 CLS
210 LOCATE 2,1
220 PRINT "Before you can enter any daily stock informat
    ion, you must decide"
230 PRINT
240 PRINT "which stocks you will be following. This prog
    ram will ask you to "
250 PRINT
260 PRINT "enter the name or symbol of ten stocks and th
    eir respective values"
270 PRINT
280 PRINT "for the high and low prices within the last 1
    2 months. If the high"
290 PRINT
300 PRINT "or low values are not known, simply enter a `
    0'.  The high and low"
310 PRINT
320 PRINT "values will automatically be updated when dai
    ly prices exceed or"
330 PRINT
340 PRINT "are less than the values in the HI/LOW file.
    If you need to change"
350 PRINT
360 PRINT "any of the information in the HI/LOW file, ch
    oose #4 CORRECT HI/LOW"
370 PRINT
380 PRINT "from the main program menu. Once you have fin
    ished entering the"
390 PRINT
400 PRINT "information in this program, you will be give
    n a choice to enter"
410 PRINT
420 PRINT "the first day's prices or to return to the ma
    in program menu."
430 PRINT
440 INPUT "Press the `ENTER' key when you are ready to c
    ontinue.",L$
450 PRINT
460 CLS: LOCATE 5,1
```

```
470 PRINT "After this first time, the ADD STOCK INFORMAT
    ION selection will not"
480 PRINT
490 PRINT "show all this text or require you to update t
    he HI/LOW file.
500 PRINT
510 PRINT "If you want to re-read this information, type
    a `Y', if not, just"
520 PRINT
530 INPUT "press the `ENTER' key. ",YES$
540 IF YES$ = "Y" OR YES$ = "y" THEN 190
550 PRINT
560 INPUT "Press the `ENTER' key again when you are read
    y to begin.",L$
570 :
580 :
1000 REM **--KEYBOARD INPUT ROUTINE--**
1010 FOR I = 1 TO 10
1020 CLS: LOCATE 5,1
1030 PRINT "Type in the name of the stock or its symbol "
1040 PRINT
1050 PRINT "The name or symbol may have a maximum of 8 ch
     aracters."
1060 PRINT
1070 PRINT "Stock #";I;:INPUT STK$(I)
1080 IF LEN(STK$(I)) > 8 THEN STK$(I) = LEFT$(STK$(I),8)
1090 GOSUB 7000: REM Remainder routine
1100 PRINT "If you are not sure of the HI or LOW value, e
     nter a `0'."
1110 PRINT
1120 INPUT "HI value ";HI$(I)
1130 GOSUB 7000: REM Remainder routine
1140 PRINT "If you are not sure of the HI or LOW value, e
     nter a `0'."
1150 PRINT
1160 INPUT "LOW value ";LOW$(I)
1170 :
1180 :
2000 REM **--CORRECTION ROUTINE--**
2010 CLS: LOCATE 5,1
2020 PRINT "1. ";STK$(I)
2030 M = VAL(HI$(I)): GOSUB 8000: REM Convert to fraction
2040 PRINT "2. HI value  = ";M;" ";F$
2050 M = VAL(LOW$(I)): GOSUB 8000: REM Convert to fractio
     n
2060 PRINT "3. LOW value = ";M;" ";F$
2070 PRINT
2080 INPUT "Is this correct ";YES$
2090 IF YES$ = "N" OR YES$ = "n" THEN 2110
2100 GOTO 2180: REM Next I
2110 INPUT "Which number is wrong ";NB
2120 IF NB = 1 THEN INPUT "Correct stock name or symbol "
     ;STK$(I)
2130 IF LEN(STK$(I)) > 8 THEN STK$(I) = LEFT$(STK$(I),8)
```

```
2140 IF NB = 2 THEN INPUT "Correct HI value ";HI$(I)
2150 IF NB = 3 THEN INPUT "Correct LOW value ";LOW$(I)
2160 IF NB < 1 OR NB > 3 THEN PRINT "INCORRECT CHOICE!"
2170 GOTO 2000: REM Ask again
2180 NEXT I
2190 :
2200 :
3000 REM **--FILE OUTPUT ROUTINE--**
3010 OPEN "HILOW.DAT" FOR OUTPUT AS #2
3020 FOR I = 1 TO 10
3030 PRINT #2,STK$(I)
3040 PRINT #2,HI$(I)
3050 PRINT #2,LOW$(I)
3060 NEXT I
3070 CLOSE #2
3080 :
3090 :
4000 REM **--RENAME FILES ROUTINE--**
4010 NAME "ADDSTOCK.BAS" AS "OLDADD.BAS"
4020 NAME "ADDREAL.BAS" AS "ADDSTOCK.BAS"
4030 CLS: LOCATE 5,1
4040 INPUT "Do you want to add the first day's stock pri
     ces (`Y' or `N') ";YES$
4050 IF YES$ = "Y" OR YES$ = "y" THEN RUN "ADDSTOCK"
4060 RUN "STKMENU"
4070 :
4080 :
7000 REM **--REMINDER ROUTINE--**
7010 CLS: VT = 2: HT = 25
7020 LOCATE VT,    HT: PRINT "*****---REMEMBER---*****"
7030 LOCATE VT +  1,HT: PRINT "YOU MUST ADD THE FRACTION"
7040 LOCATE VT +  2,HT: PRINT "AS THE LAST DIGIT."
7050 LOCATE VT +  4,HT + 3: PRINT "1/8 --------- = 1"
7060 LOCATE VT +  5,HT + 3: PRINT "1/4 --------- = 2"
7070 LOCATE VT +  6,HT + 3: PRINT "3/8 --------- = 3"
7080 LOCATE VT +  7,HT + 3: PRINT "1/2 --------- = 4"
7090 LOCATE VT +  8,HT + 3: PRINT "5/8 --------- = 5"
7100 LOCATE VT +  9,HT + 3: PRINT "3/4 --------- = 6"
7110 LOCATE VT + 10,HT + 3: PRINT "7/8 --------- = 7"
7120 LOCATE VT + 11,HT + 3: PRINT "EVEN -------- = 0"
7130 LOCATE VT + 13,HT: PRINT "****---IMPORTANT---****"
7140 LOCATE VT + 14,HT: PRINT "IF THE NUMBER HAS NO"
7150 LOCATE VT + 15,HT: PRINT "FRACTION, PLEASE ENTER"
7160 LOCATE VT + 16,HT: PRINT "A `0' AFTER THE NUMBER!"
7170 PRINT
7180 RETURN
7190 :
7200 :
8000 REM **--CONVERT TO FRACTION--**
8010 F = M - INT (M / 10) * 10
8020 M = INT (M / 10)
8030 IF F = 0 THEN F$ = ""
8040 IF F = 1 THEN F$ = "1/8"
8050 IF F = 2 THEN F$ = "1/4"
```

```
8060 IF F = 3 THEN F$ = "3/8"
8070 IF F = 4 THEN F$ = "1/2"
8080 IF F = 5 THEN F$ = "5/8"
8090 IF F = 6 THEN F$ = "3/4"
8100 IF F = 7 THEN F$ = "7/8"
8110 RETURN
```

ADDREAL

```
100 REM ***--ADD STOCK INFORMATION--***
110 :
120 :
130 REM **--VARIABLES LIST--**
140 REM STK$  = STOCK SYMBOL
150 REM HI$   = CURRENT HI PRICE
160 REM LOW$  = CURRENT LOW PRICE
170 REM DTE$  = DATE
180 REM NH$   = NEW HIGH
190 REM HL$   = NEW LOW
200 REM F$    = FRACTION
210 REM PE    = P/E RATIO
220 REM VOL   = SALES VOLUME
230 REM H     = DAILY HIGH PRICE
240 REM L     = DAILY LOW PRICE
250 REM C     = DAILY CLOSING PRICE
260 REM CR    = CORRECTED FIGURE
270 :
280 :
290 REM **--INITIALIZATION--**
300 OPEN "STOCKPTR.DAT" FOR INPUT AS #1
310 INPUT #1,PTR
320 CLOSE #1
330 PTR = PTR + 1
340 :
350 OPEN "HILOW.DAT" FOR INPUT AS #2
360 FOR I = 1 TO 10
370 INPUT #2,STK$(I)
380 INPUT #2,HI$(I)
390 INPUT #2,LOW$(I)
400 NEXT I
410 CLOSE #2
420 :
430 VT = 2: REM Vertical tab
440 HT = 25: REM Horizontal tab
450 I = 1
460 :
470 :
480 REM **--KEYBOARD INPUT--**
490 CLS
500 LOCATE 5,25
```

```
510 PRINT "Today's date is ";DATE$
520 LOCATE 7,25: INPUT "Is this correct? (Type `Y' or `N
    ') ";Y$
530 IF Y$ = "Y" OR Y$ = "y" OR Y$ = "" THEN 560
540 LOCATE 9,25: INPUT "Type in the correct date ";DTE$
550 GOTO 570
560 DTE$ = DATE$
570 CLS
580 LOCATE VT,     HT: PRINT STK$(I)
590 LOCATE VT + 2,HT: INPUT "Today's P/E ratio ";PE
600 LOCATE VT + 4,HT: INPUT "Today's volume ";VOL
610 GOSUB 7000: REM Reminder routine
620 LOCATE 22,HT: INPUT "Today's high ";H
630 GOSUB 7000: REM Reminder routine
640 LOCATE 22,HT: INPUT "Today's low ";L
650 GOSUB 7000: REM Reminder routine
660 LOCATE 22,HT: INPUT "Today's close ";C
670 :
680 :
690 REM **--CORRECTION ROUTINE--**
700 CLS
710 LOCATE VT,HT: PRINT STK$(I)
720 LOCATE VT +  2,HT: PRINT "1.   Today's P/E ratio-----
    ";PE
730 LOCATE VT +  4,HT: PRINT "2.   Today's volume--------
    ";VOL
740 M = H: GOSUB 8000: REM Convert to fraction
750 LOCATE VT +  6,HT: PRINT "3.   Today's high----------
    ";M;" ";F$
760 M = L: GOSUB 8000: REM Convert to fraction
770 LOCATE VT +  8,HT: PRINT "4.   Today's low-----------
    ";M;" ";F$
780 M = C: GOSUB 8000: REM Convert to fraction
790 LOCATE VT + 10,HT: PRINT "5.   Today's close--------
    ";M;" ";F$
800 LOCATE VT + 12,HT: INPUT "Are these figures correct
    ";YES$
810 IF YES$ = "N" OR YES$ = "n" THEN 830
820 GOTO 940: REM Figures are correct, therefore continu
    e
830 LOCATE VT + 14,HT: INPUT "Which number is wrong ";NB
840 IF NB < 1 OR NB > 5 THEN PRINT "INCORRECT NUMBER!":
    GOTO 830
850 LOCATE VT + 16,HT: INPUT "The correct figure = ";CR
860 IF NB = 1 THEN PE  = CR
870 IF NB = 2 THEN VOL = CR
880 IF NB = 3 THEN H   = CR
890 IF NB = 4 THEN L   = CR
900 IF NB = 5 THEN C   = CR
910 GOTO 690: REM Correction routine
920 :
930 :
```

```
940 REM **--EXCHANGE HI/LOW--**
950 IF H > VAL(HI$(I)) THEN HI$(I) = STR$(H): NH$ = "*"
960 IF L < VAL(LOW$(I)) THEN LOW$(I) = STR$(L): NL$ = "*
    "
970 IF VAL (LOW$(I)) = 0 THEN LOW$(I) = STR$(L)
980 :
990 :
1000 REM **--FILE UPDATE--**
1010 OPEN STK$(I) + ".DAT" AS #3 LEN = 35
1020 FIELD #3, 10 AS D$, 4 AS PE$, 6 AS VOL$, 5 AS H$, 5
     AS L$, 5 AS C$
1030 LSET D$   = DTE$
1040 LSET PE$  = STR$(PE)
1050 LSET VOL$ = STR$(VOL)
1060 LSET H$   = STR$(H) + NH$
1070 LSET L$   = STR$(L) + NL$
1080 LSET C$   = STR$(C)
1090 PUT #3,PTR
1100 CLOSE #3
1110 NH$ = "": NL$ = ""
1120 I = I + 1
1130 IF I < 11 THEN 570: REM Next stock
1140 :
1150 :
2000 REM **--NEW HI/LOW FILE UPDATE--**
2010 OPEN "HILOW.DAT" FOR OUTPUT AS #2
2020 FOR K = 1 TO 10
2030 PRINT #2,STK$(K)
2040 PRINT #2,HI$(K)
2050 PRINT #2,LOW$(K)
2060 NEXT K
2070 CLOSE #2
2080 :
2090 :
3000 REM **--FILE POINTER UPDATE--**
3010 OPEN "STOCKPTR.DAT" FOR OUTPUT AS #1
3020 PRINT #1,PTR
3030 CLOSE #1
3040 :
3050 :
4000 REM **--RETURN TO MAIN MENU--**
4010 RUN "STKMENU"
4020 :
4030 :
7000 REM **--REMINDER ROUTINE--**
7010 CLS: VT = 2
7020 LOCATE VT,     HT: PRINT "*****---REMEMBER---*****"
7030 LOCATE VT +  1,HT: PRINT "YOU MUST ADD THE FRACTION"
7040 LOCATE VT +  2,HT: PRINT "AS THE LAST DIGIT."
7050 LOCATE VT +  4,HT + 3: PRINT "1/8 --------- = 1"
7060 LOCATE VT +  5,HT + 3: PRINT "1/4 --------- = 2"
7070 LOCATE VT +  6,HT + 3: PRINT "3/8 --------- = 3"
7080 LOCATE VT +  7,HT + 3: PRINT "1/2 --------- = 4"
7090 LOCATE VT +  8,HT + 3: PRINT "5/8 --------- = 5"
```

```
7100 LOCATE VT +  9,HT + 3: PRINT "3/4 --------- = 6"
7110 LOCATE VT + 10,HT + 3: PRINT "7/8 --------- = 7"
7120 LOCATE VT + 11,HT + 3: PRINT "EVEN -------- = 0"
7130 LOCATE VT + 13,HT: PRINT "****---IMPORTANT---****"
7140 LOCATE VT + 14,HT: PRINT "IF THE NUMBER HAS NO"
7150 LOCATE VT + 15,HT: PRINT "FRACTION, PLEASE ENTER"
7160 LOCATE VT + 16,HT: PRINT "A `0' AFTER THE NUMBER!"
7170 PRINT
7180 RETURN
7190 :
7200 :
8000 REM **--CONVERT TO FRACTION--**
8010 F = M - INT (M / 10) * 10
8020 M = INT (M / 10)
8030 IF F = 0 THEN F$ = ""
8040 IF F = 1 THEN F$ = "1/8"
8050 IF F = 2 THEN F$ = "1/4"
8060 IF F = 3 THEN F$ = "3/8"
8070 IF F = 4 THEN F$ = "1/2"
8080 IF F = 5 THEN F$ = "5/8"
8090 IF F = 6 THEN F$ = "3/4"
8100 IF F = 7 THEN F$ = "7/8"
8110 RETURN
```

DSPSTOCK

```
100 REM ***--DISPLAY STOCK HISTORY--***
110 :
120 :
130 REM **--VARIABLES LIST--**
140 REM STK$    =   STOCK SYMBOL
150 REM HI$     =   CURRENT HI PRICE
160 REM LOW$    =   CURRENT LOW PRICE
170 REM DTE$    =   DATE
180 REM NH$     =   NEW HIGH
190 REM NL$     =   NEW LOW
200 REM PE      =   PRICE/EARNINGS RATIO
210 REM VOL     =   SALES VOLUME
220 REM H       =   DAILY HIGH PRICE
230 REM L       =   DAILY LOW PRICE
240 REM C       =   DAILY CLOSING PRICE
250 REM W       =   TEMP. STOCK #
260 REM F$      =   FRACTION
270 REM AV      =   AVERAGE VOLUME
280 REM AP      =   AVERAGE PRICE
290 REM CV      =   CLOSING PRICE W/O CONV.
300 REM C1      =   1ST CLOSE PRICE
310 REM C2      =   LAST CLOSE PRICE
320 REM CD      =   DIFF. BETWEEN C1 & C2
330 REM L1      =   COMMON VAR. CONV.
340 REM M       =   COMMON VAR. CONV.
350 :
360 :
370 REM **--INITIALIZATION--**
380 OPEN "STOCKPTR.DAT" FOR INPUT AS #1
390 INPUT #1,PTR
400 CLOSE #1
410 DIM STK$(20)
420 :
430 :
440 REM **--SET UP--**
450 CLS
460 LOCATE 2,26: PRINT "DISPLAY STOCK HISTORY"
470 OPEN "HILOW.DAT" FOR INPUT AS #2
480 FOR I = 1 TO 10
490 INPUT #2, STK$(I)
500 INPUT #2, HI$(I)
510 M = VAL(HI$(I))
520 GOSUB 8000: REM Convert to fraction
530 HI$(I) = STR$(M) + " " + F$
540 INPUT #2,LOW$(I)
550 M = VAL(LOW$(I))
560 GOSUB 8000: REM Convert to fraction
570 LOW$(I) = STR$(M) + " " + F$
580 LOCATE I + 3,30: PRINT I;STK$(I)
590 NEXT I
```

```
600 CLOSE #1
610 STK$(11) = "Stock Menu"
620 LOCATE I + 3,31: PRINT "11 ";STK$(11)
630 PRINT
640 LOCATE I + 5,31: INPUT "Which number ";W
650 IF W < 1 OR W > 11 THEN 5000
660 IF W = 11 THEN RUN "STKMENU"
670 :
680 :
690 REM **--TITLES--**
700 CLS
710 PRINT TAB(37) STK$(W)
720 PRINT: PRINT
730 PRINT "DATE" TAB(18) "VOL" TAB(35) "HI" TAB(50) "LOW";
740 PRINT TAB(65) "CLOSE"
750 :
760 :
1000 REM **--STOCK FILE INPUT ROUTINE--**
1010 OPEN STK$(W) + ".DAT" AS #3 LEN = 35
1020 FIELD #3,10 AS DTE$,4 AS PE$,6 AS VOL$,5 AS H$,5 AS L
     $,5 AS C$
1030 FOR K = 1 TO PTR
1040 GET #3,K
1050 PRINT DTE$ TAB(16) VOL$;
1060 :
1070 M = VAL(H$)
1080 GOSUB 8000: REM Convert to fraction
1090 H = M
1095 FOR Z = 1 TO LEN(H$)
1100 IF MID$(H$,Z,1) = "*" THEN NH$ = "*"
1105 NEXT Z
1110 PRINT TAB(32) H;F$;NH$;
1120 :
1130 M = VAL(L$)
1140 GOSUB 8000: REM Convert to fraction
1150 L = M
1155 FOR Z = 1 TO LEN(L$)
1160 IF MID$(L$,Z,1) = "*" THEN NL$ = "*"
1165 NEXT Z
1170 PRINT TAB(48) L;F$;NL$;
1180 :
1190 C = VAL(C$)
1200 IF K = 1 THEN C1 = C: V1 = VAL(VOL$)
1210 IF K = PTR THEN C2 = C
1220 CV = C
1230 L1 = CV
1240 GOSUB 9000: REM Convert to decimal
1250 CV = L1
1260 M = C
1270 GOSUB 8000: REM Convert to fraction
1280 C = M
1290 PRINT TAB(64) C;F$
1300 :
1310 AV = AV + VAL(VOL$)
```

```
1320 AP = AP + CV
1330 NH$ = "": NL$ = ""
1340 NEXT K
1350 CLOSE #3
1360 PRINT
1370 INPUT "Press the `ENTER' key to continue. ",L$
1380 :
1390 :
1400 REM **--DISPLAY SECOND PAGE--**
1410 CLS
1420 LOCATE    2,34: PRINT STK$(W)
1430 LOCATE    4,25: PRINT "Current P/E ratio  = ";PE$
1440 LOCATE    6,25: PRINT "Current high price = ";HI$(W)
1450 LOCATE    8,25: PRINT "Current low price  = ";LOW$(W)
1460 AV = AV / (K - 1)
1470 LOCATE 10,25: PRINT "Average volume     = ";AV
1480 AP = AP / (K - 1)
1490 LOCATE 12,25: PRINT "Average price      = ";AP
1500 LOCATE 14,25: PRINT "Last price         = ";C;F$
1510 L1 = C2
1520 GOSUB 9000: REM Convert to decimal
1530 C2 = L1
1540 :
1550 L1 = C1
1560 GOSUB 9000: REM Convert to decimal
1570 C1 = L1
1580 CD = C2 - C1
1590 LOCATE 16,25: PRINT "Price difference"
1600 LOCATE 17,25: PRINT "from 1st record    = ";CD
1610 :
1620 :
1630 REM **--ANOTHER STOCK--**
1640 LOCATE 22,25: INPUT "Press the `ENTER' key to conti
     nue. ",L$
1650 CLS
1660 LOCATE 2,26: PRINT "DISPLAY STOCK HISTORY"
1670 AV = 0
1680 AP = 0
1690 FOR I = 1 TO 11
1700 LOCATE I + 3,30: PRINT I;STK$(I)
1710 NEXT I
1720 PRINT
1730 GOTO 640: REM Ask for another stock history
1740 :
1750 :
5000 REM **--INCORRECT NUMBER ROUTINE--**
5010 LOCATE 22,25: PRINT "INCORRECT NUMBER!"
5020 GOTO 640: REM Ask again
5030 :
5040 :
8000 REM **--CONVERT TO FRACTION--**
8010 F = M - INT (M / 10) * 10
8020 M = INT (M / 10)
```

```
8030 IF F = 0 THEN F$ = " "
8040 IF F = 1 THEN F$ = "1/8"
8050 IF F = 2 THEN F$ = "1/4"
8060 IF F = 3 THEN F$ = "3/8"
8070 IF F = 4 THEN F$ = "1/2"
8080 IF F = 5 THEN F$ = "5/8"
8090 IF F = 6 THEN F$ = "3/4"
8100 IF F = 7 THEN F$ = "7/8"
8110 RETURN
8120 :
8130 :
9000 REM **--CONVERT TO DECIMAL--**
9010 L1 = L1 / 10: S1 = INT (L1): D1 = L1 - S1
9020 D1 = (D1 * 10) / 8: L1 = S1 + D1: L1 = INT (L1 * 10
     00 + .5) / 1000
9030 RETURN
```

DSPHILOW

```
100 REM ***--DISPLAY HI/LOW FILE--***
110 :
120 :
130 REM **--FILE INPUT ROUTINE--**
140 OPEN "HILOW.DAT" FOR INPUT AS #1
150 FOR I = 1 TO 10
160 INPUT #1,STK$(I)
170 INPUT #1,HI$(I)
180 INPUT #1,LOW$(I)
190 NEXT I
200 CLOSE #1
210 :
220 :
230 REM **--DISPLAY ROUTINE--**
240 CLS
250 LOCATE 2,1: PRINT "STOCK SYMBOL" TAB(30) "HI VALUE"
    TAB(50) "LOW VALUE"
260 FOR I = 1 TO 10
270 PRINT I;STK$(I);
280 M = VAL(HI$(I))
290 GOSUB 8000: REM Convert to fraction
300 HI$(I) = STR$(M)
310 PRINT TAB(30) HI$(I);" ";F$;
320 M = VAL(LOW$(I))
330 GOSUB 8000: REM Convert to fraction
340 LOW$(I) = STR$(M)
350 PRINT TAB(50) LOW$(I);" ";F$
360 NEXT I
370 PRINT
380 INPUT "Press the `ENTER' key when you are ready to c
    ontinue ",L$
```

```
390 :
400 :
410 RUN "STKMENU"
420 :
430 :
8000 REM **--CONVERT TO FRACTION--**
8010 F = M - INT (M / 10) * 10
8020 M = INT (M / 10)
8030 IF F = 0 THEN F$ = ""
8040 IF F = 1 THEN F$ = "1/8"
8050 IF F = 2 THEN F$ = "1/4"
8060 IF F = 3 THEN F$ = "3/8"
8070 IF F = 4 THEN F$ = "1/2"
8080 IF F = 5 THEN F$ = "5/8"
8090 IF F = 6 THEN F$ = "3/4"
8100 IF F = 7 THEN F$ = "7/8"
8110 RETURN
```

CRTHILOW

```
100 REM ***--CORRECT HI/LOW FILE--***
110 :
120 :
130 REM **--FILE INPUT ROUTINT--**
140 OPEN "HILOW.DAT" FOR INPUT AS #1
150 FOR I = 1 TO 10
160 INPUT #1,STK$(I)
170 INPUT #1,HI$(I)
180 INPUT #1,LOW$(I)
190 NEXT I
200 CLOSE #1
210 VT =  2: REM Vertical tab
220 HT = 25: REM Horizontal tab
230 :
240 :
250 REM **--CORRECTION ROUTINE--**
260 FOR I = 1 TO 10
270 CLS: LOCATE 5,1
280 PRINT "1. ";STK$(I)
290 M = VAL(HI$(I)): GOSUB 8000: REM Convert to fraction
300 PRINT "2. HI value  = ";M;" ";F$
310 M = VAL(LOW$(I)): GOSUB 8000: REM Convert to fractio
    n
320 PRINT "3. LOW value = ";M;" ";F$
330 PRINT
340 INPUT "Is this correct ";YES$
350 IF YES$ = "N" OR YES$ = "n" THEN 370
360 GOTO 520: REM Next I
370 PRINT
380 INPUT "Which number is wrong ";NB
390 PRINT
```

```
400 IF NB = 1 THEN PRINT "Type in the name of the stock
    or its symbol ": PRINT
410 IF NB = 1 THEN PRINT "The name or symbol may have a
    maximum of 8 characters.": PRINT
420 IF NB = 1 THEN INPUT "Correct stock name or symbol "
    ;STK$(I)
430 IF LEN(STK$(I)) > 8 THEN STK$(I) = LEFT$(STK$(I),8)
440 IF NB = 2 THEN GOSUB 7000: REM Remainder routine
450 IF NB = 2 THEN PRINT "Incorrect HI value = ";HI$(I):
    PRINT
460 IF NB = 2 THEN INPUT "Correct HI value = ";HI$(I)
470 IF NB = 3 THEN GOSUB 7000: REM Remainder routine
480 IF NB = 3 THEN PRINT "Incorrect LOW value = ";LOW$(I
    ): PRINT
490 IF NB = 3 THEN INPUT "Correct LOW value = ";LOW$(I)
500 IF NB < 1 OR NB > 3 THEN PRINT "INCORRECT CHOICE!"
510 GOTO 270: REM Ask again
520 NEXT I
530 :
540 :
1000 REM **--FILE UPDATE ROUTINE--**
1010 OPEN "HILOW.DAT" FOR OUTPUT AS #2
1020 FOR I = 1 TO 10
1030 PRINT #2,STK$(I)
1040 PRINT #2,HI$(I)
1050 PRINT #2,LOW$(I)
1060 NEXT I
1070 CLOSE #2
1080 :
1090 :
2000 RUN "STKMENU"
2010 :
2020 :
7000 REM **--REMINDER ROUTINE--**
7010 CLS: VT = 2
7020 LOCATE VT,      HT: PRINT "*****---REMEMBER---*****"
7030 LOCATE VT +  1,HT: PRINT "YOU MUST ADD THE FRACTION"
7040 LOCATE VT +  2,HT: PRINT "AS THE LAST DIGIT."
7050 LOCATE VT +  4,HT + 3: PRINT "1/8 --------- = 1"
7060 LOCATE VT +  5,HT + 3: PRINT "1/4 --------- = 2"
7070 LOCATE VT +  6,HT + 3: PRINT "3/8 --------- = 3"
7080 LOCATE VT +  7,HT + 3: PRINT "1/2 --------- = 4"
7090 LOCATE VT +  8,HT + 3: PRINT "5/8 --------- = 5"
7100 LOCATE VT +  9,HT + 3: PRINT "3/4 --------- = 6"
7110 LOCATE VT + 10,HT + 3: PRINT "7/8 --------- = 7"
7120 LOCATE VT + 11,HT + 3: PRINT "EVEN -------- = 0"
7130 LOCATE VT + 13,HT: PRINT "****---IMPORTANT---****"
7140 LOCATE VT + 14,HT: PRINT "IF THE NUMBER HAS NO"
7150 LOCATE VT + 15,HT: PRINT "FRACTION, PLEASE ENTER"
7160 LOCATE VT + 16,HT: PRINT "A `0' AFTER THE NUMBER!"
7170 PRINT
7180 RETURN
7190 :
7200 :
```

```
8000 REM **--CONVERT TO FRACTION--**
8010 F = M - INT (M / 10) * 10
8020 M = INT (M / 10)
8030 IF F = 0 THEN F$ = ""
8040 IF F = 1 THEN F$ = "1/8"
8050 IF F = 2 THEN F$ = "1/4"
8060 IF F = 3 THEN F$ = "3/8"
8070 IF F = 4 THEN F$ = "1/2"
8080 IF F = 5 THEN F$ = "5/8"
8090 IF F = 6 THEN F$ = "3/4"
8100 IF F = 7 THEN F$ = "7/8"
8110 RETURN
```

CRTSTOCK

```
100 REM ***--CORRECT STOCK HISTORY--***
110 :
120 :
130 REM **--VARIABLES LIST--**
140 REM STK$    =    STOCK SYMBOL
150 REM HI$     =    CURRENT HI PRICE
160 REM LOW$    =    CURRENT LOW PRICE
170 REM PE      =    PRICE/EARNINGS RATIO
180 REM VOL     =    SALES VOLUME
190 REM H       =    DAILY HIGH PRICE
200 REM L       =    DAILY LOW PRICE
210 REM C       =    DAILY CLOSING PRICE
220 REM DTE$    =    DATE
230 REM F$      =    FRACTION
240 REM M       =    COMMON VAR. CONV.
250 REM W       =    TEMP. STOCK #
260 :
270 :
280 REM **--INITIALIZATION--**
290 OPEN "STOCKPTR.DAT" FOR INPUT AS #1
300 INPUT #1,PTR
310 CLOSE #1
320 DIM STK$(20)
330 :
340 :
350 REM **--SET UP--**
360 CLS
370 LOCATE 2,26: PRINT "CORRECT STOCK HISTORY"
380 OPEN "HILOW.DAT" FOR INPUT AS #2
390 FOR I = 1 TO 10
400 INPUT #2, STK$(I)
410 INPUT #2, HI$(I)
420 M = VAL(HI$(I))
430 GOSUB 8000: REM Convert to fraction
440 HI$(I) = STR$(M) + " " + F$
450 INPUT #2,LOW$(I)
```

```
460 M = VAL(LOW$(I))
470 GOSUB 8000: REM Convert to fraction
480 LOW$(I) = STR$(M) + " " + F$
490 LOCATE I + 3,30: PRINT I;STK$(I)
500 NEXT I
510 CLOSE #2
520 STK$(11) = "Stock Menu"
530 LOCATE I + 3,31: PRINT "11 ";STK$(11)
540 PRINT
550 LOCATE I + 5,31: INPUT "Which number ";W
560 IF W < 1 OR W > 11 THEN 5000
570 IF W = 11 THEN RUN "STKMENU"
580 LOCATE I + 7,31: PRINT "Which Record? 1 to ";PTR;" ";
590 INPUT K
600 IF K > PTR THEN LOCATE 22,25: PRINT "INCORRECT NUMBER
    !": GOTO 580
610 :
620 :
630 REM **--TITLES--**
640 CLS
650 PRINT TAB(37) STK$(W)
660 PRINT: PRINT
670 :
680 :
1000 REM **--STOCK FILE INPUT ROUTINE--**
1010 OPEN STK$(W) + ".DAT" AS #3 LEN = 35
1020 FIELD #3,10 AS D$,4 AS P$,6 AS V$,5 AS H2$,5 AS L2$,
     5 AS C2$
1030 GET #3,K
1040 DTE$  =  D$
1050 PE$   =  P$
1060 VOL$  =  V$
1070 H$    =  H2$
1080 L$    =  L2$
1090 C$    =  C2$
1100 CLOSE #3
1110 :
1120 :
1130 REM **--DISPLAY FOR CORRECTION--**
1140 CLS
1150 LOCATE   2,34: PRINT STK$(W)
1160 LOCATE   4,25: PRINT "1. Date          = ";DTE$
1170 LOCATE   6,25: PRINT "2. P/E ratio     = ";PE$
1180 LOCATE   8,25: PRINT "3. Volume        = ";VOL$
1190 M = VAL(H$): GOSUB 8000: REM Convert to fraction
1200 LOCATE 10,25: PRINT "4. Day's High    = ";M;F$
1210 M = VAL(L$): GOSUB 8000: REM Convert to fraction
1220 LOCATE 12,25: PRINT "5. Day's Low     = ";M;F$
1230 M = VAL(C$): GOSUB 8000: REM Convert to fraction
1240 LOCATE 14,25: PRINT "6. Day's Close   = ";M;F$
1250 LOCATE 16,25: PRINT "0. All Correct   "
1260 LOCATE 18,25: INPUT "Which number is wrong ";NB
1270 IF NB > 6 THEN PRINT "INCORRECT CHOICE!": GOTO 1260
1280 IF NB = 0 THEN 2000: REM File output routine
```

```
1290 LOCATE 20,25: INPUT "Correct information = ";CR$
1300 IF NB = 1 THEN DTE$   =   CR$
1310 IF NB = 2 THEN PE$    =   " " + CR$
1320 IF NB = 3 THEN VOL$   =   " " + CR$
1330 IF NB = 4 THEN H$     =   CR$
1340 IF NB = 5 THEN L$     =   CR$
1350 IF NB = 6 THEN C$     =   CR$
1360 GOTO 1130: REM Ask again
1370 :
1380 :
2000 REM **--FILE OUTPUT ROUTINE--**
2010 OPEN STK$(W) + ".DAT" AS #3 LEN = 35
2020 FIELD #3,10 AS D$,4 AS P$,6 AS V$,5 AS H2$,5 AS L2$,
     5 AS C2$
2030 LSET D$   = DTE$
2040 LSET P$   = PE$
2050 LSET V$   = VOL$
2060 LSET H2$  = H$
2070 LSET L2$  = L$
2080 LSET C2$  = C$
2090 PUT #3,K
2100 CLOSE #3
2110 :
2120 :
2130 REM **--ANOTHER STOCK--**
2140 LOCATE 22,25: INPUT "Press the `ENTER' key to contin
     ue. ",L$
2150 CLS
2160 LOCATE 2,26: PRINT "CORRECT STOCK HISTORY"
2170 FOR I = 1 TO 11
2180 LOCATE I + 3,30: PRINT I;STK$(I)
2190 NEXT I
2200 PRINT
2210 GOTO 550: REM Ask for another stock history
2220 :
2230 :
5000 REM **--INCORRECT NUMBER ROUTINE--**
5010 LOCATE 22,25: PRINT "INCORRECT NUMBER!"
5020 GOTO 550: REM Ask again
5030 :
5040 :
8000 REM **--CONVERT TO FRACTION--**
8010 F = M - INT (M / 10) * 10
8020 M = INT (M / 10)
8030 IF F = 0 THEN F$ = ""
8040 IF F = 1 THEN F$ = "1/8"
8050 IF F = 2 THEN F$ = "1/4"
8060 IF F = 3 THEN F$ = "3/8"
8070 IF F = 4 THEN F$ = "1/2"
8080 IF F = 5 THEN F$ = "5/8"
8090 IF F = 6 THEN F$ = "3/4"
8100 IF F = 7 THEN F$ = "7/8"
8110 RETURN
```

DIFSTOCK

```
100 REM ***--STOCK DIF TRANSLATION--***
110 :
120 :
130 Q$ = CHR$(34): REM Quotation mark
140 :
150 OPEN "STOCKPTR.DAT" FOR INPUT AS #1
160 INPUT #1,PTR
170 CLOSE #1
180 NV = 8: NT = PTR + 1
190 REM NV = NUMBER OF VECTORS
200 REM VT = NUMBER OF TUPLES
210 :
220 OPEN "HILOW.DAT" FOR INPUT AS #1
230 FOR I = 1 TO 10
240 INPUT #1,STK$(I)
250 INPUT #1,HI$(I)
260 INPUT #1,LOW$(I)
270 NEXT I
280 CLOSE #1
290 :
300 CLS:LOCATE 2,26: PRINT "DIF TRANSLATION"
310 FOR I = 1 TO 10
320 LOCATE I + 3,25: PRINT I;STK$(I)
330 NEXT I
340 LOCATE I + 3,26: PRINT "11 Program Menu"
350 LOCATE I + 5,26: INPUT "Which Number ";NB
360 IF NB < 1 OR NB > 11 THEN 1320
370 IF NB = 11 THEN RUN "STKMENU"
380 CLS
390 LOCATE 5,15: PRINT "DIF TRANSLATION IN PROGRESS. PLEA
    SE DO NOT TOUCH!!"
400 :
410 OPEN STK$(NB) + ".DAT" AS #2 LEN = 35
420 FIELD #2,10 AS D$, 4 AS P$, 6 AS V$, 5 AS H2$, 5 AS L
    2$, 5 AS C2$
430 OPEN STK$(NB) + ".DIF" FOR OUTPUT AS #3
440 :
450 REM **--HEADER SECTION--**
460 :
470 PRINT #3,"TABLE"
480 PRINT #3,"0,1"
490 PRINT #3,Q$STK$(NB)Q$
500 :
510 PRINT #3,"VECTORS"
520 PRINT #3,"0,";NV
530 PRINT #3,Q$Q$
540 :
550 PRINT #3,"TUPLES"
560 PRINT #3,"0,";NT
570 PRINT #3,Q$Q$
```

```
580 :
590 PRINT #3,"LABEL"
600 PRINT #3,"1,0"
610 PRINT #3,Q$"DATE"Q$
620 :
630 PRINT #3,"LABEL"
640 PRINT #3,"2,0"
650 PRINT #3,Q$"P/E"Q$
660 :
670 PRINT #3,"LABEL"
680 PRINT #3,"3,0"
690 PRINT #3,Q$"VOL."Q$
700 :
710 PRINT #3,"LABEL"
720 PRINT #3,"4,0"
730 PRINT #3,Q$"HI"Q$
740 :
750 PRINT #3,"LABEL"
760 PRINT #3,"5,0"
770 PRINT #3,Q$"LOW"Q$
780 :
790 PRINT #3,"LABEL"
800 PRINT #3,"6,0"
810 PRINT #3,Q$"CLOSE"Q$
820 :
830 PRINT #3,"LABEL"
840 PRINT #3,"7,0"
850 PRINT #3,Q$"52 WK.HI"Q$
860 :
870 PRINT #3,"LABEL"
880 PRINT #3,"8,0"
890 PRINT #3,Q$"52 WK.LOW"Q$
900 :
910 PRINT #3,"DATA"
920 PRINT #3,"0,0"
930 PRINT #3,Q$Q$
940 :
950 REM **--DATA SECTION--**
960 :
970 PRINT #3,"-1,0"
980 PRINT #3,"BOT"
990 :
1000 PRINT #3,"1,0"
1010 PRINT #3,STK$(NB)
1020 :
1030 PRINT #3,"1,0"
1040 PRINT #3,"52 WK.HI"
1050 :
1060 PRINT #3,"1,0"
1070 PRINT #3,"52 WK.LOW"
1080 :
1090 PRINT #3,"-1,0"
1100 PRINT #3,"BOT"
1110 :
```

```
1120 PRINT #3,"1,0"
1130 PRINT #3," "
1140 :
1150 L1 = VAL(HI$(NB))
1160 GOSUB 9000: REM Convert to decimal
1170 HI = L1
1180 :
1190 PRINT #3,"0,";HI
1200 PRINT #3,"V"
1210 :
1220 L1 = VAL(LOW$(NB))
1230 GOSUB 9000: REM Convert to decimal
1240 LW = L1
1250 :
1260 PRINT #3,"0,";LW
1270 PRINT #3,"V"
1280 :
1290 PRINT #3,"-1,0"
1300 PRINT #3,"BOT"
1310 :
1330 PRINT #3,"1,0"
1340 PRINT #3,"DATE"
1350 :
1360 PRINT #3,"1,0"
1370 PRINT #3,"P/E"
1380 :
1390 PRINT #3,"1,0"
1400 PRINT #3,"VOL."
1410 :
1420 PRINT #3,"1,0"
1430 PRINT #3,"HI"
1440 :
1450 PRINT #3,"1,0"
1460 PRINT #3,"LOW"
1470 :
1480 PRINT #3,"1,0"
1490 PRINT #3,"CLOSE"
1500 :
1510 PRINT #3,"1,0"
1520 PRINT #3,"52 WK.HI"
1530 :
1540 PRINT #3,"1,0"
1550 PRINT #3,"52 WK.LOW"
1560 :
1570 FOR K = 1 TO PTR
1580 :
1590 GET #2,K
1600 :
1610 DTE$ = D$
1620 PE$  = P$
1630 VOL$ = V$
1640 H$   = H2$
1650 L$   = L2$
1660 C$   = C2$
```

```
1670 :
1680 PRINT #3,"-1,0"
1690 PRINT #3,"BOT"
1700 :
1710 PRINT #3,"1,0"
1720 PRINT #3,DTE$
1730 :
1740 PRINT #3,"0,";VAL(PE$)
1750 PRINT #3,"V"
1760 :
1770 PRINT #3,"0,";VAL(VOL$)
1780 PRINT #3,"V"
1790 :
1800 Ll = VAL(H$)
1810 GOSUB 9000: REM Convert to decimal
1820 H = Ll
1830 :
1840 PRINT #3,"0,";H
1850 PRINT #3,"V"
1860 :
1870 Ll = VAL(L$)
1880 GOSUB 9000: REM Convert to decimal
1890 L = Ll
1900 :
1910 PRINT #3,"0,";L
1920 PRINT #3,"V"
1930 :
1940 Ll = VAL(C$)
1950 GOSUB 9000: REM Convert to decimal
1960 C = Ll
1970 :
1980 PRINT #3,"0,";C
1990 PRINT #3,"V"
2000 :
2010 NEXT K
2020 :
2030 PRINT #3,"-1,0"
2040 PRINT #3,"EOD"
2050 :
2060 CLOSE #2,#3
2070 CLS: LOCATE 5,1
2080 FILES
2090 PRINT: PRINT
2100 PRINT "DIF TRANSLATION COMPLETE!"
2110 PRINT
2120 INPUT "Press the `ENTER' key when ready to continue
     ",Z$
2130 GOTO 300: REM Menu
2140 :
2150 :
9000 REM **--CONVERT TO DECIMAL--**
9010 Ll = Ll / 10: Sl = INT (Ll): Dl = Ll - Sl
9020 Dl = (Dl * 10) / 8: Ll = Sl + Dl: Ll = INT (Ll * 10
     00 + .5) / 1000
9030 RETURN
```

Appendix

GEMS OF MISCELLANY

In working with BASIC and file manipulation on the IBM Personal Computer, a number of pieces of information simply did not fit within the structure of this book. I feel I would be remiss to exclude them; therefore, this first section of the Appendix will cover what might be called Gems of Miscellany. It is not my intent to duplicate all the information presented in various IBM manuals. Instead, I hope to highlight information of particular value and encourage you to turn to your IBM manuals when you need additional help.

A. ADDITIONAL DOS COMMANDS

Besides the DOS commands of DIR, FORMAT, and TYPE covered in the text, a number of other commands are worth mentioning. The most important is the COPY command. With this command, a copy of any DOS file can be made. There are a number of parameters that can be used with this command, but the most common form is to copy a file from one drive to another:

A> COPY INVMENU.BAS B:

The above command will copy the file INVMENU.BAS from the diskette in drive A (the default drive in this case) to the diskette in drive B. Another use of this same form is to make a backup copy of an entire diskette's contents:

    A> COPY *.* B:

This example will copy every file on the diskette in drive A onto the diskette in drive B. As you can see, this is a very versatile command, and the more experience you have with it, the more useful it can become. I would encourage you to read carefully through the DOS manual on this and other commands. Try out the various examples on diskettes and files that can be used for experimentation.

The CHKDSK command checks the status of the disk and reports back the amount of disk space used and available. The COMP command will compare one file against another and report the differences in the two. This command is useful when you have made a copy of a file and wish to be certain that the two files are identical. DISKCOMP compares the entire contents of one diskette with the contents of another. Again, it is most useful when checking a copy that has been made. DISKCOPY will make an exact copy of a diskette, but extensive use of this command is discouraged for some rather obscure reasons. ERASE and DEL remove or delete files from the diskettes. Their use, especially with the wild card characters, should be done with great care! I once wiped out three hours of work collating files from various diskettes with one careless use of the ERASE command and the *.

The last command I will mention is the REN (for rename) command. With this command, you can change the names of files while still in DOS. There are other commands, and depending upon your use of the computer, you may or may not find need of them. You should also notice that a number of these commands duplicate functions available from BASIC:

    DOS   BASIC
    DIR ---------- FILES
    REN ---------- NAME
    DEL ---------- KILL
    ERASE -------- KILL

B. ADDITIONAL BASIC FILE COMMANDS

Besides additional DOS commands, there are a number of BASIC file manipulation commands or functions that either are more advanced in their use or outside the scope of an introductory book on

IBM BASIC files. BLOAD and BSAVE are used to load and save binary files. MERGE is a very powerful command that can be used to build a library of utility modules. The UPPER CASE CONVERSION ROUTINE is an example of a routine that can be saved as a file on a utility disk and then MERGEd into any program you want. Care must be taken so that these utility routines do not duplicate any line numbers already in your program.

CHAIN is useful if you have variables created in one program that you want to use in another program. The CHAIN command allows the programmer to move those variables between programs. Again, care must be taken so that the two programs do not share the use of the same variable name for different purposes. An example of this shared use would be the use of K as a counter for a FOR-NEXT loop in one program and as the value of a file pointer in the other program. CHAINing two such programs could cause real problems for the user and/or programmer.

C. BASIC STATEMENTS, FUNCTIONS, AND COMMANDS NOT USED

There are a number of very powerful BASIC statements, functions, and commands available to the IBM programmer that have not been used in this book. Their use was often purposely omitted to make the programs easier to explain, or more portable. If you have reached this point and have followed all the examples given in the book, I would encourage you to experiment with some of these other BASIC statements, functions, or commands. Suggestions include: INKEY$, INPUT$, INSTR, LOC, LOF, SPACE$, STRING$, SWAP, WHILE—WEND, WRITE#. In addition, there are all the statements, functions, and commands available for working with graphics. (A future book will deal with these.)

D. ADDITIONAL BASIC PROCEDURES

IBM has provided the user with many options in working with BASIC. Program files may be saved in a "protected" manner by using a comma and the letter P after the normal SAVE procedure.

SAVE "DSPSTOCK", P

This protected manner does not mean that the file is protected from erasure. Rather, it means that the program cannot be loaded and either listed or changed. It can only be run, and no way has been provided to unprotect a "protected" program file. For this reason, I would not suggest much use of this feature.

When you load BASIC or BASICA there are several parameters that can be used to override the default values. BASIC and BASICA normally allow only three files open at the same time and a maximum length of 128 bytes for random file records. Both of these limitations can be changed by using the F and S parameters when either form of BASIC is initiated.

    A>BASIC/F: 5/S: 512

The above command will load BASIC, allow five files to be opened at the same time, and provide a 512 byte buffer. The IBM manual suggests the use of this 512 byte buffer when using random files as a means of increasing performance.

E.   BATCH FILES

Typing the above sequence each time you want to bring up BASIC can soon become quite annoying and, when combined with a BAT (BATCH) file, unnecessary. Batch files will execute a number of commands one after the other automatically. BAT files can be created by using the copy command. To create a batch file that will automatically execute the above BASIC command sequence, do the following: (1) take a diskette that has been properly formatted with the /S (system) option (see Chapter 2), (2) copy BASIC.COM on to it if not already there (again, see Chapter 2), and (3) type:

    A>COPY CON: AUTOEXEC.BAT
    BASIC/F: 5/S: 512
    F6 (Press the F6 key)
    ENTER (Press the ENTER key)

The disk drive should come on and the message "1 file(s) copied" should appear.

If all of the above has been done correctly, then your diskette can be inserted into drive A, the system can be booted (in either way), and BASIC will automatically be loaded with the files option set to 5 and the buffer or /S option set to 512. No other typing is necessary.

If you do not want the process to be automatic for some reason (e.g., the date and time requests are bypassed by this method, unless specifically included in the BAT file), you can create a batch file that will execute only when the file name is typed. For example, instead of using the file name AUTOEXEC.BAT, you can use BAS512.BAT, or some other descriptive file name. Then, when the system is booted, the normal sequence of events occurs until you type BAS512. At that point, BASIC, with the above mentioned options, will be loaded. There are a lot of possible uses for these batch files, with their potential limited only by the needs or imagination of the user.

F. TAPE FILES

I have included this section on tape files for those without disk drives. IBM BASIC is a device-oriented BASIC. This means that sequential access files can be stored on cassette tape without much program modification. Only one sequential access file can be open at a time. Since IBM cassette BASIC views the printer, keyboard, and screen as output file devices also, a maximum of four output devices are possible. The program modification would generally come in the area of informing the user when to turn the tape recorder on and off or including the necessary program instructions using the MOTOR statement to accomplish the same task.

All the above presupposes that you have been able to obtain the necessary cable connection between the IBM system unit and a cassette tape recorder. As of this writing, I have not heard of anyone selling such a cable, and the only individuals I know using the cassette recorder with their IBM have had the cable especially made for them.

The only other thing to be concerned about in translating to tape sequential access programs developed for disk systems is the use of BASIC statements, functions, or commands that are not available in cassette BASIC. The following is a list of the reserved words that are not available to cassette BASIC users:

CHAIN	CIRCLE	COM	COMMON
CVI	CVS	CVD	DATE$
DRAW	FILES	GET	KEY
KILL	LOC	LOF	LSET
RSET	MKI$	MKS$	MKD$
NAME	ON COM	ON KEY	ON PEN
ON STRIG	PAINT	PLAY	PUT
RESET	STRIG(n)	SYSTEM	TIME$
VARPTR$			

I am not certain that this is a complete list, but I believe it contains most of the BASIC reserved words *not* available to cassette users. The sequential access programs presented in this book should be able to be used on tape without modification other than that noted above.

PROGRAM LIST

Index

257